A Guide to
CURRICULUM MAPPING

This book is dedicated to my husband, Johnny Lee Hale.

Twenty-five years ago we made a covenant.
To love and to cherish, for better or worse,
for richer or poorer, in sickness and in health.

I am thankful for the experiences that have embraced and tested our vows.
I look forward with joy to the coming years with our eyes fixed on the One we love.

A Guide to
CURRICULUM MAPPING

PLANNING, IMPLEMENTING, and SUSTAINING the PROCESS

JANET A. HALE

Foreword by
Heidi Hayes Jacobs

CORWIN PRESS
A SAGE Company
Thousand Oaks, CA 91320

For information:

Corwin Press
A SAGE Company
2455 Teller Road
Thousand Oaks, California 91320
www.corwinpress.com

SAGE Ltd.
1 Oliver's Yard
55 City Road
London EC1Y 1SP
United Kingdom

SAGE India Pvt. Ltd.
B 1/I 1 Mohan Cooperative Industrial Area
Mathura Road, New Delhi 110 044
India

SAGE Asia-Pacific Pte. Ltd.
33 Pekin Street #02-01
Far East Square
Singapore 048763

Printed in the United States of America.

Library of Congress Cataloging-in-Publication Data

Hale, Janet A.
A guide to curriculum mapping: planning, implementing, and sustaining the process / Janet A. Hale.
        p. cm.
Includes bibliographical references and index.
ISBN 978-1-4129-4891-3 (cloth)
ISBN 978-1-4129-4892-0 (pbk.)
    1. Curriculum planning. 2. Teacher participation in curriculum planning.
I. Title.

LB2806.15.H348 2008
375'.001—dc22   2007031654

This book is printed on acid-free paper.

07   08   09   10   11   10 9 8 7 6 5 4 3 2 1

Acquisitions Editor:	Cathy Hernandez
Editorial Assistants:	Megan Bedell and Cathleen Mortensen
Copy Editor:	Sarah J. Duffy
Typesetter:	C&M Digitals (P) Ltd.
Proofreader:	Andrea Martin
Indexer:	Kathy Paparchontis
Cover Designer:	Michael Dubowe
Graphic Designer:	Karine Hovsepian

Contents

List of Figures ix

Foreword xiii
   Heidi Hayes Jacobs

Preface xv
   A Resource for Teachers and Administrators xv
   Overview of the Contents xvi

Acknowledgments xix

About the Author xxiii

1. How Do We Need to Think, Act, and Meet Differently? 1
   Thinking Differently: Planned Versus Operational Curriculum 1
   Acting Differently: Verification Versus Speculation 3
   Meeting Differently: A Collegial Forum 6
   Conclusion 8
   Review Questions 9

2. What Are the Four Types of Curriculum Maps? 11
   Four Types of Curriculum Maps 11
   Curriculum Map Elements: An Overview 20
   Conclusion 23
   Review Questions 23

3. What Should We Consider
Before Developing Curriculum Maps? 25
   First Consideration: Exploring Personal and
      Collaborative Understanding of Curriculum Design 26
   Second Consideration: The Ongoing
      Nature of Mapping Reviews 30
   Third Consideration: A Mapping Sequence
      That Is Right for Your Learning Organization 32
   Conclusion 37
   Review Questions 38

4. What Elements Are Commonly
Included in Curriculum Maps? 39
   Curriculum Map Alignments and Elements 39
   Writing the Elements 42

Conclusion   97

Review Questions   98

Descriptive or Not Descriptive?
    That Is the Question! (Math Focus)   99

Descriptive or Not Descriptive?
    That Is the Question! (Language Arts Focus)   101

Skill Versus Activity (Math Focus: Primary Grades)   103

Skill Versus Activity (Various-Discipline Focus: Upper Grades) 105

Assessment Versus Evaluation   107

**5. What Should We Know Before Creating Diary
Maps or Projected Maps?**   **109**

Points to Ponder   109

Implementation Considerations   113

Conclusion   119

Sample Projected/Diary Maps   120

Review Questions   129

Conducting an Initial Read-Through:
    Facilitator Explanation and How-To Guide   130

Conducting an Initial Read-Through:
    Team Member Explanation and How-To Guide   139

Initial Read-Through: Collaborating to Create Quality Maps 142

Initial Read-Through Card Shuffle Debrief   144

**6. What Should We Know Before
Creating Consensus Maps and Essential Maps?**   **145**

Map Type Differentiation   145

Developmental Considerations   155

Conclusion   157

Sample Consensus Maps and Essential Maps   158

Review Questions   158

7. How Should We Be Using Our Created Curriculum Maps? **163**

Conducting Data-Driven Reviews   163

Investigating the Curriculum   170

Conclusion   180

Review Questions   180

**8. What Data Is Often Incorporated When Refining
Curriculum Maps?**   **181**

Additional Map Data   181

Essential and Supporting Questions   188

Conclusion   197

Review Questions   197

**9. How May Interpreting Standards Influence Our
Curriculum Design?**   **199**

Standards and Curriculum   200

Breaking Apart Standards   201

Determining Power Standards 209
Conclusion 214
Review Questions 214

10. What Should We Consider Regarding Technology? 217
Commercial Online Mapping Systems 217
Mapping System Considerations 219
Conclusion 229
Review Questions 229

11. What Should We Focus on
When Planning Our Implementation? 231
Systemic Change and Curriculum Mapping 232
Vision 232
Skills 243
Resources 245
Incentives 251
Action Plans 253
Conclusion 255
Review Task 255

12. What Roadblocks and Brick Walls
May We Encounter Along the Way? 257
Practical Advice From Practitioners 258

Glossary of Terms 283
Curriculum Mapping 283
Types of Maps 283
Map Elements 283
Alignments 285
Seven-Step Review Process 285
Common Review Focuses 287
Curriculum Mapping Intra-Organizations 287
Miscellaneous Terms 288

References 289

Index 293

List of Figures

1.1	10 Tenets of Curriculum Mapping	4
1.2	Verbal Claim Versus Data-Based Evidence	5
2.1	Four Types of Curriculum Maps	12
2.2	Levels of Detail in Curriculum Maps	13
2.3	Social Studies Essential Map Month	15
2.4	Social Studies Consensus Map Month	16
2.5	Social Studies Diary Map Month	17
3.1	Mental Model Shifts Through Systems Thinking	28
4.1	Map Type and Common Initial Map Elements	41
4.2A	Recommended Unit Name Norms	44
4.2B	German I Diary Map Month Including Unit Name Only	45
4.3	Numerals Versus Number Words	45
4.4A	Recommended Content Norms	48
4.4B	German I Diary Map Month Including Unit Name, Content, and Onset of Intra-Alignment Coding	50
4.5	Compare-and-Contrast Learning Continuum	52
4.6	State Standards Translated to Skill Expectations	55
4.7	Target Modality Aligned to Assessment Types	56
4.8	Verbs That Need Targets to Provide Clarity	57
4.9	Vague Versus Quality Content–Skill Set Intra-Alignment	59
4.10A	Recommended Skills Norms	60
4.10B	German I Diary Map Month Including Unit Name, Content, Skills, and Intra-Alignment Letter Coding—Content to Skills	63
4.11	Vague Versus Quality Assessment Names	66
4.12	Measurable Skill Verbs and Matching Assessment Types	70
4.13A	Recommended Assessment and Evaluation Norms	72
4.13B	German I Diary Map Month Including Unit Name, Content, Skills, Summative and Formative Assessments, and Letter–Number Intra-Alignment Coding	77
4.14	German I Diary Map Month Including Unit Name, Content, Skills, Summative and Formative Assessments, Standards, and Intra-Alignment Coding	83
4.15	Consensus Map and Diary Map Resources Comparison	85
4.16A	Recommended Resources Norms	86
4.16B	German I Diary Map Month Including Unit Name, Content, Skills, Summative and Formative Assessments, Standards, Resources, and Intra-Alignment Coding	88

4.17	Non-Normed Diary Map Excerpts	90
4.18	Quality Written Map Sample Month	92
4.19	Moving Toward Writing a Quality Map Sample Month	93
4.20	Laundry List Map Sample Month	94
4.21	Intermediate Science Map Month Before Revision	95
4.22	Intermediate Science Map Month After Revision	96
5.1	Diary Map and Projected Map Differentiation	110
5.2	Diary Map Element Implementation Timeline	115
5.3	Primary Mathematics Projected/Diary Map Month	121
5.4	Primary Reading Projected/Diary Map Month	122
5.5	Intermediate Science Projected/Diary Map Month	123
5.6	Middle School Physical Education Projected/Diary Map Month	124
5.7	Middle School Computer Keyboarding and Processing I Projected/Diary Map Month	126
5.8	High School Visual and Performing Arts: Semester 2 Projected/Diary Map Month	128
6.1	High School Communication Arts Consensus Map Month—Year One	148
6.2	High School Communication Arts Consensus Map Month—Year Two	149
6.3	Relationship of Operational and Planned Learning Evidence	150
6.4	Pinnacle Peak School District and Solarium School District Configurations	153
6.5	Articulation Review Sample Focuses	156
6.6	Overlapping Vertical Team Configurations	157
6.7	Environmental Science Essential Map Month	159
6.8	Environmental Science Consensus Map Month	160
6.9	Grade 6 Library Science Essential Map Month	161
6.10	Grade 6 Library Science Consensus Map Month	162
7.1	Five Review Meeting Principles	164
7.2	Seven-Step Review Process	166
7.3	Content Listings: Repetitions or Meaningful Spiral	171
7.4	Grade 6 Mathematics Test Item	175
7.5	Grade 7 Process Vocabulary Terms	177
7.6	Grade 7 Language Arts Diary Map Month	179
8.1	Kindergarten Mathematics Diary Map Month	183
8.2	Prekindergarten Thematic Unit Diary Map Month	185
8.3	High School Counselor Diary Map Month	189
8.4	Essential Question and Spiraled Science Supporting Questions	192
8.5	Life Science Unit Diary Map Month	194
8.6	U.S. History Unit Diary Map Month (Five-Week Unit)	195
8.7	What Type of Question?	198
9.1	Standard Statement	201
9.2	Breaking Apart Standard Statement Coding	205
9.3	Growth: Plants Unit of Study	209
10.1	Commercial Mapping System Contacts	218
10.2	Mapping System Capabilities	220

10.3   Mapping System Questions   221
10.4   Learning Organization Support Questions   226
11.1   Potential Prologue Timeline   239
11.2   Curriculum Mapping Coordinator's Projected Map Month   242
11.3   Elementary Literacy School Improvement Plan Consensus
        Map—First Grading Period   246
11.4   Elementary Principal Professional Development Diary
        Map Month   248

Foreword

The group of teachers from southern California was huddled around Janet, sitting cross-legged outside on the grass intently listening to her every word. She was clear, warm, and steady in her choice of words as she explained the meaning of the previous workshop on curriculum mapping for them. Here was a gifted coach and a group of committed educators making meaning and determining next steps at the annual Curriculum Mapping Institute in Park City, Utah. That was the first time I met Janet Hale. The intensity, focus, and fun emerging from the group's members were a natural by-product of their discussion and the help of their guide, Janet. I took a moment to listen, and I found that I was learning, too.

Years have passed since that first meeting, and Janet continues to guide, to coach, and to translate ideas into meaningful and rigorous practice. This book is based on a myriad of Janet's experiences in both public and private districts and dioceses across the United States as she has deepened and opened up mapping to thousands of educators. Janet has added to the model that I developed and published in *Mapping the Big Picture: Integrating Curriculum and Assessment K–12* (Jacobs, 1997). When I coteach workshops with Janet, I find that she stretches and challenges my thinking while showing loyalty and collegial respect. Janet is a remarkably energetic teacher and particularly connects directly to those who are at the beginning levels of their mapping journey. That is why this book is so important and so necessary.

Curriculum mapping promotes a significant transition into 21st-century solutions to age-old problems of articulation and instruction. It is a new form of communication relying on software and the Web to foster immediate review by the individual teacher and by targeted clusters of K–12 teachers vertically and across grade levels and departments. I have often said that mapping is a coin with two sides: (1) the maps themselves, which can be viewed from a wide angle and close up, classroom to building to district, and (2) the seven-stage curriculum-mapping review process. What Janet has done is to break down both sides of the coin into highly specific steps in order to assist the novice mapper and to refine the work of the more experienced curriculum-mapping staff.

Viable education models need multiple perspectives and voices to provide practitioners with tools for purposeful adaptations to actual settings. Given how mapping asks each teacher and administrator to self-disclose operational practice and review collaboratively with colleagues, the characteristics of a specific site, a specific faculty, and specific learners are critical for success. What

I think Janet has done particularly well is to give each of you the very tools you will need to adapt to your own school setting.

She begins her book with a straightforward question: "How do we need to think, act, and meet differently?" It is an essential question for all educators to consider as they approach the challenges of shifting from dormant ways of putting together curriculum to the dynamic process that mapping instigates. Janet helps the reader see that the process will not be business as usual. Throughout the book she encourages you to stretch by considering and reflecting on each key element on a map. Practical to the core in its tone, this book gives sound advice on how to group personnel to make the best decision in mapping reviews. Janet has developed powerful and specific ideas, new and different angles to the field of curriculum mapping that deserve careful attention. Her point of view and strategies are backed up with deep and wide-ranging experience.

In the curriculum-mapping model (Jacobs 1997, 2004b), there are many components—writing quality maps, providing feedback to others, organizing your staff to begin the review process, and setting up ongoing curriculum councils and cabinets. This book will help you more deeply understand those components.

Just as in any cartography shop, the curriculum-mapping model presents a full range of different kinds of maps, with different names, that serve different purposes. Janet has expanded and elaborated on these types with a specific set of definitions for each. This is potentially a great way to facilitate communicating with others about the level of detail and intent behind each mapping document.

I find that as school faculties work with my model, a genuine epiphany occurs when they see that alignment is carried out on two levels in our maps—internal and external. We want to internally align the key elements on a map: essential questions, content, skills, and assessment. In addition, we want to externally link these elements to the overarching standards and proficiencies targeted for learners. This is a challenging and critical phase in the mapping model. One of Janet's finest contributions to the field is the step-by-step methods she provides to coach mappers through the alignment-review process.

With imagination and serious reflection, Janet has generated a detailed book with exercises, worksheets, staff development activities, and sample maps to assist any staff developer or curriculum designer. Once again, I feel like I am learning from Janet, just like those teachers clustered around her on a July workshop day.

—Heidi Hayes Jacobs

Preface

Mapping is a verb. It is active.

—Heidi Hayes Jacobs

Given the educational pressures of the 21st century, many learning organizations are turning to curriculum mapping to better serve students' ongoing curriculum and instructional needs. Simply stated, *curriculum mapping* is a calendar-based process involving a teacher-designed curriculum, collaborative inquiry, and data-driven decision making. Reasons to begin mapping are logical and to the point. Ensuring successful implementation and sustainability is not as straightforward. Curriculum mapping involves a complex process; it is not a quick-fix model. If a learning organization is dysfunctional, curriculum mapping will not be its saving grace.

Using data-based decision making and keeping students' best interests in mind are at the heart of curriculum mapping, which is symbolized by Jacobs's (2004b) concept of the *empty chair*:

> We begin the workshop or meeting by placing an empty chair in clear view of all participants. We envision the first name of an actual child who attends the school. . . . All work that day must focus on Johnny, and all comments and questions are welcomed as long as they are in his best interest. We may disagree about what is in his best interest, but we do not lose the student as our perspective. (p. 2)

Curriculum mapping is not a spectator sport. It demands teachers' ongoing preparation and active participation. There must also be continual support from administrators who have a clear understanding and insight into the intricacies of the mapping process. While there are no absolutes regarding planning and implementation steps, the information, scenarios, and map samples shared throughout this book are intended to provide the necessary clarity to put curriculum mapping into action.

A RESOURCE FOR TEACHERS AND ADMINISTRATORS

A Guide to Curriculum Mapping specifically focuses on the basics regarding various aspects of Jacobs's model that need to be addressed before implementation.

Administrators and teachers involved in the planning process, as well as teachers joining in the process upon implementation, will find this book beneficial. The information I share is based on Jacobs's ongoing work (1989, 1997, 2004b, 2006a) and my personal curriculum mapping consulting and training experiences. The applications I suggest are recommendations, not edicts.

Personal interpretation plays a role in a reader's understanding. I recommend that you do not read this book in isolation. Form a book study group, correspond with colleagues via e-mail, or meet with a fellow associate in your school or office. Each chapter concludes with review questions designed to ignite collegial conversation regarding key points.

OVERVIEW OF THE CONTENTS

While each chapter has a specific focus, you will soon discover a connectedness between the shared information. The chapters build to a crescendo that asks the reader to contemplate critical components that affect a learning organization's planning and implementation.

Chapters

Chapter 1 includes the 10 Tenets of Curriculum Mapping and provides thoughtful insight regarding how a learning organization may need to think, act, and meet differently to ensure teacher-designed curriculum and decision-making processes.

Chapter 2 defines the four types of curriculum maps and presents an overview of the key purpose for each type of map. A sample month of each map type is included to aid visual clarification.

Chapter 3 points out three critical considerations that need to be addressed before starting a mapping initiative. Mapping asks teachers to be the leaders in designing the curriculum, keeping record of the curriculum, and making ongoing data-driven decisions regarding the designed and recorded curriculum. If teachers are not used to performing such roles, a learning organization must consider how to change the current culture and climate to match what is necessary for curriculum mapping to reach sustainability.

Chapter 4 is an extensive resource for writing quality maps. It addresses in detail the wording, format, and intra-alignment norms for the most common initial map elements: content, skills, assessments, resources, and standards.

Chapter 5 provides reflection points before asking teachers to design Diary Maps or Projected Maps. Reading this chapter, along with Chapter 6, reveals that the decision-making process regarding where to begin is a multifaceted deliberation.

Chapter 6 informs readers of the purposes for creating Consensus Maps and Essential Maps. It emphasizes specific points regarding the process for designing shared-agreement, collaborative maps.

Chapter 7 offers insight into the use of Jacobs's Seven-Step Review Model (1997) to formally address problems and concerns relating to curriculum and learning environments. Common review focuses, such as identifying gaps and finding repetitions, are addressed.

Chapter 8 supports the reality that curriculum maps are never considered finished. Refining existing maps' data concerning student learning and instruction is the natural next step once teachers are comfortable with mapping the initial elements. Strategies, modifications, activities, and essential questions are among the refining elements presented in this chapter.

Chapter 9 includes two collaborative procedures: breaking apart standards and determining power standards that support the process of designing Consensus Maps and Essential Maps. Incorporating either procedure may influence the designing of planned learning expectations and outcomes.

Chapter 10 addresses the selection of a Web-based mapping system. Since most learning organizations choose to purchase a subscription to a mapping system, this chapter includes an extensive list of questions to ask prospective companies to aid in the decision-making process.

Chapter 11 concentrates on five critical components that affect successful implementation and sustainability: vision, skills, resources, incentives, and action plans. If any one component is not firmly in place, a learning organization's mapping initiative may waver or ultimately fail. I recommend reading *all* preceding chapters before reading this one because the considerations shared in this chapter are built upon information shared in the previous chapters.

Chapter 12 brings this book to a close by providing perspectives from practitioners who have personally experienced implementing a curriculum-mapping initiative. Their candor is a testament to their willingness to put into action what is shared throughout *A Guide to Curriculum Mapping*.

Glossary of Terms

This section provides a quick reference for common terms associated with curriculum mapping.

Sample Curriculum Map Months

Various chapters contain sample curriculum map *months*. Providing sample months versus entire school-year maps is intentional because, given the total number of pages permitted, it was not feasible to provide school-year long maps. Be assured that when reading a map month the visual and contextual representation provides the same key points as if reading an entire school year of months.

Curriculum maps are *live* and *interactive* when viewed in a Web-based mapping system. The sample map months in this book are static and therefore will not be able to convey the full scope of the interconnected map database you can experience when viewing maps within a mapping system.

Finally, each sample map month is visually displayed in a Microsoft Word table. Since each commercial mapping system has a slightly different configuration, using a table can generically convey the information appropriately without needing to be concerned with specifics regarding each mapping system.

Acknowledgments

I cherish the notes on napkins, ponderings on paper, and e-mail exchanges filled with don't-forget-to-mention points shared by those who believed in my dream to someday write this book. While I cannot adequately thank everyone I need to in just a few pages, please know my thankfulness lives on forever in my heart.

Professionally

- *Heidi Hayes Jacobs*—Thank you for writing the Foreword. I cherish your kind words and generosity. I admire your zeal for knowledge, learning, and globally challenging educators to reach for the unexpected. I am blessed to call you my colleague and my friend.

- *Cathy Hernandez*—As my acquisitions editor you have been so kind and, above all, so patient. Working full-time oftentimes made it difficult for me to meet deadlines. I truly appreciated your flexibility. I want to thank you for your clear direction and sound advice. Both led me to find the gems amidst the mire.

- *Sarah J. Duffy*—Being a copy editor has its challenges, especially when assisting a writer who struggled with diagramming sentences in junior high. Your assistance in making my writing clear and readable was invaluable.

- *Jenn Reese*—Thank you for shepherding my work through the publishing process, from final draft to printed book! Working with you was a pleasure, and I appreciate your tremendous expertise.

- *The Reviewers*—Your suggestions were heard and recommendations heeded. While your comments were sometimes painful, they caused me to reach deep within. I hope you someday have the opportunity to read the revised version.

- *Sylvia Flagg*—Thank you for being one of the first pairs of eyes to read my original draft and provide constructive feedback. Your insights at the beginning carried me through to the end.

- *Valerie Lyle*—When I think of you, I think of passion and persistence. Your wisdom and direction for what was working well, and what wasn't, was a godsend. Thank you for your encouraging e-mails and cards that kept me going during the most trying times.

- *Beth Beckwith*—Thank you for always being available—days, nights, and weekends—to lend me a listening ear. I am grateful for your assistance in developing the mapping system questions in Chapter 10 and proofing my technology terms throughout the chapters.

- *Karen Agnew, Janet Boyle, Steve Kovach, Alice Learn, Jennifer Pickell, Matthew Shockley, Brian Smith, Cynthia Stevenson, Kathy Tegarden, Jeanne Tribuzzi, Brandon Wiley*—Thank you for sharing your candid insights documented in Chapter 12. Your experiences as curriculum-mapping practitioners provide a wonderful context for those just starting their journey. I have learned much from each one of you and I am grateful that mapping brought us together.
- *Michael McCabe*—Your joy for the written word is contagious. I always appreciate your frankness when sharing your insights and opinions. I want to express my gratitude for encouraging me, one paragraph at a time.
- *Rachelle Cracchiollo*—Thank you for believing in me so many years ago. I appreciate the opportunities you gave me to write books, develop seminars, and train teachers across the nation and around the world.
- *Jane Snyder*—I knew that if I ever did write this book, I wanted to thank you. Your mention of two words, *curriculum mapping,* long ago when I was working with you in Ames, Iowa, has delightfully enriched my life. Thank you!

Personally

- *Ret. Colonel Norman "Dean" Schanche*—You raised your daughter to believe that learning is never ending. Thank you for buying me an encyclopedia set in an era when my schoolmates had to walk to the library to hold the world in their hands.
- *Margaret Hale*—I could never, ever have asked for a more wonderful mother-in-law. Thank you for loving me both in actions and in words. When I am on the road you feed Johnny, bring special treats for our spoiled dog children, straighten up the house, prune the plants, and wash all of my sweaters and skirts by hand. I look forward to our goodnight phone calls that let me know you love me whether I am at home or abroad.
- *The Branson Babes*—Your thoughts and prayers carried me through the entire writing process. When I had moments of self-doubt, you believed in me. Hopefully we can spend more time together now. Of course, I'll be the driver. Who wants to sit in the front seat?
- *Rondi Faretta*—Thank you for the countless incredible massages you gave me to relieve my tension and stress. Your encouraging words also touched me deeply (pun intended).
- *My Pool Buddies*—You have taught me much about love, forgiveness, and loyalty. Thank you for these life lessons.

Humorously

- *Belgian Mini Chocolate Chips*—Thank you to the culmination of innovators and inventors that led to the creation of such delightful morsels of comfort that were consumed in breads and cookies; sprinkled over ice cream; and on occasions of greatest frustration, eaten straight from the bag!

Most Important

Thank *you*, the reader, for your commitment and willingness to be a risk taker. Any time you read an educational book, who knows where the learning may lead? My hope is that you find the answers you have been searching for by reading this book. I want you to know that I pictured you in my mind as I wrote each page. Although our paths may never cross, it is my sincerest hope that the road you choose to travel, both professionally and personally, is filled with times of comfort, times of challenge, and especially times of magnificent memories.

> *Two roads diverge in the woods,*
> *And I—I took the one less traveled by,*
> *And that has made all the difference.*

—Robert Frost

PUBLISHER'S ACKNOWLEDGMENTS

Corwin Press gratefully acknowledges the contributions of the following reviewers:

Eugene Bartoo, Professor of Education
University of Tennessee, Chattanooga, TN

Rose-Marie Botting, K–5 Science Curriculum Specialist (Retired)
Broward County Schools, Fort Lauderdale, FL

Gabrielle Charest, Coordinator of Professional Development
Sequoia Union High School District, Redwood City, CA

Lorraine Gilpin, Assistant Professor of Teaching and Learning
Georgia Southern University, Statesboro, GA

Kate Glenn, Literacy Specialist
Tempe Union High School District, Tempe, AZ

Robert Kutter, Curriculum and Staff Development Specialist
Grey Eagle, MN

Victoria S. McConnell, Eighth-Grade Science Teacher
Colonel Richardson Middle School, Federalsburg, MD

John Michalski, Seventh-Grade Science Teacher
East Hanover Middle School, East Hanover, NJ

Carol Mickley, Sixth-Grade Teacher
Southern Lehigh Middle School, Center Valley, PA

Denise Mullen, Social Studies Department Chair
James Monroe Middle School, Albuquerque, NM

About the Author

 **Janet A. Hale** is an educational consultant and trainer who specializes in curriculum mapping and travels extensively to work with rural, urban, and inner-city learning organizations. She enjoys assisting newcomers to the curriculum-mapping model, supporting implementation procedures, aiding struggling initiatives, and advising those ready for advanced mapping. Her experiences as an elementary, middle, and high school teacher, combined with a master's degree in leadership with an emphasis in curriculum, are an asset when helping teachers and administrators just starting or already engaged in the mapping process.

Since 1988 Janet has developed a variety of national educational seminars and trainings. She has written an assortment of educational supplementary materials and has presented in conferences sponsored by the Association of Supervision and Curriculum Development, the International Reading Association, and the Association of Christian Schools International.

Janet resides in Tucson, Arizona, where she enjoys bird, reptile, and wild animal watching with her husband, Johnny, and their four-legged Schnauzer children. She can be contacted via e-mail at teachtucson@aol.com or by phone at 520-241-8797. You may also enjoy visiting her Web site, www.CurriculumMapping101.com.

How Do We Need to Think, Act, and Meet Differently?

Times change, and we change with them too.
—Owen's Epigrammata

Curriculum mapping causes systemic change within a learning organization. Change in an organization's actions affects its individual members. Conversely, change in the individual member's actions affects the whole. Curriculum mapping perceives all members of a learning organization as leaders. The members closest to the students are the teachers. Curriculum mapping empowers teachers, with administrative support, to be the curriculum leaders. As leaders they do not look to others to solve problems; instead they look to one another to confront and solve problems as a team (Heifetz 1994).

THINKING DIFFERENTLY: PLANNED VERSUS OPERATIONAL CURRICULUM

Substantial amounts of time, money, and energy are spent to meet federal, state, and local curriculum mandates and directives. Guidelines, scope and sequences, frameworks, course descriptions, and measurement criteria are often developed to aid in defining students' planned-learning expectations.

While planning learning is needed and valid, a predicament occurs when data comparison begins. When assessment results and other forms of data can only be compared to planned-learning documentation, accuracy in accessing problems or solutions gives way to speculation or conjecture. If teachers are asked to evaluate why students underperformed on a state assessment, and there is no recorded documentation by each teacher of what was actually learned, the conclusions drawn will lack precision.

Two Perspectives

Curriculum mapping views curriculum from two perspectives. The first is the *planned learning* curriculum. Planned learning may or may not actually become reality. Therefore, a second view is necessary. The *operational* curriculum represents learning that truly happened.

A teacher's operational curriculum documentation is called a *Diary Map* (Jacobs 1997). Planned learning curriculum is documented using a variety of map types, each with a unique purpose: (a) an individual teacher's *Projected Map*, (b) a school site team's *Consensus Map*, or (c) a districtwide *Essential Map*. A learning organization's curriculum maps are accessed by using a Web-based mapping system. Each teacher and administrator has a personal log-in name and a password. Some systems provide guest passes that allow students, parents, and the community to view planned learning maps.

Jacobs (2006a) acknowledges that "curriculum mapping is formal work" (p. 115). Designing curriculum maps, and conducting formal mapping reviews (addressed in Chapter 7), takes a deep commitment of time and effort. If planning and implementation are well thought out, the endeavor will be a successful one. Jacobs (2004b) defines a mapping initiative's success as having "two specific outcomes: measurable improvement in student performance in the targeted areas, and the institutionalization of mapping as a process for ongoing curriculum and assessment review" (p. 2).

A Student's Journey

According to Marzano (2003), to master every discipline's state standards, a student's K–12 educational journey would take 23 academic school years. What he proved statistically, teachers know in reality. Teachers have to make decisions about what learning to omit. Unless teachers are diary mapping, a learning organization has no documentation of what each teacher has excluded.

Teachers have various reasons for omitting specific learning. What one teacher values, another may not. What one is comfortable teaching, another is not. What one deems necessary to study in depth, another does not. Environmental factors may also play a role in omission. An unexpected weather front that closes down a district for three weeks or the discovery of asbestos in a school's ceilings that causes classes to be moved to another campus for two months will affect the outcomes of planned learning expectations.

While not intended to do so, a curriculum based solely on planned learning documentation may end up providing students with Swiss-cheese educations. Parents of triplets ask that Johnny, Jane, and Julissa be separated upon entering Kindergarten. If there is no collaborative, teacher-designed planned learning and no documentation of each teacher's operational learning, there is a chance that the triplets will experience three different K–12 curricula. This is not to say that curriculum mapping demands the triplets' teachers teach the same exact learning at the same exact time in the same exact way. It simply points out that students need teachers to document both the collaboratively planned learning and each individual teacher's operational learning to best serve students and provide an equitable education for all.

10 Tenets of Curriculum Mapping

In any field of study, curriculum mapping included, there are principles that drive perception, communication, and how business is conducted. These principles, or tenets, provide consistency and flexibility in a learning organization's actions (see Figure 1.1).

These tenets are paramount to how a learning organization may need to think differently than it has in the past. When a learning organization begins to think differently, it begins to act differently.

ACTING DIFFERENTLY: VERIFICATION VERSUS SPECULATION

Curriculum mapping is not meant to be an action that teachers simply go and do. This complex initiative cannot be grasped simply by attending an inservice or two. It takes instruction, exploration, experience, and adequate time before a learning organization's members begin to act differently using documentation of what actually happened as well as what is planned.

Evidence Versus Claim

To impact improved student learning, teachers and administrators must commit to using data-driven evidence rather than verbal claims. Diary Maps provide the evidence of each teacher's operational learning. Figure 1.2 provides three examples of how this type of curriculum map can significantly impact curriculum decision making.

Data-Driven Collaborations and Decision Making

Curriculum maps are a form of data-based evidence that influences curricular dialogue and decision making. The sample on page 6 is just one example of how teachers may rethink or redesign a curriculum based on map evidence rather than on speculation.

Figure 1.1   10 Tenets of Curriculum Mapping

1. Curriculum mapping is a multifaceted, ongoing process designed to improve student learning.

2. All curricular decisions are data driven and in the students' best interest.

3. Curriculum maps represent both the planned and the operational learning.

4. Curriculum maps are created and accessed using 21st-century technology.

5. Teachers are leaders in curriculum design and curricular decision-making processes.

6. Administrators encourage and support teacher-leader environments.

7. Curriculum reviews are conducted on an ongoing and regular basis.

8. Collaborative inquiry and dialogue are based on curriculum maps and other data sources.

9. Action plans aid in designing, revising, and refining maps.

10. Curriculum-mapping intra-organizations facilitate sustainability.

Figure 1.2   Verbal Claim Versus Data-Based Evidence

Verbal Claim No Diary Maps	**Data-Based Evidence** With Diary Maps
We always teach biomes around this time of year. Why change now? It doesn't really matter anyway as long as the students learn it sometime during the year.	From the evidence found by reviewing two years of Diary Maps, each one of us teaches biomes at various times starting in January and ending in May. The new state science assessment will be given during the first week of April. The state testing blueprint shows that 45% of the test will be based on environmental science. We need to reach an agreement on which quarter or month we will focus on biomes. Then our next step will be to determine what the key learning must be in that unit.
I really enjoy teaching *Where the Red Fern Grows*. It was my favorite book when I was in sixth grade. There is a really good movie I like to show my students at the end of the unit. They have to decide how the movie producer and director modified the book's story line.	Even though I enjoy teaching *Where the Red Fern Grows*, based on our reading-resources mapping review, the data reveals that this book is being used as a reading text in Grades 6, 7, and 8. After looking at the state standards that address fictional text, and the fact that the Grade 8 state assessment uses mostly fictional excerpts, I have to admit that my teammates and I may need to stop using *Where the Red Fern Grows* in sixth grade as one of our core texts. I have been thinking that it actually fits best in seventh grade. . . . If we do decide that this book will no longer be part of sixth-grade learning, I have some great lessons, activities, and a final project for the grade that ends up using it.
Students don't like to solve linear equations. They never listen to me when I explain how to solve them. They think math is a boring subject.	By reviewing the anonymous student survey completed by 105 of our middle school students, I found an interesting discrepancy. Question 3 asked: *Which subject do you believe is the most important to learn in school to be successful as an adult?* Seventy-five percent of the students selected mathematics. Question 9 asked: *Which subject is your least favorite in school?* Ninety percent of the students responded mathematics. This is both profound and alarming! It's not that they are not interested in the subject; they obviously hold mathematics in high regard. We need to review our Diary Maps to see when and to what depth we are teaching critical concepts. Then we need to zoom in and discuss our presentation styles. The way we are teaching may be a part of what I thought was an apathy issue until I read the survey results.

A Secondary Experience

A high school conducted a mapping review wherein teachers were grouped across grade levels and disciplines. One review team consisted of teachers from both the mathematics and the science departments.

A curriculum revelation occurred for one science teacher involved in the review. While reading his team's Diary Maps before attending a small-group meeting, he discovered a course prerequisite anomaly. He taught an advanced placement (AP) science course. The Algebra I course had always been the prerequisite. Upon reading the maps he discovered that the content and skills learned in Algebra I are not sufficient. For years he'd been thinking that he was simply reteaching what students had forgotten. He now had evidence to the contrary. The students actually did not learn what was needed until Algebra II.

He shared his discovery with his small-group review team. Their conversation centered on the map-data evidence. The two departments met as a large group and eventually came to agreement on making an official change to the AP science course's prerequisite requirements. Starting with the following school year, Algebra I and Algebra II would be the prerequisite courses.

This transformation instantly affected the science teacher's class schedule because he had been teaching two AP science course periods. The science department collaboratively determined an appropriate replacement course.

When a learning organization starts to think differently, it will begin to act differently. To act differently, teachers must begin to meet differently.

MEETING DIFFERENTLY: A COLLEGIAL FORUM

A *forum* is defined as a public meeting place involving discussion among experts. Teachers are experts; they must be provided ample time and opportunities to discuss their questions of public interest—the students. Unfortunately, many schools and districts are constructed, both in physical layout and in time management, in such a way that meeting in horizontal (same grade level), vertical (series of grade levels), like (same discipline), or mixed (two or more disciplines) configurations on a regular basis is nonexistent or so infrequent that the meetings are ineffective. In fact, many learning organizations still function similarly to how schools and districts were designed to function in the 1890s (Jacobs 2006b).

For curriculum mapping to be an effective tool, meeting often with a preplanned focus and advanced preparation is imperative. While meeting face-to-face is important, if the ability to do so across grade levels or for mixed disciplines is not possible at the onset of a mapping initiative, the use of 21st-century technology, including an online mapping system, is indispensable.

Web-Based Mapping

Curriculum mapping advocates the use of a Web-based mapping system because it expedites curricular design and alignment (Gough 2003; Jacobs 2003a, 2003b, 2004a; Kallick and Wilson 2004; Udelhofen 2005). A mapping system provides instant access to the entire learning organization's curriculum with the click of a mouse. Without having to travel to a particular campus to meet in person, a review team can enter the mapping system and instantaneously view what the planned or operational curriculum is on any campus.

A mapping system's current and archived curriculum maps provide users with an interrelational database. Individual and collaborative map reviews are often conducted using a system's search and report features. What previously may have taken hours to scan and search for by having to read a series of paper-document maps manually now literally takes seconds within a mapping system. A variety of comparison reports allow teachers to access map data from different school years, grade levels, and disciplines that significantly aid collaborations and decision making.

Throughout the remaining chapters, I refer to the necessity of using a mapping system to support the mapping process. Considerations regarding the purchase of a commercial system, or what must be considered for constructing a self-generated one, are addressed in Chapter 10.

Advanced Preparation

If a learning organization conducts rote meetings, oftentimes the wrong people are meeting at the wrong times for the wrong reasons (Jacobs 2006b). As a guest at many meetings, I have often observed that 5 to 10 minutes are lost while everyone gets settled. Another 5 to 10 minutes vanish while announcements that could be made via e-mail are shared. When the meeting finally turns to data review, teachers scramble to make sense of the presented data because they were not provided an opportunity to review the information prior to meeting. This approach is reactive and counterproductive (Costa and Kallick 2000).

Curriculum mapping asks for advanced personal preparation. This is a critical phase, or step, in the seven-step review process (Jacobs 1997). While Chapter 7 addresses each step in depth, it is important to note here that curriculum mapping asks teachers and administrators to individually review pre-selected data before meeting. Based on a predetermined focus, all in attendance will have taken personal notes as part of the preparation process (Jacobs 1997). When this reflective phase is honored, the quality of conversation and decisions made is deeper and more dynamic.

Working Collegially

Beyond teachers making decisions based on map evidence and advance preparation, curriculum mapping also requires full disclosure (Jacobs 2006b). Meeting differently involves a teacher's willingness to openly reveal and discuss details pertaining to personal learning environments, including (a) what is being learned, (b) when it is learned, (c) how learning is measured, and (d) how learning is taught. While many teachers are willing to do so with ease, it has been my experience that full disclosure is difficult for some. How these teachers display their discomfort varies depending on the past and current culture and climate within the learning organization. Barth (2006) addresses these manifestations metaphorically as the "elephants in the room [that takes on] the various forms of relationships among adults within the schoolhouse" (pp. 9–10). Barth categorizes teachers' work-related behaviors into four relationships:

- *Parallel play* relationships exist when teachers function in close proximity but do not share what they are doing with one another and have no desire to do so.
- *Adversarial* relationships happen when teachers purposefully withhold beneficial information from one another regardless of the information's ability to aid student progress. These teachers will do whatever is necessary to not participate.
- *Congenial* relationships appear friendly on the surface. They interact in positive ways as long as it remains superficial. These teachers do not like to be placed in any professional situation that causes them to have to critically examine what they do or why they choose to do it.
- *Collegial* relationships represent teachers who actively work together to advance one another's educational performance and students' success. They perceive each other as colleagues who collectively strive for better solutions and best practices. They are active learners. These teachers read, attend, discuss, and deliberate. They do not rest on past or present laurels. They are willing to sacrifice and learn anew if it aids in improving their students' learning.

Of course, the ultimate desire is for all members of a learning organization to be involved in collegial relationships. But the reality is that a learning organization may experience reluctance or resistance from teachers who function within the remaining types of relationships. If teachers are not used to functioning in collegial relationships and fully disclosing their curricula and practices, meeting differently may initially pose a problem. It is critical at the preplanning and execution phases to consider what needs to take place in order to encourage teachers to be collegial collaborators.

CONCLUSION

Curriculum mapping is an ongoing process that asks teachers and administrators to think, act, and meet differently to improve their students' learning. Teachers are responsible, with administrative support, for (a) designing and documenting both the planned and the operational learning using a Web-based mapping system; (b) making collegial curriculum decisions based on evidence rather than claim; (c) meeting in horizontal, vertical, and mixed- and like-discipline configurations to better understand student learning needs;

(d) preparing in advance by reviewing maps and other databases before meeting; and (e) fully disclosing one's learning curriculum and practices as part of the mapping process.

For some, this set of requirements may cause drastic changes in the way curriculum documentation and decision making currently takes place in a learning organization. For others, it may mean only minor adjustments. For many, it will lay somewhere in between.

REVIEW QUESTIONS

Based on your learning organization's past and present culture and climate, discuss your answers to the following questions with a partner or in a small group.

1. What are your thoughts or reactions to the 10 Tenets of Curriculum Mapping? What tenets are you most intrigued by? Concerned with? Why?

2. Has your learning organization historically made curriculum decisions based only on planned-learning documents? If yes, why do you think so? If no, are both the current and archived operational curriculum documentation accessible to all?

3. Has your learning organization historically designed or selected curricula based on administrative decision making? If yes, what do you perceive will need to change? How will the changes guarantee and encourage all teachers to become curriculum designers?

4. If you had to explain what is meant by *curriculum mapping is a process*, what would you emphasize as critical to the process given how your school and/or district currently functions?

5. Does your learning organization function most often based on data-based evidence or verbal claim? If it depends on the situation, what variables seem to affect the situation?

6. Does your school or district set agendas for curriculum meetings ahead of time that include a predetermined focus or purpose? Do those in attendance review the preselected data individually and make personal notes prior to meeting?

7. What is the collaborative rapport in your grade level or department, school, and/or district? Do teachers function most often in parallel play, adversarial, congenial, or collegial relationships? Does it depend on who is involved in the meeting dynamics? What do you perceive needs to change to encourage teachers to consistently function in collegial relationships regardless of group dynamics?

2

What Are the Four Types of Curriculum Maps?

Knowledge is of two kinds. We know a subject ourselves,
or we know where we can find information.

—Samuel Johnson

*C*urriculum, in Latin, means a course or path run in small steps. *Curriculum map* is a generic term used to refer to a document that represents a small step in a student's learning path. Since a student's path involves numerous teachers over a journey of 13+ years, it is advantageous when teachers have instant access to the maps that represent each small step.

Curriculum maps are never intended to be regarded as static documents. They are the living, breathing database of a learning organization's current and past curricular history that serve as a catalyst for ongoing curriculum dialogue and decision making (Jacobs 2004b).

While coordinators and administrators often map professional development and administrative roles, the explanations in all chapters preceding Chapter 10 focus on teachers mapping student learning. Regardless of whether a map represents administration, professional development, or student learning, it can be classified as a specific type of map.

FOUR TYPES OF CURRICULUM MAPS

There are four types of curriculum maps. As mentioned previously, a *Diary Map* represents the students' operational curriculum; it is the only type of map that

11

documents actual learning. Although there is some variation in the names used for each of the remaining three types of maps by the mapping system companies, the common terms used are *Projected Map, Consensus Map,* and *Essential Map.* These curriculum maps represent students' planned learning. Figure 2.1 provides a brief overview of each map type and its purpose.

Figure 2.1 Four Types of Curriculum Maps

Type of Map	Level of Map	Recording Period	Recording Person(s)	Purpose of Map
Diary Map	School site	Monthly, after instruction	Individual teacher	A teacher independently records or updates map elements that have actually been a part of students' learning based on national, state, local, or self-generated standards.
Projected Map	School site	Monthly, before instruction	Individual teacher	A teacher independently records or updates map elements that represent students' planned learning based on national, state, local, or self-generated standards.
Consensus Map	School site	Monthly or by grading periods, before instruction	Two or more teachers by grade level, department, or cross-disciplinary or interdisciplinary team	Teachers collaboratively reach agreement concerning compulsory planned learning expectations for a given discipline or course based on national, state, district, or self-generated standards.
Essential Map	Districtwide	Monthly or by grading periods, before instruction	Task force representing all schools and consisting of both teachers and administrators	A task force collaboratively reaches agreement regarding mandatory planned learning expectations for a given course or series of courses based on national, state, district, or self-generated standards.

When traveling, road maps become more specific the closer you get to the main destination. The main destination in curriculum mapping is the empty chair—the students in a particular classroom and course of study (Jacobs 2004b). In curriculum mapping, the concept of *more specific* translates to *more detailed* data within each type of map. An Essential Map has the least amount of detail, whereas the Projected Map and the Diary Map have the most detail representing monthly learning. A teacher's daily lesson plans contain the greatest amount of information or level of detail (see Figure 2.2).

Figure 2.2   Levels of Detail in Curriculum Maps

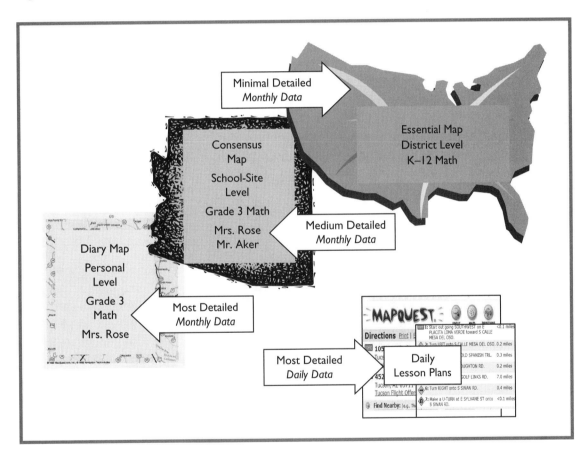

A Visual Comparison

Figures 2.3 to 2.5 provide a visual snapshot of one month of learning at three different map levels. Notice that the data included in the Essential Map remains in the Consensus Map and the Diary Map. With each level, greater detail regarding learning expectations is included.

Essential Map

This planned learning map documents required learning throughout a learning organization. There are two imperatives when implementing this type of map:

- An Essential Map is never meant to be designed exclusively by administration. A curriculum-mapping tenet states that teachers are involved in designing the curriculum. If a teacher-based task force is not involved in the design of an Essential Map, there will be a high probability of little or no teacher buy-in since they may feel neither trusted as leaders nor honored as curriculum designers.
- An Essential Map is never meant to contain excessive detail. This takes away from the autonomy of a school site or an individual teacher. This map is not intended to be a scripted day-by-day or week-by-week pseudo pacing guide or record of lesson plans. When correctly designed, an Essential Map informs schools of the obligatory learning determined to have the greatest impact on ensuring student learning success.

When an Essential Map is published within a selected mapping system and is ready for implementation, a school-site teacher team replicates the appropriate grade level or course as a Consensus Map, using the Essential Map's data as the baseline for student learning, and includes additional planned learning, as represented in Figure 2.4.

Consensus Map

The term *consensus* indicates collective agreement. For this type of map, curriculum agreement takes place within a particular school site. For example, if a district has four elementary schools, it would have one Essential Map and four Consensus Maps.

A Consensus Map can be designed by teachers with or without other types of maps in existence. If an Essential Map exists, it serves as the foundation for a school site's Consensus Map. If no Essential Map exists, but Diary Maps do, teachers come to agreement on planned learning by reviewing the existing Diary Maps and revisiting the appropriate standards to design the Consensus Map. If no maps exist, a teacher team may design a Consensus Map by (a) reviewing current or past school- or district-generated curriculum documents that can be adapted to a map element structure and/or (b) enlisting the *breaking apart standards* procedure, which is explained in Chapter 9.

When Consensus Maps are designed without incorporating data from Essential Maps, they are not considered complete when first drafted. A critical step in the design process is to conduct vertical comparison reviews across grade levels or courses. Grade-level or course-specific teams review the drafted Consensus Maps to ensure no gaps, repetitions, or absences are present in the planned learning. Once the Consensus Maps are published and in use, teachers can still expect times of revision and refinement. Ongoing adjustments often

(Text continues on page 19)

Figure 2.3   Social Studies Essential Map Month

Month	Content	Skills	Assessment	Standards
September	*(First Quarter)* A. U.S. Geography: 5 Themes Resources --Chapter 1 B. U.S. Regions: Division Formation Resources --Chapter 2	A. Explain each theme's attributes: location, place, human-environmental interactions, movement, regions B. Identify each region's divisions: *Region 1 (Northeast)* Division 1 (New England) Division 2 (Middle Atlantic) *Region 2 (Midwest)* Division 3 (East North Central) Division 4 (West North Central) *Region 3 (South)* Division 5 (South Atlantic) Division 6 (East South Central) Division 7 (West South Central) *Region 4 (West)* Division 8 (Mountain) Division 9 (Pacific)		A. G5.2.2 (I) B. G6.3.2 (I) G5.2.2 (I)

Figure 2.4 Social Studies Consensus Map Month

Month	Content	Skills	Assessment	Standards
September	**THIS IS YOUR LAND, THIS IS MY LAND** A. U.S. Geography: 5 Themes Resources --Chapter 1 --U.S. Maps/Various Types *Primary Source Kit* B. U.S. Regions: Division Formation Resources --Chapter 2 --U.S. Maps/Various Types *Primary Source Kit*	A1. Explain orally and in writing each theme's attributes: location (relative, absolute), place (human, physical), human–environmental interactions (adapt, modify, depend), movement (people, goods, ideas), regions (formal, functional, perceptional) A. Identify visually and in writing 5 major land forms: mountain, plateau, plain, peninsula, valley A. Identify visually and in writing 3 major water forms: ocean, lake, river B1. Identify visually and in writing each region's divisions: *Region 1 (Northeast)* Division 1 (New England) Division 2 (Middle Atlantic) *Region 2 (Midwest)* Division 3 (East North Central) Division 4 (West North Central) *Region 3 (South)* Division 5 (South Atlantic) Division 6 (East South Central) Division 7 (West South Central) *Region 4 (West)* Division 8 (Mountain) Division 9 (Pacific) B. Evaluate visually and in writing why divisions are geographically formed as they currently are based on 5 themes	A1. SAME 5 Short-Answer Attributes Test (Evaluation: Rubric) A1. COMMON 2-Minute Oration (Evaluation: Rubric/Peer Commentaries) B1. SAME 20-Item U.S. Division Identification Map Quiz	A. G5.2.2 (I) G4.3.1 (D) G4.3.2 (D) ELA5.7.1(R) B. G6.3.2 (I) G5.2.2 (I)

Figure 2.5   Social Studies Diary Map Month

Month	Content	Skills	Assessment	Standards
September	**THIS IS YOUR LAND, THIS IS MY LAND** *EQ: How does locality change perception?* *SQ: How do the geography themes relate to environmental planning?* A. U.S. Geography: 5 Themes Resources --Chapter 1, pp. 21–33 --U.S. Maps/Various Types *Primary Source Kit* --*From The Land's Eye* Video B. U.S. Regions: Division Formation Resources --Chapter 2, pp. 35–45 --U.S. Maps/Various Types *Primary Source Kit*	A1. Explain orally and in writing each theme's attributes: location (relative, absolute), place (human, physical), human-environmental interactions (adapt, modify, depend), movement (people, goods, ideas), regions (formal, functional, perceptional) A2. Identify visually and in writing 5 major land forms: mountain, plateau, plain, peninsula, valley A3. Identify visually and in writing 3 major water forms: ocean, lake, river B1. Identify visually and in writing each region's divisions: Region 1 *(Northeast)* Division 1 (New England) Division 2 (Middle Atlantic) Region 2 *(Midwest)* Division 3 (East North Central) Division 4 (West North Central)	A1–C2. FOR Essential Question Essay (Evaluation: Peer Review/ Rubric) A1. SAME 5 Short-Answer Attributes Test (Evaluation: Rubric) A1. COMMON 2-Minute Oration (Evaluation: Rubric/Peer Commentaries) A2–A3. 20-Item Identification Quiz B1. SAME 20-Item U.S. Division Identification Map Quiz B2. Regions Poster Presentation (Evaluation: Peer Review/Rubric)	A. G5.2.2 (I) G4.3.1 (D) G4.3.2 (D) ELA5.7.1(R) ELA4.3.1(R) B. G6.3.2 (I) G5.2.2 (I)

17

Figure 2.5 (Continued)

Month	Content	Skills	Assessment	Standards
	--Teacher-Created Regions Treasure Hunt PowerPoint/ Handout --http://www.enchantedlearning .com/usa/statesbw/regions.shtml (*Regions Lesson Plans*)	*Region 3 (South)* Division 5 (South Atlantic) Division 6 (East South Central) Division 7 (West South Central) *Region 4 (West)* Division 8 (Mountain) Division 9 (Pacific) B2. Evaluate visually and in writing why divisions are geographically formed as they currently are based on 5 themes		
	C. U.S. Regions: Cultural Resources --Teacher-Created Regions Handout --Small-Group Internet Research/Note Taking	C1. Identify visually and in writing 9 major cultural regions: New England, Mid-Atlantic States, South, Midwest, Southwest, Rocky Mountains, Pacific Northwest, West, Hawaii, Alaska, based on each region's states C2. Differentiate in writing each region's distinctive foods, traditions, recreation	C1. 10-Item Identification Test C2. Region Comparison Essay (Evaluation: Rubric)	C. G6.3.4 (I) ELA4.3.1(R)

take place during the first few years of publication, especially when Essential Maps are later published because this may affect a particular school site's established Consensus Maps.

Projected Map and Diary Map

These two map types are in fact the *same map* in that they provide data regarding an individual teacher's learning environment. They are differentiated simply by real time (i.e., calendar months) and purpose.

Let's say it is February. Mrs. Murnighan's Grade 5 mathematics curriculum map includes detailed data for each month of the school year. The data for September through January is referred to as her Diary Map. Mrs. Murnighan has reviewed the data each month and has made certain that the information included accurately reflects the operational learning for the current school year up to January. The detailed data for the current month through June is referred to as her Projected Map since these months currently provide evidence of the planned learning for the remaining months of the school year.

If a teacher designs a personal map without the existence of other types of maps, the teacher will base student learning on grade-level or course-appropriate national, state, or local standards and, if applicable, established curriculum guidelines. If a Consensus Map exists, a teacher's personal map will be based on the collaborative map's data, as represented in Figure 2.5.

Curriculum Maps Versus Lesson Plans

Now that we are writing maps, do we still have to write lesson plans? Teachers often ask me this question when they are initially learning how to write a curriculum map. Remember, maps are recorded by months, not days. A curriculum map is focused on recording the *what*, *when*, and if desired, a brief overview of the significant *how*s. Curriculum maps are not meant to replace lesson plans; maps are meant to inform a learning organization about the big picture of student learning (Jacobs 1997). Lesson plans include the intimate details regarding how a teacher specifically and strategically plans to have students experience the learning. Curriculum maps are learning summaries.

I do not know of a school or district that no longer requires teachers to write lesson plans after a mapping initiative begins. I have seen changes, though, in teacher requirements. A few examples include (a) tenured teachers not having to turn in weekly lesson plans, but still needing to have their lesson plans available for informal administrative review or substitute-teacher access, while nontenured or probationary teachers still have to officially turn in their lesson plans; (b) when recording or revising a Diary Map, each teacher including three or four lesson plans that truly enhance the students' learning process; and (c) teacher teams creating collaborative lesson plans and observing one another teaching the lessons to provide peer coaching opportunities.

CURRICULUM MAP ELEMENTS: AN OVERVIEW

The number of elements included in a curriculum map varies depending on factors such as (a) the type of map; (b) the length of time teachers have been mapping; (c) collaborative decision making regarding revisions or refinements to existing maps; and (d) past, present, and future curriculum initiatives.

Common Initial Map Elements

When introduced to the concepts of curriculum mapping and designing curriculum maps, teachers commonly begin by recording the following initial elements:

- **Content:** What students must *know*
- **Skills:** What students must *do* in relation to the knowing
- **Assessments:** *Products or performances* that measure the knowing and doing
- **Evaluations:** *Single or multiple criteria* that appraise students' abilities regarding a given assessment or series of assessments
- **Standards:** *Proficiency targets* that serve as a framework for the knowing and doing
- **Resources:** *Textbooks, materials,* and *references* that aid in the instruction of the knowing and doing
- **Intra-Alignment:** While not a literal element (i.e., does not have a specific column or field within a mapping system's recording template), this is a critical *visual component* that provides coherency between the included elements

Common Additional Map Elements

The following are the most common elements that may be integrated into curriculum maps after teachers have become comfortable with mapping the initial elements:

- **Strategies:** *Specific criteria* that enable students to improve learning
- **Modifications/accommodations:** Content, skill, or assessment *adjustments* made for general education students or special needs students
- **Activities:** *Experiences* or *lessons* that lead students toward independent mastery of learning expectations
- **Essential questions:** *Conceptual learning* questions that can be *generalized* beyond specific learning topics
- **Supporting questions:** *Conceptual learning* questions that address a *specific topic* focus

Both the common initial and additional elements are not meant to be perceived as a sequential requirement. If a school has had professional training in designing units of study based on essential questions and supporting questions and is currently using these questions in instruction and assessment, they should be included when the teachers initially begin to write maps. The point that needs to be stressed here is that teachers experience a learning curve when being trained regarding the wording, format, and intra-alignment of the map elements. At the onset of a mapping initiative, less is more.

Intra-aligned content, skills, assessments, and standards are the elemental cornerstones (Jacobs 1997). Chapter 4 comprehensively explains these common initial elements as well as the inclusion of evaluations and resources. Chapter 8 addresses refining map data by including one or more of the additional elements.

One Discipline at a Time

Along with not overloading the number of map elements teachers are initially required to map, make sure to not overload teachers with the number of disciplines or courses to map when initially implementing the mapping process. For the first year, if teachers are asked to create a Projected Map or a Diary Map, it is recommended that each teacher maps one grade-level discipline (elementary), one grade-level or course period (junior high school/middle school/high school), one grade-level discipline or course (specialists), or one pull-out period or one or two specific students (special education) to gain personal confidence in writing and recording the map elements.

Districtwide Discipline Focus

If curriculum mapping is a districtwide initiative, it is recommended that one discipline be selected as the first districtwide focus. The simplest discipline to systemically map is mathematics due to its somewhat natural learning progression. The most difficult to systemically map is language arts. The multifaceted composite of reading, writing, listening, and speaking makes agreement on how to map this discipline complex.

The selection of a districtwide discipline focus does not mean that only those teaching the discipline participate in the mapping process. Everyone who works directly with students needs to learn to map. For environments such as special education, counseling, or support services, what is mapped may vary and is best determined once all teachers and support staff have learned how to write a quality map that includes the common initial elements. Everyone needs to personally internalize (a) the mapping procedures, (b) how to write a quality map, (c) how to record the map elements within a mapping system, and (d) how to use a mapping system's data-retrieval features to drive curriculum decision making. All disciplines will eventually have a turn at being a districtwide focus.

Selecting an initial districtwide discipline to begin the process of ensuring a spiraled curriculum void of gaps, repetitions, and absences will have design implications. For example, while elementary teachers are only mapping mathematics, at the middle school and high school levels, some teachers are mapping mathematics while others are mapping various disciplines. Therefore, it may take four to five years to vertically map and align the collective disciplines of mathematics, science, social studies, and language arts since the elementary teachers are at a slight disadvantage. To expedite the vertical-articulation process, once teachers have internalized how to design and write maps, some larger learning organizations have elementary teachers divide up the yet-to-be-mapped disciplines and each grade level designs Consensus Maps first before recording Projected Maps or Diary Maps for the additional disciplines.

Specialists including art, music, physical education, library science, technology, and trade professions should start learning how to write a quality map by mapping one grade level or course at the onset of a mapping initiative. At some point the specialist teachers will need to discuss designing collaborative planned learning maps. For example, if a learning organization is small and has one art teacher in the elementary school, one in the middle school, and one in the high school, these three teachers can work together to design Consensus Maps for each school site. If a learning organization is large and there are two art teachers in each of four elementary schools, two art teachers in each of two middle schools, and three art teachers in one high school, these fifteen teachers may collaboratively design K–12 Essential Maps that include the mandatory learning regardless of school site. Each school site's art teachers will then use the appropriate Essential Map data as the foundation for the school-specific Consensus Maps.

Special Education

The decision about whether to have teachers with small or large case loads of Individualized Education Plan (IEP) students write maps in the initial phase of a curriculum-mapping initiative is one that each learning organization will have to make on its own. Since they will be a part of collaborative teams that will be using the maps, it is important for special education teachers to be a part of the initial learning process to become familiar with (a) the purposes of mapping; (b) the map types and how-tos for mapping the elements, (c) usage of the selected mapping system, and (d) participation in mapping reviews.

While special education teachers are asked to learn to write a map, which student or students are mapped on an ongoing basis will vary per teacher. One teacher may choose to map a resource or a support pullout group of students, while another teacher may choose to map one fully included student. In the case of the latter, some special education teachers prefer to add the student's modifications and accommodations directly to the included general education teacher's map, while others prefer to write a personal map to reflect the student's learning. I have observed special education teachers who prefer to map student behavior expectations rather than academia. I have also observed special education teachers who serve a unique student population, and although their students are not directly involved in the mainstream, they were and remain wholeheartedly committed to learning about mapping, designing maps, and being involved in mapping reviews. They do not actually write maps since their students' learning consists of basic life skills such as using the restroom or dressing oneself unassisted, but they are intimately involved in their schools' curriculum reviews and decision-making processes.

I consistently find that special education teachers truly appreciate having an instantly accessible mapping system that contains the general education students' planned and operational curriculum. Many use the mapping system often as a resource for planning IEP students' learning needs and participating in discussions about what is in their students' best interests.

CONCLUSION

There is no one way to do curriculum mapping "right." Curriculum mapping is intimate work. What may be the best implementation process for one learning organization may not work for another. Determining how to begin the mapping process can therefore seem overwhelming. Decisions regarding implementation should not be made alone. Chapter 3 recommends conducting a prologue that includes a joint decision-making process. In addition, Chapters 5 and 6 provide insight into implementation considerations for the various types of curriculum maps that may affect the decision-making process.

Regardless of the map type or types selected, teachers must experience ownership in designing and documenting students' planned and operational small steps. Adapting the French novelist Marcel Proust's famous saying, curriculum mapping encourages a voyage of discovery that consists not in seeking new landscapes, but in having new eyes.

REVIEW QUESTIONS

Here are questions to ponder regarding what has been presented in this chapter. Share your answers and thoughts with a partner or in a small group.

1. You have been asked to describe the name and purpose of each type of curriculum map. What will you say? (Try to do so first without looking back through this chapter. If you want to double-check your responses, Figure 2.1 provides a quick reference.)

2. Since lesson plans are not equivalent to curriculum maps, how will you address this potential concern within your learning organization when implementing your mapping initiative?

3. You recently heard that a neighboring school district is going to start curriculum mapping in the fall and is asking each teacher to map every discipline or course taught during the first year of implementation. What is your advice for this district's administration?

4. During a teacher training focused on learning how to diary map the common initial elements, you overhear the following verbal exchange:

   Teacher A: I think this will be great once we get maps in the system and can all see what the others have been doing!

   Teacher B: Why do I have to record all this information in a personal map? I know what I do with my students. If a teacher wants to know what has happened in my room, he or she can find me and ask.

   How would you personally respond to Teacher B, given what you have read in Chapters 1 and 2?

3

What Should We Consider Before Developing Curriculum Maps?

*But the bravest are surely those who have the
clearest vision of what is before them, glory and
danger alike, and yet notwithstanding go out to meet it.*

—Thucydides

Curriculum mapping asks teachers to be curriculum designers. A learning organization's curriculum design is oftentimes not the primary responsibility of teachers; more often it is the responsibility of the administration, with input from selected teachers. Since asking all teachers to play an active role in designing curriculum may challenge how a learning organization currently functions, this chapter focuses on three critical considerations that need to be contemplated before curriculum mapping is implemented.

The first consideration addresses the necessity of functioning as an open and participatory design community. All teachers are expected to be engaged in the design, revision, and refinement of student learning and instructional practice (Jacobs 1997, 2004b). Given these expectations, the establishment of a consortium of teachers and administrators involved in a preplanning and learning phase is imperative.

The second consideration focuses on the fact that curriculum maps are never considered *done*. Finality is not a concept found in curriculum mapping. This must be explicitly acknowledged from the outset of a mapping initiative. Teachers must be aware up front that they will be conducting ongoing curriculum reviews and continually questioning whether the current learning expectations, assessments, and teaching practices are in students' best interests. The results of such collaborations may affect immediate or future map documentation.

The third consideration offers insight into selecting the map or maps to begin the documentation process. Every learning organization has its own history, culture, climate, and current issues that may affect the selection process.

FIRST CONSIDERATION: EXPLORING PERSONAL AND COLLABORATIVE UNDERSTANDING OF CURRICULUM DESIGN

A teacher generally works *independently* in his or her instructional environment. Mapping calls for teachers to work *interdependently* to collectively improve student learning. This requisite is customary in various collaborative models (DuFour, DuFour, and Eaker 2005; Jacobs 1997, 2004b, 2006a; Lezotte and McKee 2002; Schmoker 1999, 2006; Wiggins and McTighe 1998). Mapping is a team effort.

Administrators are critical team players in curriculum mapping. I find that most teachers are willing to be curriculum leaders and designers, and to work interdependently, but become frustrated early on or even give up if there is inadequate administrative support. While district-level support is necessary, in order to achieve successful implementation and sustainability, every principal involved must express explicit and implicit support for school-site teachers by doing the following:

- learning the complexities of mapping to ensure deep, personal understanding
- providing regular and adequate time for teachers to learn and engage in the mapping model
- keeping teachers focused on the beliefs and ideals of the process and why mapping was initially implemented
- being optimistic and, when necessary, flexible
- encouraging, monitoring, and celebrating both the small and large increases in the design and use of maps
- continually expanding one's personal knowledge of curriculum, instruction, and assessment (Marzano, Waters, and McNulty 2005)

Without these six requisites securely in place, a mapping initiative's success, while well intentioned, may ultimately fail.

A Teacher-Designed Curriculum

Any team must be mutually aware of its goals. For curriculum mapping, a major ongoing goal for improving student learning and performance is to design vertically articulated, rigorous curriculum. It is therefore imperative that teachers and administrators have a mutual understanding of what constitutes the curriculum.

In curriculum mapping, textbooks, kits, and materials are not perceived as the curriculum. They are resources that enable or enhance the curriculum and the learning process. Curriculum mapping recognizes teacher-determined concepts, content, skills, and assessments aligned to strategically analyzed national, state, local, or self-generated standards as the curriculum. Depending on past initiatives and professional development, this may be a small or large shift in thinking for a learning organization's teachers.

In the late 20th century and into the 21st century, many schools and districts unintentionally began to misrepresent curriculum. When a textbook-adoption cycle takes place, oftentimes the administration asks a few select teachers to be intensively involved in the selection process. Eventually a textbook or kit series, and possibly supplementary materials, get finalized and ordered. When these materials are delivered, all the teachers in the learning organization are literally told, or perceive, that they have now been given new curriculum. This is a misnomer. They have been given new resources.

It is of the essence that administrators and teachers are informed up front that mapping the curriculum does not equal copying a textbook's main teaching points or listed standards connections. If this takes place, curriculum maps would need major revamping during every adoption cycle to match the new textbook's representation of learning. If teachers instead learn how to break apart standard statements and translate them into map elements (see Chapter 9), once a map is recorded in a mapping system, all that needs to be revised after a textbook adoption cycle is the resource listings within the map. While this makes sense, initially it may be difficult for some teachers to avoid the urge to literally map the textbook. It may therefore take some time for teachers and administrators to grasp and understand the process of creating a teacher-designed, standards-based curriculum.

Curriculum Mapping Is Built on Mutual Trust and Respect

Mutual trust and respect in the learning process and in each other plays a major role in establishing an interdependent learning community. Although many teachers embrace opportunities for individual and collaborative curriculum reflection and design, some find this requisite emotionally unnerving. To address the potential emotional concerns of some teachers, prior to implementing curriculum mapping, it is wise to have administration at all levels publicly acknowledge what has and has not gone well in past and present initiatives. This is not meant to be a blame game or gripe session. It is a public forum to face the realities of what may not be said overtly, but lurks covertly and can hurt a new initiative's chances for success. Discussion points may include (a) pent-up tensions over past failures, (b) concerns about present-day issues and problems, (c) factors that may need to be adjusted or established to promote a reflective-inquiry culture that includes support from those mistrusted in the past, and (d) sharing one another's deepest hopes and desires for academic and social success for all students and teachers (Senge et al. 2000).

Public acknowledgment does not guarantee instant or massive buy-in. Factors influencing cautionary attitudes may include the number of failed or died-a-slow-death initiatives, treatment of those who displayed uneasiness during implementation of previous initiatives, and the number of current initiatives teachers are struggling to effectively sustain while simultaneously being required to participate in a new initiative (Fullan 2001a).

Fullan's third point is significant. There is much to learn when curriculum-mapping implementation begins. Some will catch on quickly. For others the learning process will be a struggle. Most teachers want to do well what is being asked of them. Therefore, they will be concerned about their performance. Many will wonder if the curriculum maps will be used to measure their ability to teach. Therefore, it is important to make an explicit statement that curriculum maps will never be used in this manner. Learning organizations have mandated procedures to determine a teacher's aptitude. Maps do not need to be added to the already established protocols. Even though verbal acknowledgment is given, some teachers will want reassurance in writing. It is recommended that school-site and district administrators provide written documentation that no curriculum maps, regardless of stage of development, will ever be used for teacher evaluation or punitive purposes. If maps are misused in this way, it will instantly destroy any trust or confidence that may have existed.

Second-Order Change

Curriculum mapping involves systemic, or second-order, change. Marzano, Waters, and McNulty (2005) state that "incremental [first-order] change fine tunes the system through a series of small steps that do not depart radically from the past. Deep [second-order] change alters the system in fundamental ways, offering a dramatic shift in direction and requiring new ways of thinking and acting" (p. 66). Second-order change causes members of a learning organization to make a series of personal and collective mental model shifts.

Kallick (2006) incorporates Senge et al.'s (2000, pp. 80–83) Systems Thinking Model in her explanation of the mental shifts that teachers and administrators make to internalize a new initiative. The series of shifts take approximately three to four years before reaching Level IV (see Figure 3.1).

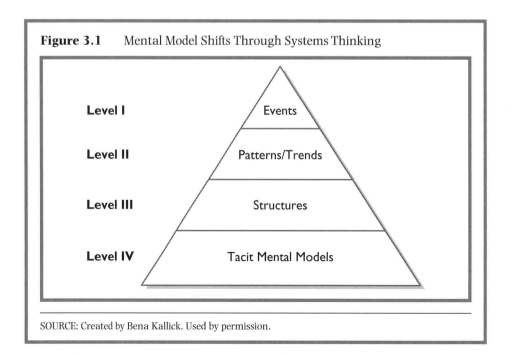

Figure 3.1 Mental Model Shifts Through Systems Thinking

SOURCE: Created by Bena Kallick. Used by permission.

Level I: An initiative begins through a series of presentations that often include professional development inservices, faculty trainings, small-group discussions, and hands-on workshops. The learning organization's members may not mentally connect the purpose of the various meeting experiences at this time. Instead, each event may appear isolated or unrelated.

Level II: After a significant succession of meetings providing opportunities to mentally, physically, emotionally, and verbally explore current, implicit mental models through reflection and inquiry, members begin to make mental connections between the previous meeting experiences and new expectations. These experiences begin to merge into a pattern or trend. From this point on, members continue to make instantaneous connections between the learning and doing experiences.

Level III: After an extensive period of time during which formal and informal experiences regarding the established pattern or trend take place, members begin to mentally and emotionally reconfigure the experience repetitions into a new mental model structure. This new structure creates synergy between the initial unrelated series of events and the growing pattern or trend. This new mental model begins to feel natural rather than awkward, as it did in Levels I and II.

Level IV: The pattern or trend now shifts to an implicit, or tacit, mental model wherein subconscious thought generates conscious actions. The new way of thinking is now a deep belief and has become an integrated and seamless component of the culture and professional lifestyle of the members of the learning organization.

Time for Preplanning

It is important to consider how teachers and administrators will ultimately reach Level IV. Time must be dedicated to preplanning how curriculum mapping will be established throughout a learning organization. Jacobs (2004b) refers to this preplanning time as a *prologue*.

One purpose for conducting a prologue is to educate a foundational group of teachers and administrators so that they can gain personal and collective confidence in conveying curriculum-mapping concepts to others. Chapter 11 addresses in more detail the two types of curriculum-mapping intra-organizations that work closely with all the teachers throughout a learning organization: a districtwide Curriculum Mapping Cabinet and a school-site Curriculum Mapping Council (Jacobs 1997, 2004b, 2007).

It is recommended that a mapping prologue last approximately half a school year, if not a full school year. Besides learning (a) the purpose for each type of curriculum map, (b) how to write a map including the common initial elements with consistency and quality using a selected mapping system, (c) how to conduct the process of breaking apart standards and determining power standards (Chapter 9), and (d) how to conduct formal curriculum reviews using the mapping system's search and report features and other databases, the cabinet and council members need to address the following questions:

- Based on the first districtwide focus, what will be the first type of map designed by teachers? What considerations will need to be addressed for specialists and special learning environments?

- How will curriculum mapping's short- and long-range action plans (also discussed in Chapter 11) be implemented?
- Who will be responsible for providing teachers with step-by-step and sustained professional development?
- What needs to occur to guarantee that all teachers reflect individually and collaboratively as they continually question and deliberate curriculum and instructional practice?
- How can current meeting structures, both within individual schools and throughout the learning organization, eventually be modified or changed to support monthly or weekly early-release days, late-start days, or full professional development days to provide teachers with the necessary time to design maps and meet in various review team configurations?

During the prologue the cabinet and council members are engaged in learning as much as they possibly can about mapping and the mapping process. Learning organizations that do not conduct a prologue or adequate preplanning often struggle when implementation begins. When a learning organization takes the time to conduct a prologue, it is more likely to be successful in institutionalizing curriculum mapping.

SECOND CONSIDERATION: THE ONGOING NATURE OF MAPPING REVIEWS

When curriculum mapping first began in the mid-1980s, the work was primarily focused on creating documents that defined the learning content, the length of time spent on the learning content, and the relationship between learning content and district assessments (English 1980). Curriculum mapping dynamics now include the following:

- asking each teacher to individually document students' operational learning each school year
- documenting evidence of both the ongoing planned and the operational learning by months
- aligning learning expectations to standards and assessments
- using a mapping system that interrelates map data
- working with other teachers to agree upon collective planned learning
- conducting ongoing reviews via collegial collaborations (Jacobs 1997, 2004b)

Udelhofen (2005) states that without these six factors in place, learning documentation is "an inconsistent, fragmented curriculum that does not optimize grade-to-grade, cross-content area learning experiences" (p. xix).

A Teacher-Examined Curriculum

Curriculum maps equal data. Curriculum mapping equals ongoing data-driven decision making using various types of maps and other forms of data sources (Jacobs 2004b). Depending on a formal or informal mapping review's focus, maps may be used comparatively in any of the following ways (or combination thereof):

- maps to maps
- maps to previously created curriculum guides and guidelines
- maps to national, state, or local standards and ancillary documents
- maps to national, state, local, or school-site test results
- maps to student work samples
- maps to student, teacher, parent, or college surveys

Jacobs (2004b, 2006b) refers to map comparisons as a diagnosis–prognosis relationship. Teachers, like doctors, diagnose their students' needs and determine the best prescriptions. Curriculum maps serve as current and archived patient records. To aid in this process, Jacobs (1997, 2004b) advocates using a Seven-Step Review Model. Each of the steps, as well as suggested review focuses, is detailed in Chapter 7.

The following example provides another case of how teachers begin to think, act, and meet differently when reviewing data and making curriculum decisions using curriculum maps.

In late April a six-member Grade 10 science team decided to conduct a curriculum review. Based on their desire to examine potential cross-disciplinary learning in mathematics and science, the team chose to focus on data recorded in Grade 6 through Grade 10 mathematics and science Consensus Maps within their mapping system.

Because of time constraints, the science team decided not to bring together the 22 mathematics and science teachers for an in-person meeting. Instead they decided to meet in a Web-based forum. To prepare for the meeting and conduct the review, the science team took several steps:

- individually read through the appropriate map data
- met in three-person teams to discuss their individual findings based on a potential cross-disciplinary focus
- met as a large-group comparison team to discuss small-group findings
- generated four discussion questions for the mathematics and science teachers' forum
- sent an e-mail invitation outlining the following:
  o the focus and purpose for conducting the science and mathematics map review
  o large-group findings based on map data evidence
  o four discussion questions
  o suggested mapping system's reports that can be used to view significant map comparison findings
  o the cyberspace e-meeting date and time

In early May 18 teachers attended the Web-based meeting hosted by the science team. Conversation was rich and invigorating. The participating teachers shared with their respective departments the collective decisions that had been made. Revision or refinements were made to Consensus Maps for the following school year once they were officially archived and rolled over to the new school year.

This review example is not meant to convey that curriculum mapping demands that meetings and reviews be held in cyberspace. It simply reveals that with the capabilities of Web-based mapping systems, electronic meeting forums, and other expansions in technology such as instant messaging and video conferencing, the potential for meeting forums has advanced and will continue to do so with ongoing innovations. Cyberspace meetings will never fully replace face-to-face meetings, though, since body language, facial expressions, and proximity play a significant role in collegial conversations.

THIRD CONSIDERATION: A MAPPING SEQUENCE THAT IS RIGHT FOR YOUR LEARNING ORGANIZATION

During the prologue, time will be spent on deciding which type(s) of map should be the first to be recorded within a selected mapping system. If you attend a regional or national curriculum-mapping workshop or conference, you will soon realize that there is no single right answer. It is an intimate decision to make, and it must be an appropriate one for your learning organization. While it is worthwhile to listen to and learn from what others have chosen to do, the final decision for your learning organization must be one that reflects both its current and future concerns, problems, and issues that the mapping process will aid in addressing.

Use the Proper Map Name

When discussing the initial map selection, make certain that all involved in the process refer to each map by its proper name rather than using the generic term *curriculum map*. Each map name's adjective—*essential, consensus, projected, diary*—conveys the purpose for each map type's documentation. For example, if someone suggests that teachers should first develop a Consensus Map, it conveys that teachers should work in teams to design one map that represents agreed-upon planned learning for one specific course at one specific school site. If someone else suggests that each teacher should first learn how to write a Diary Map, it conveys that one person will design one personal map that documents what has been learned in one specific course in one specific classroom or learning environment.

What Should Come First, the Egg or the Chicken?

Oftentimes, a Diary Map or a Consensus Map is selected as the initial map choice. I am often asked, "Which one is really the best to begin mapping?" I always remember the first time I connected this question to an infamous question and remarked that what is being asked is "What should come first, the egg or the chicken?" While it may sound a bit cliché, it really is apropos.

The first time I used this analogy I was working with a large district's recently created Curriculum Mapping Cabinet. It was time to discuss the selection of an initial map type, yet some of the cabinet members were still struggling with conceptualizing each map's purpose in relation to the protocols for designing each map type.

I shared that each teacher recording a Diary Map is similar to each teacher laying an egg. In other words, each teacher is personally responsible for writing map data within a mapping system. Since there is no such thing as team diary mapping, some teachers may struggle with having to individually accomplish the task of writing a personal map. On the flip side, having each teacher internalize how to write the map elements is critical for constructing mental understanding.

Individually writing a map does not require that a teacher do so without support. Support must be provided regardless of what type of map teachers are initially learning to design. Meeting forums may include hands-on lab times; one-on-one mentoring; or buddy systems wherein small groups of teachers work simultaneously but do not map the same grade level, discipline, or course to keep with the integrity of personally designing a map.

If teachers are asked to initially design Consensus Maps, it is similar to creating a chicken. A teacher team comes to agreement on what the chicken will look like and how it will behave. In other words, they agree on what will be taught and when it will be taught during the school year based on analyzing the standards and breaking them apart into content and skill statements.

Since the mapping process is just beginning, teachers will have no data from Diary Maps that document what each teacher values; therefore, specific protocols for designing a Consensus Map must be established. If the teachers function in collegial relationships, creating a chicken runs smoothly. If there is quite a bit of strife or mistrust among teachers, it may be better to start with diary mapping and slowly move toward collaborative map design.

I concluded my comparative analogy by sharing that, regardless of the initial map type selected, eventually other types will follow. If Diary Maps are first, they will eventually be put, metaphorically speaking, into one basket and aid teachers in designing a Consensus Map. If a Consensus Map is designed first, each teacher will in turn lay an egg, a Diary Map, based on the agreed-upon learning contained in the Consensus Map.

A few moments passed as the teachers and administrators discussed the analogy with one another. Then a district administrator added, "I get it now. . . . I can see in a few years we will form a teacher-led task force to design the chicken coop, the Essential Map, by reviewing all of our school site's chickens!"

Everyone laughed and acknowledged that they were beginning to see the relationship between all the map types. Conversation continued, and eventually the cabinet selected the map type that they deduced was the best choice for their district given past and present cultures, current teacher relationships, recent state and local testing results, and existing districtwide and school-site initiatives.

Map Selection Examples

Since not everyone can attend curriculum-mapping conferences or workshops to network and hear firsthand what various learning organizations have chosen to do, the examples in the following three boxes highlight why it is important to carefully consider the mapping sequence that is appropriate for your learning organization and to plan in advance for professional development, adequate time to map, and differentiated support to aid teachers during the initial stages of learning to design curriculum maps. The first example is one in which I was personally involved. The remaining two were shared with me during a National Curriculum Mapping Institute.

Example 1

A district asked for help in determining why its relatively new mapping initiative was wavering. Two administrators had been given the districtwide task of implementation. They had attended several curriculum-mapping conferences and workshops and had read a variety of curriculum-mapping materials.

At the beginning of the school year, they conducted an initial full-day, districtwide curriculum-mapping overview inservice for all teachers and administrators and a full-day, small-group rotation training per school site on how to enter a Diary Map in the district's selected mapping system.

The elementary school teachers were instructed to diary map mathematics. The middle school and high school teachers were instructed to diary map one course taught. Specialists and resource teachers also were asked to select one course or grade level to diary map.

I asked how much time and support was provided for each teacher to enter the Diary Map elements. The administrators told me that each teacher was given a 30-minute, student-free time slot once a month and could use a classroom computer or go to a technology lab to enter the data. If teachers had questions they could call either administrator at the district office since there was no on-site support.

I shared that 30 minutes once a month is not adequate when initially learning how to write a Diary Map's elements, and not having on-site support is problematic.

I then asked if they had formed Curriculum Mapping Councils and a Curriculum Mapping Cabinet. They said they knew about these intra-organizations, but had not given much thought to establishing them. They admitted feeling burdened being the only two in the district trying to make mapping happen. They decided it would be a good idea to revisit the need for establishing these organizations.

The next question proved the most revealing as to why their initiative was having implementation difficulties. When asked how many other new initiatives were started at the same time as curriculum mapping, the administrators said that it was anywhere from four to eight, depending on school site, grade level, and discipline. This explained why teachers were visibly and verbally expressing signs of stress and revolt over having to map. The problem was not mapping; it was simply an overload of professional expectations.

After further conversation focusing on this district's needs, I proposed modifications to the original action plan, including having teachers delay diary mapping and begin learning the collaborative process for designing Consensus Maps. I also suggested that art, music, and physical education teachers shift their focus to designing Essential Maps.

Given the current climate and culture, allowing teachers to bond and support one another in the learning process was the right choice. For the remainder of the school year, and into the first half of the next school year, teachers collegially designed Consensus Maps. In the spring, teachers began to use the Consensus Maps as the basis for Projected Maps and Diary Maps. Teachers involved in the specialists' Essential Map design process continued working throughout the school year.

Curriculum mapping eventually became institutionalized in this district. By the middle of the second year, a districtwide Curriculum Mapping Cabinet and site-based Curriculum Mapping Councils were in place and functioning well.

The cabinet and council members recently formed a task force to design districtwide mathematics Essential Maps using data from the site-based Consensus Maps. All teachers continue to play active roles in curriculum design and use the maps continuously to drive curriculum decision making.

Example 2

After conducting a prologue, a large district chose to start its mapping initiative by asking teachers to diary map to ensure that each teacher personally grasped how to write the common initial map elements, learned how to use the mapping system, and became familiar with conducting informal mapping reviews. The district provided twice-a-month, half-day, small-group professional development trainings at each school site led by Curriculum Mapping Council members. Each training session had a planned focus. Teachers knew the purpose and outcome of each training in advance.

Before the close of the first year of mapping, teachers were surveyed via e-mail and asked if they wanted to use the next school year to improve the quality of the first-year Diary Maps or start diary mapping a new discipline. The Curriculum Mapping Cabinet discussed the survey results and approved the majority vote. Ninety-eight percent of the teachers wanted to continue mapping the initial discipline or course and improve map quality based on self-determined revision goals. This decision instantly boosted teachers' self-confidence and trust in the fact that their voices were being heard and honored.

During the next school year, while teachers revised map quality they also received training in conducting formal reviews to locate gaps, repetitions, and absences in the curriculum using the maps and the mapping system. They commented that learning about the review process and discovering how to use the mapping system's search and report features deepened their understanding of how mapping can aid them in improving student learning and performance. Some teachers also showed interest in learning

(Continued)

(Continued)

the process for designing Consensus Maps, so differentiated professional development training was implemented for these teachers.

Starting in the summer of the second implementation year, the district began conducting a weeklong summer workshop that included various curriculum-mapping modules. The modules were conducted by Curriculum Mapping Council members and some administrators. The workshop was mandatory for newly hired teachers; anyone else choosing to attend received a stipend. Minisession topics included mapping basics; how to use the mapping system; the map elements' wording, format, and intra-alignment norms; conducting reviews; creating Consensus Maps; and district-vision round tables.

Currently, teachers in this district continue to (a) participate in ongoing reviews and refine student learning based on curriculum maps, which now include Essential Maps, Consensus Maps, and Projected/Diary Maps; (b) develop and implement common assessments; and (c) collaboratively evaluate student work samples. Some schools have formed professional learning communities and use specific and strategic, measurable, attainable, results-oriented, and time-bound (SMART) goals along with map data to aid in improving student learning.

Example 3

It was the beginning of May, and a district's Curriculum Mapping Cabinet was discussing next steps. During the current school year, all teachers and administrators were engaged in monthly curriculum-mapping book and video study groups to learn curriculum-mapping basics without officially beginning to map. The cabinet agreed that these meetings laid a solid foundation and created a comfort level before implementing curriculum mapping. This was evident in a survey completed by both teachers and administrators.

During this exploratory year, district-level administrators had been working on how to reconfigure teacher meeting time allotments without disrupting class time so that there would be ample time for teachers to map and to meet in the coming school year. The administrators created a proposal and presented it to the Board of Education. The proposal was approved for a one-year trial. Starting in the fall, a weekly early-release day was built into the master school calendar. Every Thursday students would be released 90 minutes early. To meet legal requirements of teacher-to-student time, the four remaining weekdays would be extended by 22.5 minutes. Bus schedules were adjusted to meet the new requisites.

During May each school conducted a full faculty meeting in which cabinet members facilitated discussion regarding what teachers proposed would be the best map type to begin the mapping process in the following school year, given short- and long-range curriculum goals and current test results. At the end of each meeting, teachers and administrators were given an entry code to participate in an online, next-steps mapping survey.

After evaluating the survey data, the cabinet's action plan consisted of a concurrent five-point process:

- Mathematics Consensus Map will be designed by teacher teams at the individual school sites.
- Teachers not teaching mathematics will select appropriate courses for which to begin the process of developing Consensus Maps.
- Special education teachers and resource specialists will select a grade-level or department team to work with on the development of a Consensus Map.
- Art, music, physical education, and library science teachers will individually design a Projected Map/Diary Map for a particular grade level to enable them to move toward designing Essential Maps.
- Due to drastic dips in achievement scores, K–12 language arts Essential Maps will be designed and drafted by a districtwide task force.

For this district, a five-point plan was the right choice. Since every teacher and administrator had been actively engaged in a prelearning year and knew there would be weekly meeting time, buy-in was high and teachers were excited about the mapping process.

The Curriculum Mapping Cabinet continued to meet twice a month for the remainder of that summer to prepare for the various map type focuses and to learn both basic and advanced features of the recently selected mapping system. The cabinet also planned mapping system training rotations so that all teachers could be introduced to the mapping system's basic features during the first month of the upcoming fall semester. The final summer step for the cabinet was to support the development of each school site's Curriculum Mapping Council.

CONCLUSION

Curriculum mapping is a worthy endeavor. Studies have proven that, when implemented properly, curriculum mapping positively impacts student performance based on teachers' intimate involvement in designing and improving curriculum and personal instructional practice (Jacobs 2004b; Kercheval and Newbill 2001). However, it must also be acknowledged that there are learning organizations wherein the term *curriculum mapping* has left a bitter taste due to one or more of the following variables: a misconception that mapping is a simple, first-order change; poor or no preplanning or prologue; non-use of a Web-based mapping system; inadequate time to map; non-use of developed maps to conduct curriculum reviews; lack of school-site administrative support; and no ongoing professional development.

Jacobs (2004b) states that "as a genuine 21st-century shift in our practice, mapping requires knowledge and courage," and she adds that "after the prologue, [there is] no epilogue" (p. 8). The remaining chapters in this book are dedicated to addressing each facet of the mapping process so that you can gain the knowledge and clear vision necessary to set a direction for your learning organization's curriculum-mapping journey.

REVIEW QUESTIONS

Given your learning organization's past and present curriculum initiatives, both failed and flourishing, plus the desire to move toward a teacher-designed curriculum, discuss your responses and answers to the questions below with a partner or in a small group.

1. How would you fill in the blanks?

   Before I read this chapter I thought _____;
   now I realize _____.

   Be ready to share insight into your responses.

2. Given the educational, social, and emotional histories of our school or district, I currently perceive that establishing a cohesive, collegial, teacher-designed curriculum environment will be *easy/moderate/difficult* (select a word or make up one of your own) to establish.

   What is the evidence or data that supports your response? What specific factors do you recognize need to be established or modified to create synergy between *independent* and *interdependent* curriculum decision making?

3. My school/district has had *no/marginal/adequate/extensive* (select a word or make up your own) professional development in teacher-led curriculum design. Therefore, I believe that our teachers will _____ when introduced to curriculum mapping's concept of asking teachers to design the curriculum.

   What evidence-based data are you using to support your selected word choice and fill-in-the-blank statement?

4. Given your learning organization's overt and covert cultures, current dynamics of teacher leadership, and multilevel administrative support, which of the three considerations discussed in this chapter do you identify as being the easiest to implement? Which do you perceive will be the most difficult or challenging? Why?

What Elements Are Commonly Included in Curriculum Maps?

"Excellent!" Watson cried.
"Elementary," said Holmes.

—Sir Arthur Conan Doyle

Sherlock Holmes is infamous for putting together separate elements and analyzing their connections. The same process occurs when writing and reviewing curriculum maps. Since curriculum maps are oftentimes accessed, read, and discussed *without* the map writer or writers present, consistency in wording, format, and intra-alignment contribute significantly to the quality and clarity regarding accurate map data interpretation throughout a learning organization.

CURRICULUM MAP ALIGNMENTS AND ELEMENTS

Jacobs (1997) refers to a map as "a brief description of the *content* . . . a description of the processes and *skills* emphasized; and the nature of the *assessment*" (p. 62, emphasis added). These three elements aligned to one another, standards, and relevant resources comprise the most common initial map elements. The words *brief, emphasized,* and *nature of* convey that a curriculum map is a succinct summation of planned or operational learning.

Four Categories of Alignment

Alignment is a term that is often used in education. Regarding curriculum mapping, there are four alignment categories. The first alignment is the connection between elements within a map's individual month or unit and is referred to as *intra-alignment.* This type is most often visually documented using a letter–number coding process.

The second alignment is element comparison throughout a map's school year of months or units and is referred to as *horizontal intra-alignment.* This type is visible using specific search and report features in a mapping system that highlights element data within one map.

The third alignment includes element comparison of multiple maps representing one grade-level discipline or one specific course and is referred to as *horizontal inter-alignment.* This type is visible using specific search and report features in a mapping system that compare specific elements in a series of like maps.

The fourth alignment is a comparison of elements in a series of grade levels' like- or mixed-discipline maps and is referred to as *vertical inter-alignment.* This type is also visible using specific search and report features in a mapping system that compares elements in a series of like- or mixed-discipline maps.

As Jacobs (1997) notes, "skills are not taught in a vacuum. They are addressed in application to content, and they are evidenced in a product or performance by the learner" (p. 4). To ensure a rigorous, aligned curriculum, teachers are encouraged to conduct curriculum reviews to evaluate maps based on all four alignment categories. When learning to write a map, teachers initially focus on the concept of intra-aligning map elements within a specific month or unit and will therefore be the alignment focus within this chapter.

Elements Included in Each Type of Map

Elements included vary slightly depending on the type of map. Figure 4.1 features the most common elements incorporated at the onset of a mapping initiative.

As each year progresses, revision and refinement to existing elements, as well as incorporating additional elements, are components of the ongoing mapping process.

When Learning to Write
Curriculum Maps: A Cautionary Note

Each teacher needs to develop a personal cognitive understanding of how to write the elements. Cognition cannot be handed to someone. It must be experienced (Jensen 2000). As Erickson (2002) comments, "writing is thinking—and the arrangement of words on paper to effect instructional improvement in the classroom is a sophisticated task" (pp. 3–4).

Early on in the map-writing learning process I am often asked, "Aren't there maps already written somewhere that we can just go and copy? It would be much easier that way." Yet a teacher would not allow his or her students to copy

Figure 4.1   Map Type and Common Initial Map Elements

Type of Map	Initial Elements
Projected Map **Diary Map** An individual's recording at each school site Includes greatest amount of detail and data	*Personal summation of planned and operational learning* • Content • Skills • Summative assessments (also known as assessments *of* learning) • Significant formative assessments (also known as assessments *for* learning) • Standards • Resources
Consensus Map A teacher team's recording at each school site Includes midrange amount of detail and data	*Collaborative, compulsory planned learning* • Content • Skills • Common and/or same assessments (only included if collective agreement) • Benchmark assessments (if schoolwide and appropriate to course) • Standards • Resources (only included if collective agreement and available to all teachers teaching the course)
Essential Map Teacher-led task force recording for districtwide incorporation Includes least amount of detail and data	*Collaborative, mandated planned learning* • Content • Skills • District benchmark or state-mandated assessments (appropriate to course) • Standards • Resources (only included if available to teachers districtwide)

another student's work when learning a process or when taking a test. The teacher would say that is cheating. Equally inappropriate is copying someone else's map when trying to learn how to write the map elements.

Most mapping systems provide users with an ability to conduct searches for curriculum maps worldwide. While this affords access to an incredible exchange of learning models and curriculum designs, the ability to view others' maps is not meant to encourage a copy-and-paste procedure that causes map-writing learners to skip critical steps of self-actualization and understanding. One way in which viewing online sample maps proves beneficial, though, is it enables teachers as learners to evaluate a map's quality and clarity when trying to interpret the map's data, without the map writer(s) present, based on the norms shared in this chapter and the sample map months featured throughout this book. Reviewing existing maps online can spark dialogue about the necessity for a learning organization to write quality maps.

WRITING THE ELEMENTS

This is a lengthy chapter. It is recommended that you read through its pages incrementally to allow time to absorb each element's explanation. Please do not assume that you will remember absolutely everything by reading through the information once. Since writing is a process, it will take time to learn and remember all that recording a quality map entails.

Following each element's explanation, you will find two figures. The first, referred to as Figure 4.2A, presents bulleted information and examples regarding the element's recommended format, wording, alignment, and distinctive features. You will find that some bulleted statements repeat what is shared in previous paragraphs. This is intentional. Collectively, the A figures are meant to be used as a quick-reference tool when actually writing a map. The second figure after each element's explanation, Figure 4.2B, is a sample Diary Map month that grows in detail with each added element. The sample month begins with only one element and ends with all five initial common elements. Please do not study the map contextually; instead, focus intently on the wording, format, and visual intra-alignment as they expand with each added element.

A variety of sample Projected/Diary Map months that include the common initial elements are located near the end of Chapter 5. As you study each element and observe its wording, format, and intra-alignment being added to the sample German 1 Diary Map month in this chapter, you may also want to study the additional sample map months to note how each element is written in a variety of grade levels and disciplines.

Just as a reminder, all of the sample map months use a generic table template. When recording a map in a mapping system, the elements will be written in the same way or a similar manner. The one process that varies depending on the system used is the elements' visual intra-alignment.

Unit Name

If you don't recall *unit name* being mentioned in Figure 4.1, you are correct. It needs to be mentioned here because some mapping systems require a map's recording process to begin with writing a unit name. When writing a unit name, record each word in all capital letters to distinguish the unit name from the map elements.

If throughout a school or district teachers do not currently base learning on a unit-design model, determining unit names may be based on discipline-specific standards' strands, concepts, themes, and/or topics such as the following:

- NUMBER SENSE
- PROBABILITY AND STATISTICS
- GEOGRAPHY OF SOUTH AMERICA
- ECONOMICS: NORTH AMERICAN TRADE
- LANGUAGE: CRITICAL ANALYSIS
- PERSONAL HEALTH: DRUG AWARENESS

or a broad term or phrase befitting the learning contained within a unit:

- 1776
- BIOMES
- PYRAMID DESIGN
- 1920s ART CONTRIBUTIONS
- SPRING DANCE RECITAL

Most unit-driven mapping systems do not allow duplicate unit names within an academic year's curriculum map. To distinguish between spiraled unit names within a given school year wherein each unit's content, skills, assessments, standards, and resources vary or expand as the school year progresses, teachers either incorporate a *sequential numbering system* such as Roman numerals (e.g., NUMBER SENSE I, NUMBER SENSE II, NUMBER SENSE III) or include a *signifier* after the base unit name (e.g., LITERARY ELEMENTS, LITERARY AUTHOR STUDY, LITERARY 19TH-CENTURY CLASSICS).

If unit names are needed from the onset or planned to be incorporated in the future, it is advised that consistency in a learning organization's base set of unit names be determined or developed early on within various disciplines and throughout all grade levels by either the curriculum-mapping cabinet or discipline-specific task forces. This will save a lot of time and frustration when wanting to inter-align curriculum across grade levels and courses. Having similar unit names or key words included within the unit names aids significantly in a mapping system's ability to search and find desired data quickly.

When developing consistency by establishing unit names, it is probably easiest to do so with mathematics because you can use state standards' names such as *number operations, geometry, algebra,* and *data analysis.* Sometimes discipline-specific teachers prefer theme or concept names rather than topic names. For example, K–12 social studies teachers may choose to base unit names on the National Council of Social Studies theme strands such as *culture; time, continuity, change; people, places, environments;* and g*lobal connections.* Recently I observed a K–12 task force of science teachers brainstorming and determining unit names that could be used throughout the learning organization. Words such as *systems, environments,* and *reproduction* were on their potential list. I have also seen teachers develop unit names based on cross- and interdisciplinary design using overarching themes or concepts. For example, *systems* are found in social studies, mathematics, social studies, technology, and a variety of other disciplines.

It is also wise to explore determining consistent unit names before teachers get into a habit of naming units in extremely creative ways, which will make it difficult to find pertinent data when searching in a mapping system. It is best when the selected unit names are viewed as a recommended norm that may be enhanced to provide clarity for map reader. For example, if SYSTEMS is selected as one of the K–12 science unit names, a teacher may choose to name a unit SYSTEMS: HUMAN BODY to indicate the unit's specific focus within the *systems* concept.

There may also be times when a single, cross-, or multidisciplinary unit's learning expectations may not accurately fit any of the established unit names' terms or phrases. If this is the case, the teacher(s) will need to generate an appropriate unit name that accurately represents the expectations within the unit(s) of study.

Criteria

Figure 4.2A addresses unit name wording, format, intra-alignment, and distinctive features.

Figure 4.2A Recommended Unit Name Norms

	Reference Points

Wording	• A unit name serves a purpose similar to a book's title. It is written as a broad statement or simple phrase representing the information within.
	
	Examples:
	
	    MODERN CREATIVE DANCE
	    GEOMETRY AND SPATIAL SENSE III
	    NUMBER COMPUTATION: ADDITION/SUBTRACTION
	    HUMAN DEVELOPMENT: PRENATAL TO BIRTH
	    ANCIENT MESOPOTAMIA

Format	• A unit name is written in all CAPITAL LETTERS to differentiate it from the map elements. • **Boldface** a unit name if the mapping system allows or when using a table template.

Alignment	• If the mapping system requires a unit name, it will automatically display the name for map readers.
	• If the mapping system does not require a unit name, or when using a table template, a unit name can still be included. The unit name is written within the content field directly above the unit's first content listing.
	
	Examples:
	
	    PLANET EARTH
	        A. Layers: Crust, Mantle, Core
	        B. Movements: Convection Currents, Volcanic Eruptions, Ice Flows
	        C. Geologists: Structural Geologists, Stratigraphers, Geomorphologists
	
	    NUMBER SENSE I
	        A. Number Recognition: 0–10
	        B. Number Sets: 0–10

Distinctive Features	• If a mapping system does not require a unit name, or when using a table template, and more than one unit is included in one month, each unit name and its corresponding content listing(s) are written vertically within the content field.
	
	Example of one month containing two units of study:
	
	    EXPOSITORY READING
	        A. Informational Text Purposes: Inform, Instruct, Guide, Direct, Show
	        B. Stated or Implied Main Idea: Textual, Visual
	
	    FICTIONAL READING
	        C. Historical Fiction Text: Fact Versus Fiction

Figure 4.2B   German I Diary Map Month Including Unit Name Only

Month	Content	Skills	Assessment	Standards
September	**GUTEN TAG**			

Use of Numerals in Maps

Before continuing with the map element explanations, a mention of recording numeric amounts is appropriate. Regardless of the element, the numbers 0 through 9 are written as numerals rather than as words. (The only exception is when students are literally learning to read or write a number word or words.)

The use of numerals versus words serves a purpose. Readers' eyes can scan and find numerals more easily and quickly than number words when reviewing curriculum maps. Figure 4.3 provides a visual example of elements written both ways. Your eyes can scan and locate the numeric data (middle column) more quickly than the number word data (right column).

Figure 4.3   Numerals Versus Number Words

Element	Numeral	Number Word
Unit Name	**POST–COLD WAR: BIG 3 POWERS**	**POST–COLD WAR: BIG THREE POWERS**
Content	Fractions: 1/2, 1/4	Fractions: One-half, One-fourth
Skill	Identify visually 5 parts of a friendly letter: date, opening, body, closing, signature	Identify visually five parts of a friendly letter: date, opening, body, closing, signature
Assessment	7-Sentence Paragraph	Seven-Sentence Paragraph
Resource	4-Square Graphic Organizer	Four-Square Graphic Organizer

Content

Content is what students must *know.* Collegial conversation regarding what constitutes the act of knowing is worthwhile since this term has multiple meanings, the most common of which include the following:

1. To perceive or understand as fact or truth; to apprehend clearly and with certainty: *I know the situation fully.*

2. To have established or fixed in the mind or memory: [*I*] *know a poem by heart. Do you know the way to the park from here?*

3. To be cognizant or aware of: *I know it.*

4. To be acquainted with (a thing, place, person, etc.), as by sight, experience, or report: [*I*] *know the mayor.*

5. To understand from experience or attainment: [*I*] *know how to make gingerbread.*

6. To be able to distinguish, as one from another: [*I*] *know right from wrong.* (Random House 2006)

Depending on the discipline and prior curriculum-design experience, teachers may perceive content differently. The two most common interpretations are topic-based and concept-based learning. Some state standards' disciplines have a tendency to be topic-based while others, such as social studies and science, have a tendency to be concept-based (Erickson 2007). Unless a learning organization has had training in a conceptual-learning design model (Erickson 2002, 2007), or backwards design model (McTighe and Wiggins 2004; Wiggins and McTighe 1998), content learning has a tendency to be topic-based. For example, if a curriculum map's HUMAN BODY unit contains content such as Bones and Muscles, Healthy Eating Habits, or Personal Hygiene, the learning is topic based. If the unit has content listings such as Structure, Functions, or Symbiotic Connections, the learning is concept based. Mention of these two interpretations is not a declaration that one is correct and the other is not. There are other types of content learning such as works, issues, and problem-based learning (Jacobs 2002). Regardless of curriculum design preference, within a curriculum map, the term *content* refers to what students must specifically know at a given time (e.g., particular month or months) within a school year (horizontally) and in relation to learning that takes place over a period of years (vertically). Over time, as a learning organization expands its understanding of content learning, maps are always open to revision or refinement to reflect what is currently valued.

Regardless of interpretation, what students must know is noun-focused learning. Verb-focused learning indicates skill, or doing, ability or action expectations. (The exception to this rule occurs most often in physical education and the performing arts.) Critical to curriculum design and writing map elements is teachers' being able to differentiate the knowing (content) and the doing (skills). I have read many maps wherein skills are written as content and vice versa. While learning how to write a map, investigating and discussing the differentiation between these two elements and their relationship ensures accuracy in map design, map writing, and most important, student learning.

Read the following content expectations. Which two are not accurate content listings?

1. Right Brain Drawing: Tasks, Functions

2. Identify Parts of a Plant

3. Engine Test Measurements: Horsepower, Torque, Work, Rate, Volumetric Efficiency

4. Compute Coefficients

If you said the second and fourth items, you are correct. They begin with a skill *ability* or *action* verb (identify/compute). For these listings the question becomes, "What is it the students have to specifically *know?*" To provide this clarity, the map writer or writers need to revise these content listings by (a) not including a verb and (b) including a descriptor after the appropriate key noun or noun phrase. Descriptors are usually separated from the noun or noun phrase by a colon, as the first and third items above demonstrate.

To revise the second item, a map writer may choose to rewrite the content as follows:

- Plant Parts: Roots, Stems, Leaves, Flowers, Fruits, Seeds

To revise the fourth item, the writer may choose to rewrite the content like this:

- Coefficient of Variation: Distribution Attribute

Now the writers have provided map readers with specifics regarding what students must know.

Immediately following this chapter's Review Questions is an exercise called Descriptive or Not Descriptive? That Is the Question! It can be used to stimulate thought and conversation about writing quality content listings. The disciplines used in the exercise may not be your area of expertise. Don't be disappointed. The purpose of the exercise is to study how content listings need to be worded. An answer key follows each discipline's section of the exercise.

Book Titles

Writing book titles as content expectations warrants comment. It goes back to the question "What is it that students must know?" If a content listing is *Animal Farm,* map readers conclude that students must know the intellectual significance of this particular work, including the political ramifications based on its satirical allegory of Soviet totalitarianism. If students must know reading strategies such as context clues, main and supporting characters, plot and subplots, or multiple settings, the appropriate term or terms are what need to be the content listing, and the book title should be included as a resource. If, in fact, students are expected to know specific English, social studies, and potentially other discipline-specific knowledge contained within this classic literature selection, it would be most appropriate to design a cross- or interdisciplinary unit of study titled ANIMAL FARM and the appropriate content and skills included within.

Criteria

Figure 4.4A addresses content wording, format, intra-alignment, and distinctive features.

Figure 4.4A Recommended Content Norms

	Reference Points

Wording	• Content listings represent what students must specifically know for a given month or unit. They are typically written as a *noun/noun phrase: descriptor.*
	• Verbs are occasionally used as descriptors, but not to indicate what students must do. For example, the first quality example below contains five verbs. These verbs relate to what the noun phrase *informational text* does for a reader, not what students do with informational text.
	
	Quality examples:
	    Informational Text Purposes: Inform, Instruct, Guide, Direct, Show
	    WWII: Key Causes for U.S. Entry
	    Cheer Motions: Ready Position, Lunge, High V, Low V
	
	Inappropriate use of verbs in content listings:
	    Read Informational Text
	    Explain Key Causes of WWII
	    Execute Cheers
	
	Unique verb-focused content listings occur occasionally in physical education and other performance-based courses. For example, a unit may appropriately include the following:
	    BASKETBALL
	        A. Full-Court Game: Rules
	        B. Ball Handling: Dribble, Control, Protect, Pivot
	        C. Passing: Chest/Bounce, Jab Step/Pull Back, Ball Fakes

	• Descriptors play a vital role in acknowledging the specific knowing expectations within a given month or unit. Including descriptors significantly increases a learning organization's ability to find gaps, repetitions, and absences during curriculum reviews.
	
	Vague content listings (general nouns/no descriptors):
	    Graph Data
	    Poetry
	    Geography

	Reference Points
	Quality content listings (specific nouns: descriptors): Double-Bar Graph: Up to 3 Variables Haiku Poetry: Syllabication U.S. Geography: Northeast Region
Format	• The first letter in each word of a content listing is capitalized, similar to a chapter title in a table of contents. • A content listing's key noun or noun phrase is followed by a colon and an appropriate descriptor. Examples: Earth's Moon: 8 Sequential Phases Metaphors: Extended, Mixed, Dead Texas: Panhandle Plains, Prairies, Piney Woods, Lakes Sir Isaac Newton: 1665–1704 Key Contributions Square Roots: Principal and Regular

Alignment	• Intra-alignment for the included map elements is based on each content listing within one month or, for individual-unit mapping systems, one unit.
	 • Intra-alignment is visually represented using a letter-number coding process.* A sequential alphabet coding precedes each content listing.
	 • Each coding letter is capitalized and followed by a period and one space after the period before content listing begins.
	
	 Example:
	
	 ITALIAN RENAISSANCE
	
	     A. Florence: Major Influences
	
	     B. Alliances: Treaty of Lodi
	
	     C. Innovations: 15th-Century Contributions
	
	 *Note: One commercial mapping system has a distinctive method for creating intra-alignment. While a map writer or writers' mental process is the same as the letter–number coding process, visual alignment is achieved using a specific system feature and procedure.
	
	 • The intra-alignment letter–number coding restarts with a capital letter A for every new month, or in some mapping systems, every new unit.
	 • Since learning does not instantly stop on the last day of a month, for month-based mapping systems, if the previous month's last content listing is continued as the first content listing in the new month, it will receive the letter A in the new month and notation is made regarding the continued learning.

(Continued)

Figure 4.4A (Continued)

	Reference Points

	Example:
	
	September's third content listing below is preceded by a capital C. In the following month, October, the same content listing is preceded by letter A, and a continued learning notation is made in parentheses.
	
	September's Content Listings
	    A. Initial and Final Phonemes: /t/ /l/ /m/
	    B. Prepositions: Under, Over, Through
	    C. Story Elements: Main Character, Setting
	
	October's Content Listings
	    A. Story Elements: Main Character, Setting (Cont. from Sept.)
	    B. Initial and Final Phonemes: /d/ /r/
	
	Vague representation of continued-next-month content learning is not recommended:
	October's Content Listings
	    See September

Distinctive Features	• It is important to remember that content listings written using a noun or noun phrase followed by descriptors truly provide needed clarity for horizontal and vertical curriculum design.
	
	Content listings that do not provide clarity:
	    3-D Shapes
	    Speech
	
	Content listings that do provide clarity:
	    3-D Shapes: Cone, Sphere, Pyramid
	    Ceremonial Speech: Eulogy

Figure 4.4B German I Diary Map Month Including Unit Name, Content, and Onset of Intra-Alignment Coding

Month	Content	Skills	Assessment	Standards
September	**GUTEN TAG** A. Alphabet: Letter Name, Pronunciation B. Masculine/Feminine/Neuter Nouns: Classroom Environment C. Time: Calendar, Seasons			

Skills

Skills are what students must do in relation to the knowing (content). Skills are cognitive *ability*, physical *action*, or a combination of both. They are written beginning with a capital letter and have no period at the end of the statement. (I mention this now so you will not wonder why all the skill statement examples have no periods.) There are three parts to a well-written skill statement: measurable verb, target, and descriptor. Read the following skill statements:

- Compare in writing 3 elements, line, stanza, meter, using traditional/ nontraditional forms of poetry
- Identify aurally and orally between ½ notes, ¼ notes
- Justify in writing effects of economic ebb and flow in relationship to target audience sales

Now read them again with each of the three parts identified in parentheses after the appropriate portion:

- Compare *(measurable verb)* in writing *(target)* 3 elements, line, stanza, meter, using traditional and nontraditional forms of poetry *(descriptor)*
- Identify *(measurable verb)* aurally and orally *(target)* between ½ notes, ¼ notes *(descriptor)*
- Justify *(measurable verb)* in writing *(target)* effects of economic ebb and flow in relationship to target audience sales *(descriptor)*

Each part plays a significant role in conveying what students must do. The verb represents a specific action or ability that can be distinctively measured using appropriate assessments and evaluations. The target conveys the manner or mode, in other words, how the action or ability will be formally and possibly informally measured. The descriptor provides details in relationship to the aligned content. Before discussing each skill statement part in detail, the difference between a skill and an activity must first be addressed.

Skill Versus Activity

A skill represents ability or action competency, not an activity leading toward competency. At first, some may find it difficult to differentiate the two. One reason may be that learning is a continuum. There are times when learning begins as content, becomes part of a skill, and later is incorporated into an activity. This transformation of learning can take place in one school year or over a period of years. Figure 4.5 provides an example of a potential compare-and-contrast learning continuum.

Figure 4.5   Compare-and-Contrast Learning Continuum

Map Element	Curriculum Map Recording
Learning begins as *content*.	Compare/Contrast: Similarities/Differences
After students exhibit consistency in the concept of compare-and-contrast, the content transforms into a *skill* action or ability.	Compare and contrast in writing 3 domestic policy roles of presidency
Students eventually generalize the action or ability and utilize it during various *activities* that aid in new content and skill learning.	Compare and contrast resources for average daily intake of water by woodland animals. 3- to 4-member teams compare and contrast 18th-century Native American tribes' food, crops, and water harvesting procedures.

Activities are practice experiences that lead to mastery of a primary skill or skill set. For example, students may use a secondary skill of visually identifying key characteristics of three leaf types to aid in the primary skill focus of classifying.

When writing a skill statement, the measurable verb must correctly inform map readers of the skill expectation. If the initial verb does not represent the intended ability or action, misinterpretation is highly likely. The following examples are snippets from two teachers' personal experiences while trying to internalize writing quality measurable-verb skill statements. Both examples ring true of the learning curve that some teachers experience in trying to accurately convey student learning expectations when writing skill statements.

High School Communication Arts

Recorded Skill Statement

Walk around the room and interview classmates while focusing on 3 techniques: eye contact, restating of questions, clarifying responses

The initial verb is *walk*. When this teacher was asked if students were learning the skill of walking, she laughed, rolled her eyes, and said, "No, of course not!" When asked if she thought the intended measurable verb was contained within her original statement, she scanned the text, sighed, and answered, "Yes ... *interview*." She quickly realized that she had another word that was not appropriate regarding the skill expectation. She realized that *classmates* was part of the activity. She acknowledged that the skill ability is to be able to interview anyone.

Her Revised Skill Statement

Interview orally people focusing on 3 techniques: eye contact, restating of questions, clarifying responses

Grade 5 Social Studies

Recorded Skill Statement

Role-play the Boston Tea Party

The initial verb is *role-play.* When this teacher was asked if role-playing was the primary learning expectation, he thought for a moment, shook his head, and said, "No, not really. They had to justify the ramifications of how this American colonist protest against Great Britain helped ignite the American Revolution." He acknowledged that the role-play was an activity to engage students in group discussion about this historic event from multiple perspectives.

His Revised Skill Statement

Justify in writing ramifications of Boston Tea Party in relationship to igniting American Revolution from multiple perspectives

Be aware that a verb may be appropriate as a skill's measurable verb in one discipline, but not in another. For example, the verb *play* in music is often a measurable skill:

- Play all note and rest values as encountered in a repertoire individually and with others

Whereas in math or science, the verb *play* most likely represents an activity:

- Play multiplication games
- Play Chemical Compounds Jeopardy

Teachers need to have multiple opportunities to explore the differentiation between skills and activities in relationship to curriculum design and writing curriculum maps. Participating in the Skill Versus Activity exercise at the end of this chapter may help ignite collegial conversation.

Nonmeasurable Verbs

As mentioned previously, the initial skill verb is critical for accurately conveying what students must do. The term *measurable* literally means "able to be measured." The following verbs cannot, in and of themselves, be measured and therefore may not begin a skill statement in a curriculum map:

- *demonstrate*
- *understand*
- *know*
- *show*
- *use*

Demonstrate is the act of exhibiting. Standards, also known as *proficiency targets*, and related documents often start standard statements with this directive. Consequently, clarity regarding specific student learning expectations can be misleading, as in the following:

- Demonstrate the associative property of multiplication

The above proficiency target implies that by the end of the school year, or by the state testing date, students will be able to independently do the following:

- Change grouping of 3 factors using parentheses to represent the same product

While the measurable verb *change* is not explicitly stated in the standard proficiency target, it is implied. Map data is meant to be explicit and requires teachers to contemplate and state in a map what is clearly being expected of students.

Understand is an important concept when designing assessments that measure students' ability to cognitively connect one or more content-skills sets. The question first must be: What is it that students must do in order to understand? When teachers translate what students must understand into measurable verbs and design quality skill statements aligned to content, assessment design instantly likewise becomes easier due to the clarity of the explicit learning expectations.

Show is similar to the term *demonstrate*. It is related to the act of exhibiting. The question becomes: What is it that needs to be exhibited? When the desired actions or abilities are written as measurable verb-based skill statements, appropriate assessments likewise become easier to design to best match the learning expectations.

Figure 4.6 provides examples of various standard proficiency targets that incorporate nonmeasurable verbs and teachers' translations into explicit measurable skill expectations.

The term *use* is unique. In Figure 4.6's last translation, *use a calculator* (i.e., press the correct keys to produce an outcome) *to determine slope* is not the primary learning focus. In the reworded statement, the translation clarifies for map readers that teachers agreed that for their students the primary learning is an ability to determine.

As with the previous proficiency target, the following standard statement's primary learning measurable verb is located within the statement:

- Use the following to interpret historical data: timelines—B.C.E. and B.C./C.E. and A.D.; graphs, tables, charts, and maps

The measurable verb is *interpret*. To employ this ability, specific types of various graphic organizers (timelines, graphs, tables, charts, maps) that contain historical data are expected to be used. For this standard statement, what is critical to curriculum design, especially when creating a Consensus Map or an Essential Map, is the teachers' collegial reflection and dialogue regarding the expected depth and breadth of students' ability to interpret graphically displayed historical data given age, maturation, and prior academic knowledge. Likewise, while

Figure 4.6   State Standards Translated to Skill Expectations

State Standard	What Students Must Be Able to Do
Understand how voice can affect a writer's work and a reader's interpretation	*Identify* 3 common characteristics of voice: who is speaking (not necessarily author), who is being spoken to (audience), how written words are used to set tone for audience (emotion)
	Justify why people have favorite authors using primary sources
Know that the sun is one of many stars in the Milky Way galaxy and that stars differ in size, temperature, and color	*Define* chemical components of a star as a ball structure of mostly hydrogen/helium gases
	Compare and *contrast* stars based on 3 single or combined attributes: size, temperature, color
	Extrapolate why scientists believe there is a range of stars in Milky Way galaxy using self-selected research data
Show how the three branches of government function through a system of checks and balances	*Compare* and *contrast* the roles of legislative, executive, judicial branches as set forth by U.S. Constitution
	Justify purpose for separation of governmental power
	Sequence processes for checks-and-balances scenarios wherein a particular branch exerts legal power
Use a calculator to determine slope	*Determine* slope with/without using a calculator

this statement includes explicit learning expectations, there is much to be discussed regarding what is also implied.

There will be times when a mandated proficiency target's initial verb is explicit and appropriate, and therefore does not need to be altered for clarification:

- Tune instrument using a tuner or other pitch reference
- Recite short poems or stories with appropriate expression
- Draw a geometric figure showing specified properties, such as parallelism and perpendicularity
- Compare ways people lived in colonial times with how people live today (e.g., housing, food, transportation, school)
- Describe how advertising influences health behavior
- Identify elements of a story, including characters, setting, and key events

Targets

The second part of a well-written skill statement is the target. The target references for map readers the manner or mode by which students' assessment(s) will be conducted in relation to the measurable verb(s). Some measurable verbs need targets, while others do not. You may have noticed that the six items listed above are actually grouped in two sets of three. The first three initial verbs do not need targets since each verb itself indicates explicitly how students will be measured (i.e., tune [*aurally*], recite [*orally*], draw [*in writing*]). The second three verbs need targets added textually to express the mode(s) by which students' independent abilities or actions will be measured.

The most common targets include *in writing, orally, visually, aurally, kinesthetically, manipulatively,* and *manually.* Read the following two skill statements:

- Identify 7 key parts: spark plug, valves, piston, piston rings, connecting rod, crankshaft, sump
- Identify visually and orally 7 key parts: spark plug, valves, piston, piston rings, connecting rod, crankshaft, sump

Which skill statement enables readers to accurately visualize the actions expected of students when it is time for an informal or formal assessment? The first skill statement leaves it up to map readers to infer. The second skill statement clearly conveys the required modes.

When an included target, such as *in writing,* follows a skill statement's measurable verb, it does not imply that students will never practice or participate in learning using other modes. Most classroom activities include a variety of learning modes such as small- or large-group discussions (orally), hands-on experiences (kinesthetically, manipulatively, manually), or listening to a teacher/others discuss a topic or issue or hearing an object producing sound (aurally). Since a curriculum map's content–skills–assessment relationship represents the big picture of learning, the skill statements' target modes need to match the manner(s) in which the recorded intra-aligned assessments measure the learning. Study the two examples in Figure 4.7.

Example 1's assessments appropriately measure visual and written modes. Example 2's assessment does not appropriately measure kinesthetic, aural, and oral modes. Although these examples are simplistic, they make the point that assessments must thoughtfully and accurately measure both the content–skill expectations and the manner in which the expectations are measured.

Figure 4.7   Target Modality Aligned to Assessment Types

Example 1		
Content	*Skills*	*Assessments*
A. Animal Groups: Vertebrates, Invertebrates	A1. Distinguish visually and in writing characteristics between 5 with-backbone members (fish, amphibians, reptiles, birds, mammals) and 6 without-backbone members (sponges, coelenterates, echinoderms, worms, mollusks, arthropods) A2. Classify visually and in writing various animals based on backbone/no-backbone criteria	A1-A2. 20 Animal Identification Quiz A1-A2. Partner Comparison Lab (Evaluation: Teacher Ob/Student Note Taking/Checklist)
Example 2		
Content	*Skills*	*Assessments*
A. Musical Patterns: Whole, Half, Quarter Rhythm	A1. Differentiate aurally and kinesthetically beat divisions A2. Sing in unison and in rounds to call/response songs	A1-A2. 10 MC Test

As mentioned previously, some measurable verbs are self-explanatory regarding how an ability or action will be measured (e.g., write, illustrate, draw, orate, tune). Certain disciplines' measurable verbs naturally imply that learning will be measured in writing. For example, in mathematics *solve, calculate, find,* and *figure* are most often measured using written responses and therefore do not need the target *in writing* included after these four measurable verbs in a mathematics map. *Read* is another unique measurable verb. It is assumed that this verb is accomplished silently in conjunction with the skill statement's descriptor or other skill statement(s) unless otherwise indicated by using the target *orally* after the verb (e.g., Read orally timed passage; Read numerals in sequence and isolation). Figure 4.8 includes a sample list of verbs that, regardless of discipline, need a target mode or modes after the measurable verb to provide map readers with clarity regarding how the learning will be or has been measured.

Figure 4.8   Verbs That Need Targets to Provide Clarity

Classify	Differentiate	List
Communicate	Discriminate	Match
Compare	Distinguish	Organize
Contrast	Estimate	Predict
Convert	Evaluate	Prioritize
Correlate	Explain	Produce
Criticize	Generalize	Prove
Critique	Identify	Recognize
Define	Infer	Sequence
Describe	Interpret	Summarize
Determine	Invent	Support

Regarding target modes, consideration must be given to courses that do not fall within the conventional disciplines found in learning organizations. For example, I have worked with a technical high school that offered courses in such disciplines as grounds keeping, auto mechanics, cabinetry, and media. One of the teachers at this school wrote the following skill statement:

- Edit electronically audio/video components using movie production software

This teacher included all the parts of a quality written skill and therefore conveyed well to map readers the student learning expectation. For the students in this particular course, the mode for editing is electronic. A student may leave this class and go to a language arts class wherein he or she is expected to edit in writing using a corrective pen. Both courses emphasize the conceptual action of editing, but with different modes.

When writing a skill statement, targets are written directly after the measurable verb, not after the descriptor:

- Differentiate visually and orally front/back field positions

Versus

- Differentiate front/back field positions visually and orally

Since a target relates directly to the measurable verb, it is easier for map readers to locate this information when it comes directly after the verb. Every once in a while it may seem awkward to include the target directly after the verb:

- Tell in writing time on analog and digital faces

Even so, it is recommended that teachers stay consistent with the established norm of measurable verb, target, descriptor.

Descriptors

The third part of a well-written skill statement is the descriptor. It adds critical clarity and enhances the learning expectation relationship between a skill or skill set and the aligned content learning. A skill statement's descriptor should not be identical to the content descriptor's text. This simply duplicates information and does not assist map readers. Figure 4.9 compares vague versus quality content–skills recordings. Notice that the skill descriptors in the quality column provide new information regarding the content–skills intra-alignment relationship.

If teachers choose to start a skill statement with the verb *apply*, there must be a descriptor that indicates to what the action or ability learning is being applied. For example, a teacher may write the following:

- Apply one-point linear perspective

Apply one-point linear perspective *to what?* The skill statement needs a descriptor to provide map readers with clarity and accuracy in understanding the student learning expectations. This teacher may choose to revise the skill statement to read:

- Apply one-point linear perspective to drawing scenes using chalk and pencil media

When first learning to write a map, some teachers may have difficulty in differentiating content descriptors from skill descriptors and therefore record nouns in a skill statement that are actually content learning. Here is an example:

Content

- Time: Clocks

Skill

- Tell in writing time to 1/2 hour, 1/4 hour

Figure 4.9 Vague Versus Quality Content–Skill Set Intra-Alignment

Vague Intra-Alignment Content–Skill Statement Descriptors	Quality Intra-Alignment Content–Skill Statement Descriptors
Content Addition *Skill* Solve addition problems	*Content* Addition: 2 Digits With Regrouping *Skills* Solve horizontal and vertical problems Solve 2-step word problems
Content Oral Presentation: Research *Skills* Research topic Present research paper Use visual aids	*Content* Oral Presentation: Web-Based Research *Skills* Summarize in writing and orally 4 key points based on self-selected topic and thesis statement Elaborate in writing and orally at least 3 subpoints per key point using visual aid or aids to enhance presentation
Content Fossils *Skill* Study fossils	*Content* Fossils: Formation *Skills* Identify visually and in writing 4 key conditions/processes necessary for fossils to form: insulation, sedimentation, permineralization, uplift Explain in writing how biostratigraphic correlation aids in determining rock ages including faunal succession (animals), floral succession (plants)

In actuality the concept of *time related to quantity* is the content (i.e., half or quarter hour). Here is a revision that indicates to map readers the intended content and aligned skills:

Content

- Time: 1/2 hour, 1/4 hour

Skills

- Tell in writing time on analog and digital faces using numerals, colon
- Identify in writing time period using A.M., P.M. symbols
- State orally when a given analog or digital time is half past, quarter past, quarter to the hour

The revision makes clear to map readers, and teachers as curriculum designers, the current learning expectations for the students. For curriculum maps to truly be a strategic tool that aids in designing a rigorous curriculum, it is best in the long run if teachers learn to pay attention to detail from the onset of a mapping initiative.

Skill Statements Are Not About the Teacher

A skill statement represents what students, not the teacher, are responsible for doing. A Kindergarten teacher recorded the following skill statement in her Diary Map:

- Introduce orally short /u/ sound

This skill statement conveys to map readers that the kindergarteners introduce the sound. When this fact was brought to this teacher's attention, she realized that she wrote all of the skill statements from the perspective of her actions, not those of the students. She revised this particular skill statement to read:

- Produce orally short /u/ sound

Since all skill statements are about the students, they do not need to begin with *The students will. . . .* Each skill statement starts with the measurable verb.

Criteria

Figure 4.10A addresses skill wording, format, intra-alignment, and distinctive features.

Figure 4.10A Recommended Skills Norms

	Reference Points
Wording	• Skills represent what students must do in relationship to what students must know (content) regarding learning abilities or actions. • A skill statement begins with a measurable verb. *Demonstrate, understand, know, show,* and *use** are not considered measurable. • In Mathematics, Solve . . . , Calculate . . . , Find . . . , Figure . . . , do not need *in writing* included as a target. Read . . . does not need a target unless students are assessed/evaluated *orally* wherein this target would be included. • Do not begin a skill statement with *The student will. . . .* Start with the measurable verb. Examples: Identify visually and in writing 5 major land forms: mountain, plateau, plain, peninsula, valley Recognize in writing 4 common attributes of saints through the ages: servanthood, humbleness, sacrificial nature, common man Outline in writing historical development of Periodic Table of Elements Solve 2-step word problems Read orally given passage focusing on rate, tone *Use is unique. While rarely the primary learning expectation, *use* is often included at the onset of a prepositional phrase.

	Reference Points
	Examples: Construct a freestanding sculpture using 2 media Prioritize in writing potential effects of global warming using multiple graphic organizers
	• A measurable verb needs an appropriate clarifying target regarding assessment expectations if the verb is not explicit (e.g., write, draw, spell). For example, *identify* can be measured in writing, orally, visually, aurally, kinesthetically, manipulatively, or manually. Examples: Explain in writing 3 key characteristics of carnivores: organs for capturing and disarticulating prey, status as a hunter, status as a scavenger Justify visually and orally 3 benefits for a target audience being provided statistical data displayed in multiple graph formats Discriminate aurally between low- and high-pitch sound frequencies
Format	• A skill statement starts with a capital letter, but does not end with a period. • A target is written directly after the measurable verb, not after the descriptor. • Each skill statement's letter* or letter–number coding is directly followed by a period, one space, and the skill statement. Examples: A1. Blend orally 2–3 phonemes to form monosyllabic words C2. Determine visually and in writing how families have similarities and differences worldwide: food, clothing, shelter, games E. Differentiate in writing monounsaturated and polyunsaturated trans fats and health effects of each E. Compare in writing global trans fats response and regulation using self-selected primary-source documentation *Note:* The use of number coding may or may not be used in a Consensus Map or an Essential Map as it will be dependent on the inclusion or exclusion of planned assessments.
Alignment	• Continue intra-alignment coding by connecting content to skill statements by including the appropriate corresponding content alphabet coding letter in front of each aligned skill listing(s). • To intra-align content-skills to an assessment or assessments, a number sequence is added after each skill's coding letter. The number sequence starts over with the number 1 for each content coding letter in a month or unit. (*Important Note:* Since the sample German 1 Diary Map month does not yet include assessments, there will be no numbers included with the skill's letter coding at this time in Figure 4.10B.)

(Continued)

Figure 4.10A (Continued)

	Reference Points

	The following letter–number coding example represents two content–skill sets, A and B, within one unit:
	
	Unit Name and Content
	GEOMETRY III
	    A. Figure: Line of Symmetry, Turn Symmetry
	    B. Figure Transformation: Rotation, Reflection
	
	Skills
	    A1. Determine visually and in writing if a figure's halves create a mirror image by drawing straight line through center of figure
	    A2. Differentiate visually and in writing figures that follow Rule of Turn Symmetry and figures that do not
	    B1. Identify visually and in writing a rotation as a turn around a center point that causes a figure to appear different while still congruent to original figure
	    B2. Identify visually and in writing a reflection as a flip-over motion wherein every point of figure moves across a line to create a mirror or reverse image
	    B3. Prove visually and in writing that a figure's rotation and reflection can yield same image result

Distinctive Features	• A map's skill statement must be a skill, not an activity. An activity provides practice regarding scaffolding that eventually enables students to independently exhibit the skill learning expectation(s). There are times when skills may appear specific, but there should be a sense of generality to the statement. Significant activities are important for teachers to be aware of in one another's learning environments since they aid in collegial conversation and understanding each other's pedagogical practices, but are most often included in maps during map-data refinement either as attachments or in a newly added element field.
	
	Activity example:
	  • Draw a clown using small and large shapes with crayons
	
	Revised as a skill example:
	  • Draw various objects integrating small and large shapes using various media
	
	Activity example:
	  • Prioritize in writing in a small group extreme weather versus glacier retreating effects using Venn Diagram
	
	Revised as a skill example:
	  • Prioritize in writing potential effects of global warming using multiple graphic organizers

	• To provide clarity for map readers, do not repeat content terms as skill statement descriptors. Include quality skill descriptors that enhance readers' student-learning information based on the content knowledge.

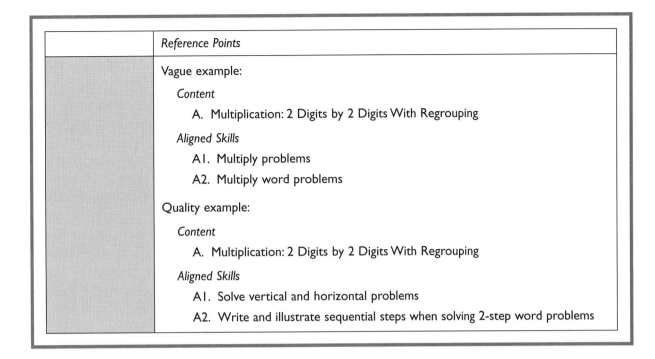

	Reference Points
	Vague example:
	Content
	A. Multiplication: 2 Digits by 2 Digits With Regrouping
	Aligned Skills
	A1. Multiply problems
	A2. Multiply word problems
	Quality example:
	Content
	A. Multiplication: 2 Digits by 2 Digits With Regrouping
	Aligned Skills
	A1. Solve vertical and horizontal problems
	A2. Write and illustrate sequential steps when solving 2-step word problems

Figure 4.10B   German I Diary Map Month Including Unit Name, Content, Skills, and Intra-Alignment Letter Coding—Content to Skills

Month	Content	Skills	Assessment	Standards
September	**GUTEN TAG** A. Alphabet: Letter Name, Pronunciation	A. Recite A–Z in and out of sequence using German pronunciation A. Pronounce and spell orally letters in translated or given German name		
	B. Masculine/ Feminine/Neuter Nouns: Classroom Environment	B. Translate orally into English German names of common objects (e.g., desk, chair, door, window, pen, pencil, paper, board, light, other single object items) using proper gender: der, die, das B. Identify orally classroom objects in German when told English name using proper gender		
	C. Time: Calendar, Seasons	C. State orally 7 days (Sunday, Monday, Tuesday, Wednesday, Thursday, Friday, Saturday), 12 months (January, February, March, April, May, June, July, August, September, October, November, December), 4 seasons (Winter, Spring, Summer, Fall) in and out of sequence C. Write 7 day names in sequence and in isolation		

Assessment

The word *assessment* evokes numerous mental models (Ainsworth and Viegut 2006; English and Steffy 2002; Marzano, Pickering, and McTighe 1993; McTighe and Wiggins 2004; Reeves 1996–2002; Stiggins et al. 2005). While experts may differ in theory or practice, collectively they ask a similar student-centered question: Are the assessments being administered *accurately* measuring what students must know and be able to do?

Jacobs (1997) remarks that "focusing on assessment through the course of the year deepens accountability" (p. 22). Is there a synergy, or coherency, between the intra-aligned content, skills, and assessments within a curriculum map? If a physical education teacher's students are learning to serve a volleyball, measuring the learning by administering a paper-and-pencil test would not be coherent. Likewise, students' ability to compose musical scores would not be best measured by a fill-in-the-blank quiz.

Ensuring that assessment types accurately measure content–skill or skill sets is critical to improving instruction, learning, and student performance. To aid in determining this synergy, an assessment name must properly define the nature (e.g., multiple choice, essay, poster, PowerPoint presentation, two-act play) of the assessment. If a teacher writes an assessment as *Chapter 8 Test*, this information does not provide map readers with insight into students' cognitive or psychomotor demands. If a teacher wants to include chapter or resource information, it can be written in parentheses after defining the assessment's attribute or attributes:

- 10 Short-Answer (Chapter 8) Test
- 25 Item (Unit 4) Exam
- 30 Item 15 MC/10 FinB/5 Constructed-Response (Chapter 3) Test
- 2 Act (Script C) Play

Although it may seem trite to include the specific number or type of items in an assessment name rather than write a generic name (e.g., test, quiz, report), when teachers begin conducting reviews focused on assessment practices, this data is invaluable and will drive collaborative conversations.

Three teachers noticed that their students did not perform as well as expected on a new selected-response district benchmark assessment. The teachers were certain that their students knew the necessary information, so what was the problem? They evaluated the actual test items and verified that it was not a content-skills learning or literacy issue. One teacher brought up the fact that the benchmark assessment had quite a few test items. They counted the test items and noted that there was a total of 55 items. They reviewed their Diary Maps and discovered that the average number of selected-response assessment items given was 20. They hypothesized that perhaps it was a fatigue issue, not a learning issue. For the next semester they committed to slowly increasing the number of test items per assessment to eventually mirror the district benchmark assessment format. When the students took the next district assessment, the scores improved.

When writing an assessment name, each word begins with a capital letter, similar to writing a proper name or a title. When recording an assessment in a map, as mentioned previously, teachers need to write the assessment as a defined name that provides a succinct depiction of the measurement. Consider the following examples:

- 20 Item Test
- Biomes PowerPoint Presentation
- Eleanor Roosevelt Essay

Notice that these assessment names do not include narratives regarding administering processes or procedures (e.g., handing out materials, completion steps, duration, feedback to students). Depending on the mapping system used, this information is either attached as a linked document or included within a provided assessment template.

Assessment Versus Evaluation

When first learning how to write a map, since there is much to remember, it is best for teachers to begin by including the assessment names and, when appropriate, key evaluation information. An assessment is the actual product or performance. The evaluation is the criteria and judgment placed on the product or performance. I have found that if teachers have not had professional development that focuses on this difference, there is often misrepresentation within the written maps. For example, teacher observation is not an assessment. It is an evaluation wherein a teacher visually judges students' product or performance based on criteria such as a checklist, a rubric, a matrix, or a grading scale.

Some recorded assessments do not need evaluation data if the defined name denotes how student learning is judged. Take a look at the following three assessment names, and determine which one needs evaluation information included:

- 10 Term Etymology Quiz
- 25 Item (MC/FinB/Matching) Test
- 2 Persuasive Mini-Essays

It is highly likely that the 10 Term Etymology Quiz is awarded 10 points per term, with a total value of 100 points. Knowing the school or district grading policy, map readers can figure out the evaluation grading scale criteria without this being indicated in parentheses. The 25 Item (MC/FinB/Matching) Test denotes a mixture of item types, yet given the total of 25 items, again each item is most likely worth four points and therefore the total possible score is 100 points. For both of these assessments, no evaluation explanation is needed unless the teacher evaluation criteria are unique. With the remaining assessment, 2 Persuasive Mini-Essays, it is unclear how the teacher evaluates the student product. Because the evaluation criteria are not clear, the assessment name needs evaluation information. Given that the teacher is in the early stages of learning to write a map, the evaluation information can initially be conveyed in parentheses after the assessment name without having to actually attach or include the literal criteria and documents involved in the evaluation process. Here is an example of the teacher's included evaluation information:

- 2 Persuasive Mini-Essays (Evaluation: Peer Review/Student-Generated Rubric)

At the onset of mapping, teachers who need to include evaluation information and documentation often do not have formalized (e.g., written) criteria. When asked how students' evaluation is determined for a given assessment, a response may be, "I just look at the work and I know." Know what? For a performance or complex product-based assessment, students should be provided written evaluation criteria prior to producing the product or performance. Some teachers may need adequate amounts of time set aside to literally create the necessary documents and evaluation information to use in the classroom and to eventually attach or include in a curriculum map.

If teachers are not ready to attach evaluation criteria and documentation when first writing maps, as previously mentioned, an assessment's evaluation clarification is summarized in parentheses directly after the assessment name:

- Core Pattern Performance Task (Evaluation: Teacher Ob/Rubric)
- Penny Hardness Lab (Evaluation: Checklist/Journal Entries)
- 5 Constructed-Response Question Test (Evaluation: Rubric)
- President Truman Oration (Evaluation: Peer Review/Checklist)
- Leaf Comparison Graphic Organizer (Evaluation: Teacher Ob/Checklist)

It is important to remember that assessment names cannot be vague. They must be accurate indications of how the intra-aligned content and skills are appropriately being measured (see Figure 4.11).

Figure 4.11   Vague Versus Quality Assessment Names

Vague Assessment Names	Quality Assessment Names
Test	30 MC Test
Quizzes	5 10-Item Short-Answer Quizzes
Report	Self-Selected Research Report (Evaluation: 5 Periodic Teacher–Student Interviews/Draft Checklist/Final Document Rubric)
Graphic Organizer	Main-Idea Comparison Graphic Organizer (Evaluation: Peer Discussion/Summary Sheet)
Homework	FOR Moon's Phases Sequential Chart (Evaluation: Small-Group Peer Review/Checklist)

To spark conversation regarding writing quality assessment names (and, when appropriate, evaluation information), it may be helpful to use the Assessment Versus Evaluation exercise found at the end of this chapter.

Summative Versus Formative Assessment

Although Diary Maps and Projected Maps are the most intimate and detailed maps, they are not meant to include every single assessment administered to students. A map is a summary of the learning expectations and assessments. When first learning how to write map elements, teachers most often focus on including *summative* assessments, which are sometimes referred to as assessments *of* learning (Chappuis et al. 2004). These performances or products are meant to provide progress information to students as well as others, such as teachers, parents, and district or state departments. They are formally graded and affect report-card outcomes or other assessment-result databases.

The second assessment category that may be included in a map is significant *formative* assessments. Black and Wiliam (1998) state that formative assessment must include formal feedback to individual students regarding "the particular qualities of his or her work, with advice on what he or she can do to improve, and should avoid comparisons with other pupils" (under "How Can We Improve Formative Assessment," ¶ 3). Stiggins et al. (2005) describe these assessments as assessments *for* learning. They are not intended to be graded; they are meant to provide instant feedback to inform and empower a student to self-determine, with teacher guidance, what he or she needs to personally and strategically improve to reach or extend beyond independent mastery.

If a teacher chooses to include a significant formative assessment, FOR (in all capital letters) is written prior to the assessment name:

- FOR Fluency Rate Reading (Evaluation: Teacher-Student Ob/Fluency Rate Chart/Feedback Form)
- FOR 2 Bias Article Essays (Evaluation: Peer Discussion/Rubric)

The all-capital FOR informs map readers that a particular assessment is formative rather than summative:

- 25 Item Test
- Cartoon Storyboard (Evaluation: Teacher Ob/Checklist/Rubric)
- FOR 10 Term Quiz
- 30 Item (MC/Matching/Short-Answer) Test
- FOR Eye Poster (Evaluation: Peer Review/Checklist/Feedback Form)

While collaborative dialogue about the practice of using formative versus summative assessments in relation to student learning success is imperative (Stiggins 2007), this topic of conversation may not take place at the onset of a mapping initiative. Therefore, when teachers are initially asked to map, they must decide if an included assessment is an assessment of learning or an assessment for learning and indicate it as such when recording the assessment name.

If a teacher values homework as an assessment and wants to include assignments in a Projected/Diary Map, the question becomes "Is the homework an assessment of learning or for learning?" Once determined, the teacher will record (a) the intra-aligned letter–number coding to link the appropriate content-skill(s) to the assessment; (b) if appropriate, include the term FOR prior to the defined name to indicate it is a formative rather than a summative assessment; (c) the assignment's defined assessment name (e.g., Note Taking/10 Page Reading Assignment, 20 Item HW Assignment, Body Contour Sketch), as opposed to simply including the generic term *homework;* and (d) if appropriate, evaluation information in parentheses or as an attachment.

When projected or diary mapping, a teacher is accountable for intra-aligning every content-skill or skill set to an assessment or assessments. There may be times when a skill or skill set may not yet be ready for summative assessment by the end of the month or unit. In this case the teacher needs to include at least one formative assessment that measures the in-progress learning and is documented appropriately in the map using the FOR term prior to the assessment name.

Benchmark Assessment

The term *benchmark* has various connotations. It literally means a point of reference. Benchmark assessments are often given after a specific period of time, such as the middle and/or end of a grading period. A benchmark assessment is meant to provide teachers with individual and collective data concerning where students have been, currently are, and need to be going regarding targeted learning.

If a district or school site administers benchmark assessments, the assessment name is written within a map in the appropriate testing month or months. If the date or dates of administering are known, they may be included in parentheses directly after the name. For example, if a benchmark assessment is given in November, an Essential Map's notation may read:

- DISTRICT BENCHMARK Writing Test (Sept. to Nov. 19)

Since a benchmark assessment can be given at a single school site or simultaneously throughout a learning organization, to differentiate the two in a Consensus Map, the term SCHOOL is often used to denote a school site–designed assessment, as opposed to a districtwide assessment:

- SCHOOL BENCHMARK Reading Test (Sept. 28)
- DISTRICT BENCHMARK Reading Test (1st Quarter/Oct. 19)

Benchmark assessments are usually administered on the same day throughout a school or a district. To best meet students' needs, a given benchmark assessment should be scored immediately by the teachers who administer it. If this is not possible, the results and actual assessment items must be returned to the teachers in a timely fashion (e.g., within a few days) to be reviewed by the teachers to plan immediately for student intervention or extension.

If a state-mandated test or exam is noted in an Essential Map or Consensus Map, the official name and testing window is included:

- AIMS State Exam (April 15–19)

Common Versus Same Assessment

Common assessments are school-site, teacher-designed, or teacher-selected assessments administered simultaneously by all teachers teaching a specific course or unit of study. These assessments may have a single-discipline, cross-disciplinary, or interdisciplinary focus. The purpose of a common assessment is to focus on specific learning expectations, not all the expectations within a course or unit of study. Therefore, collegial planning and decision making regarding the selection of what will be assessed, as well as an appropriate product or performance measurement, are determined before the assessment and evaluation criteria are selected or created.

After administering a common assessment teachers immediately score their personal students' work and then compile the individual results for collective review to aid and support all students' progress (DuFour et al. 2006). For example, three teachers each have 20 students. Collectively they are responsible for 60 students and work interdependently to ensure that all 60 students are successful. These teachers strategically plan immediate intervention and acceleration based on the common assessment results of the students' performance.

Same assessments are somewhat similar to common assessments in that teachers collaboratively determine the specific learning expectations that influence the designed or selected assessments and evaluation criteria, but same assessments are administered at the individual discretion of each teacher and, therefore, not necessarily administered simultaneously. When a teacher chooses to administer an agreed-upon same assessment, collaboration with other teachers is optional.

Agreed-upon common or same assessments appear in Consensus Maps. Evidence of planned and operational use of the assessments appears in each teacher's Projected Map and Diary Map. Reference in a collaborative map to an assessment being common or same is accomplished by writing the appropriate term in all capital letters before the assessment name. For common assessments, some teachers choose to include the planned testing date or window for administering the assessment:

- COMMON 25 MC Test (Feb. 16–18)
- SAME Dear Aunt Sally Letter (Evaluation: Checklist)
- COMMON Cell-Division Experiment Design (Evaluation: Checklist) (Nov. 8)

Bloom's Verbs

Oftentimes when teachers are learning to write a map and design curriculum, they are provided a list of verbs representing Benjamin Bloom's cognitive levels. While such a list may prove helpful to some, it is critical that the list does not become a crutch. A teacher must be able to determine the accurate measurable verb naturally or by breaking apart standards (see Chapter 9) rather than feel forced or become dependent on using a specific list of verbs.

Erickson (2007) points out that "it is time to use Benjamin Bloom's verbs where they can be most helpful—in the design of learning experiences and assessments. That is where we want students to analyze, synthesize, evaluate, and create" (p. 58). The best use of Bloom's verbs is in checking for coherence between the intra-alignment of the content skills and the assessments. Does the assessment or assessments accurately measure the verb–target-descriptor expectations? Figure 4.12 visually represents this thought process.

The center ring lists Bloom's Taxonomy classifications. The middle ring provides a sampling of measurable verbs that engage specific cognitive processes. The outer ring provides a sample set of assessment types that match the demand(s)

Figure 4.12 Measurable Skill Verbs and Matching Assessment Types

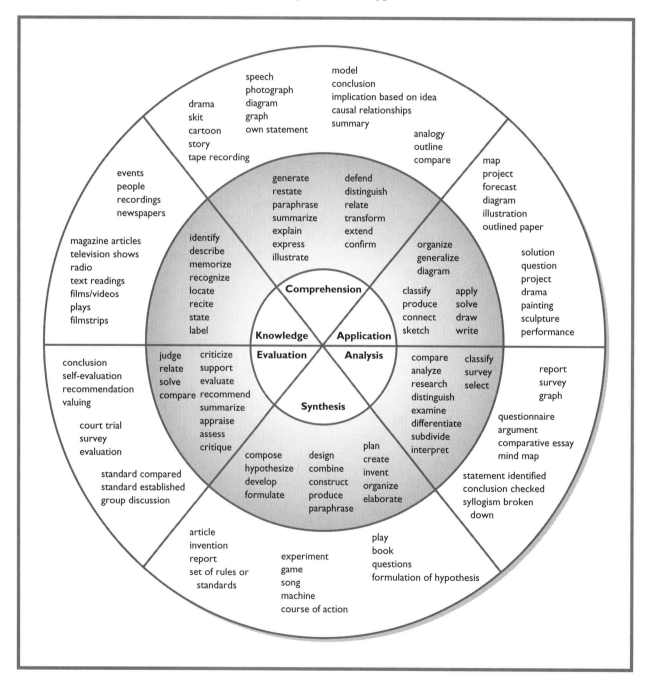

SOURCE: Adapted from the *Task-Oriented Question Construction Wheel Based on Bloom's Taxonomy* ©2004 St. Edward's University Center for Teaching Excellence (http://www.stedwards.edu/cte/media/BloomPolygon.pdf).

given the aligned cognitive processes. When focusing on one specific wedge, a synergy develops between the cognitive level, the measurable verb expectations, and the appropriate assessment measurements. This comparative process is an excellent mapping-review focus that asks teachers to evaluate the relational appropriateness of skill-statement learning to planned or actual assessments.

Do Assessments Belong in Every Type of Curriculum Map?

The answer to this question depends somewhat on the length of time a learning organization has been mapping. Over time, a Projected/Diary Map will potentially contain the greatest variety of assessment evidence: (a) personally selected assessments, (b) collaborative common or same assessments, (c) compulsory school-site benchmark assessments, (d) mandatory districtwide benchmark assessments, and (e) statewide assessments.

An important point to make is that no assessments are included in a collaboratively designed Consensus Map unless or until implementation of (a) teacher-generated or selected common or same assessments and/or (b) school-site or district benchmark assessments are agreed upon. If a state-mandated test or exam is included in an Essential Map, it will in turn appear in the course's Consensus Map at each school site. Likewise, it will appear in the Projected/Diary Map of a teacher who teaches the course. If a school has students participating in national testing or college-entrance exams, this information may be indicated in the appropriate course(s).

Essential Maps include no assessments unless districtwide benchmark assessments have been implemented or there is a desire to document state assessments and testing dates in the given course and map month(s).

Criteria

Figure 4.13A addresses assessment and evaluation wording, format, alignment, and distinctive features.

Standards

The term *standard* is used generically to express any portion or portions of a standard's thread of learning. For example, in Arizona, the technical terms used for the mathematics thread are *standard > strand > concept > performance objectives*. In Ohio, the mathematics terms are *standard > benchmark > grade-level indicators*. In this chapter, as well as in Chapter 9, a specific standard proficiency target is referred to as a *standard statement*.

Standard Statements: Level of Learning Expectations

Standards alignment is critical when designing *spiraled learning continuums* in a given school year or over a series of school years. Most mapping systems have features that enable map readers to record and review students' standards journey toward independent mastery in a given grade level or course, or series of grade levels or courses.

(Text continues on page 77)

Figure 4.13A Recommended Assessment and Evaluation Norms

	Reference Points

Wording	• An assessment is written as a name that precisely defines the assessment.
	• Common abbreviations used in assessment names include multiple-choice (MC), true/false (TF), and fill-in-the-blank (FinB).
	
	Examples:
	
	    15 Item Quiz
	    Friendly Letter
	    30 Item (MC/TF) Test
	    Anne Frank 5-Paragraph Essay

	• A precisely defined name refers to the number of items, the formatting (e.g., MC, TF, Matching, Open-Ended Response, Short Answer), and/or the clarifying adjective (e.g., Penny Hardness, Egyptian Pyramids, Attribute Block) that is written before the assessment-type noun (e.g., Quiz, Test, Lab, Presentation, Poster, Oration).
	
	Examples:
	
	    Penny Hardness Lab
	    30 MC Test
	    2 Open-Ended Newspaper Article Response Essays
	
	• Any how-tos regarding the execution of the assessment or grading information is not a part of an assessment's defined name. Depending on the mapping system used, this information may be included as an attachment or recorded in a designated area within an assessment template.
	
	Not a defined assessment name:
	
	    Each student gets the same list of vocabulary/spelling words and has to record each word in a word web. The student must include an antonym, synonym, meaning, and use each word in a sentence. This assessment is worth 100 points.
	
	Revision:
	
	10 Word Vocabulary Web
	
	(Note: After writing the assessment name, depending on the mapping system used, a teacher may write in a template or attach the explanation text as written above, as well as attach a copy of the blank word web.)
	
	• Evaluations must be included when map readers cannot determine from the assessment name how student learning is appraised. The evaluation process and documentation is either attached or included in the mapping system's provided template.
	• If a teacher is not ready to attach or include detailed evaluation data, he or she briefly describes criteria and evaluation tools in parentheses after the assessment name.

	Reference Points

	• The term *teacher observation* is abbreviated as *Teacher Ob* when included in an evaluation description.
	
	Examples:
	
	    Flag Football Game (Evaluation: Teacher Ob/Checklist)
	    Main Character Portrait (Evaluation: Rubric)
	    Common and Complex Machines Lab (Evaluation: Self-Critique/Teacher Feedback)
	    Emerald Isle Poster (Evaluation: Peer Review/Checklist)

	• It does not benefit map readers to simply repeat a word or phrase from the content-skill listings as an assessment name. The intra-alignment (letter–number) coding informs readers of what students must know and be able to do. Be specific regarding the learning measurement(s) as it will add depth to the collaborations and conversations focused on assessment practice during informal and formal reviews.
	
	Example:
	
	  Content
	    A. Time Zones: Worldwide
	
	  Skills
	    A1. Distinguish visually between latitude and longitude lines
	    A2. Determine visually and in writing time in multiple zones using longitudinal lines
	
	Vague Assessment Name
	    A1-A2. Time Zone Quiz
	
	Precise Assessment Name
	    A1-A2. 10 Zone Identification Problems Quiz
	
	Example:
	
	  Content
	    A. Patterns: No More Than 3 Attributes
	
	  Skills
	    A1. Identify visually and orally core pattern as beginning of repetitive pattern chain
	    A2. Create and extend manipulatively core pattern 3 times
	    A3. Discriminate visually and orally core pattern within self-created extended pattern
	
	Precise Assessment Name
	    A1-A3. Pattern Chain Performance Task (Evaluation: Teacher Ob/Rubric)

(Continued)

Figure 4.13A (Continued)

	Reference Points
Format	• Each word in an assessment name begins with a capital letter, similar to a proper name or title. • There is no period at the end of an assessment name or after evaluation parentheses. • When appropriate, an evaluation summary is included in parentheses directly following the assessment name with one space separating the end of the assessment name and the beginning of the parentheses. • Each assessment name's letter-number coding(s) is followed by a period, one space, and the assessment name. Example: A1-B2. Pyramid Side-Cut View Poster (Evaluation: Peer Review/Rubric)
Alignment	• When using intra-alignment coding to visually display learning coherency, content and skills are aligned to one another using letters, while content-skills are aligned to assessments using letters and numbers. • Sequential numbers are written to the right of each skill letter. Numbering returns to 1 when the content letter changes within a given month or unit. Example: *Unit* **EXPANDING THE NATION: 1800–1815** *Content* A. Louisiana Purchase: Lewis and Clark B. War of 1812: Land/Naval Engagements *Skills* A1. Analyze in writing Jefferson's instruction to Lewis concerning Northwest Passage A2. Justify in writing 4 primary participants' contributions to Corps of Discovery: Meriwether Lewis, William Clark, Sacagawea, Touissant Charbonneau A3. Map visually and in writing Lewis/Clark and Pike Expeditions B1. Analyze in writing primary and secondary effects of 8 battles: Battle of Tippecanoe, Battle of Frenchtown, Battle of York (Toronto), Battle of Lake Erie, Battle of Thames, Battle of Horseshoe Bend, Battle of Plattsburgh, Battle of New Orleans B2. Distinguish in writing strategic military decisions made by United States, Britain, Canadian British colonist leaders B3. Explain in writing Treaty of Ghent's "status quo ante bellum"

	Reference Points
	Assessments

Assessments

    A1–B3. 50 Item (MC/FinB/Short Answer) Test

    A1–A2. FOR Note-Taking Journal Entries (Evaluation: Teacher-Student Meeting/Student Self-Reflection)

    B1. Battle Comparisions Matrix (Evaluation: Teacher Ob/Rubric)

    B2. FOR Who's the Best? Debate (Evaluation: Peer Review/Rubric)

- When an assessment measures a single skill, the appropriate letter–number coding precedes the assessment name.

Examples:

    A1.

    B3.

    C2.

- When an assessment measures a series of skills within the same letter skill set, a hyphen is used between the first and last appropriate letter–number in the sequence.

Examples:

    A1–A3.

    C2–C4.

- When an assessment measures two or more nonsequential skills within the same or different letter set, a comma or commas separate the letter–number coding.

Examples:

    A2, B2, C1.

    B1, B3.

- When an assessment measures a series sequence in more than one letter-skill set, a combination of hyphens and commas is used.

Examples:

    A1–B3, C2, D1–D2.

- When an assessment measures all skills in all letter-skill sets, a hyphen is used between the first and last letter–number skills.

Example:

    A1–D3.

- If a cumulative assessment is given that encompasses all of the content–skill sets in a given month or unit, this assessment is listed first in the entire series of assessment listings, regardless of when it is actually given (as it is often the last assessment). Remember that a map is the "big picture" of a month or unit and the data within may not always be in perfect chronological order regarding content, skills, or assessments.

(Continued)

Figure 4.13A (Continued)

	Reference Points

	Examples:
	
	    A1-F2. 50 Item (MC/TF/Short Answer) End-of-Unit Test
	
	    A1, A3. FOR 2 Constructed-Response Answer Quiz
	
	• Content–skills sets' assessments are grouped with no line space between a given grouping. There is a line space or spaces only between new letter–skills sets. Given all the above possibilities, when reading a map there may be a variety of letter–number coding used to display the assessments' intra-alignment in a given month or unit.

Distinctive Features	• All skill statements must be accounted for regarding intra-alignment in a Projected Map/Diary Map. Therefore, each skill statement must be aligned to at least one summative or, if appropriate, formative assessment.
	
	Examples:
	
	    A1-A3. Full-Team Scrimmage Game (Evaluation: Teacher Ob/Checklist)
	
	    A4. FOR 2- to 4-Man Drills (Evaluation: Teacher Ob/Peer Discussion/Student Self-Reflection)

	• Recording an assessment name as *Chapter 8 Test* does not provide beneficial documentation of the assessment measurement. If teachers want to include chapter or similar resource notation, the assessment name is defined first and is then followed by the appropriate information.
	
	Examples:
	
	    A1-D4. 25 Problem (Chapter 8) Test
	
	    A1-C3. 15 MC/FB/Open-Ended Question (Unit 3) Test
	
	    E1-F2. Tectonic Plates (L 4-2) Lab

	• If using a mapping system wherein learning is recorded specifically by month, teachers can visually represent skills first measured formatively (FOR) in one month as now being measured summatively in a later month by using the appropriate intra-alignment coding from the previous month or months in parentheses before the summative assessment. Example: An October Diary Map assessment listing states: (Sept. C1-C2.) A1-A2. 25 Item Test Map readers' interpretation: This summative assessment measures September's formatively assessed C1 and C2 skills as well as October's A1 and A2 skills.

Figure 4.13B German I Diary Map Month Including Unit Name, Content, Skills, Summative and Formative Assessments, and Letter–Number Intra-Alignment Coding

Month	Content	Skills	Assessment	Standards
September	**GUTEN TAG** A. Alphabet: Letter Name, Pronunciation	A1. Recite A–Z in and out of sequence using German pronunciation A2. Pronounce and spell orally letters in translated or given German name	A1. 30 Sounds Oral Pronunciation Test A2. FOR Personal Oration (Evaluation: Teacher Ob/Checklist)	
	B. Masculine/Feminine/Neuter Nouns: Classroom Environment	B1. Translate orally into English German names of common objects (e.g., desk, chair, door, window, pen, pencil, paper, board, light, other single object items) using proper gender: der, die, das B2. Identify orally classroom objects in German when told English name using proper gender	B1-B2. Talk With Your Neighbor Simulation (Evaluation: Teacher Ob/Checklist)	
	C. Time: Calendar, Seasons	C1. State orally 7 days (Sunday, Monday, Tuesday, Wednesday, Thursday, Friday, Saturday), 12 months (January, February, March, April, May, June, July, August, September, October, November, December), 4 seasons (Winter, Spring, Summer, Fall) in and out of sequence C2. Write 7 day names in sequence and in isolation	C1. FOR 25 Word Oral Test C2. 10 Word Quiz	

If teachers simply indicate that a standard statement is addressed, it is not enough information to lead to in-depth conversation and decision making regarding students' mastery expectations. Generating a report that notes that a standard statement is addressed 23 times in a school year does not provide map readers with critical data regarding students' step-by-step journey unless the report also informs readers of the students' level of expectation for each standard statement.

A mapping system feature, configured slightly differently depending on the system used, allows map writers to designate the current level of learning expectation for a given standard statement addressed in a month or unit. Most systems' level-of-learning-expectation terms are *introduce* (I), *develop* (D), *mastery* (M), and *reinforce* (R). When recording the map elements in the system, teachers click on or check a small box that indicates the selected level of learning for each intra-aligned standard statement.

To determine a standard statement's level of learning expectation, teachers must consider that the journey toward mastery may progress over a few weeks, months, a full school year, or possibly longer.

Consider the following standard statement:

- Read and write numerals up to 100

A teacher knows that the high-stakes state testing is administered in mid-April. Therefore, to ensure success for all students, each student must independently master this standard statement no later than the beginning of April. The teacher uses a backwards-planning design regarding both the *explicit* and *implicit* content-skills learning requirements in the standard statement. Based on this design process, starting with September, the beginning of the school year, the teacher records the following in a Projected Map within a mapping system:

Content

A. Number Recognition: 0–25

Skills

A1. Read orally numerals in sequence

A2. Write numerals in sequence

Assessments

A1. Individual Performance Task (Evaluation: Teacher Ob/Checklist)

A2. 26 Item Test

Standard

A. Read and write numerals up to 100 (I)

The teacher intra-aligned this month's content-skills learning to the standard statement using the content's letter coding and indicates that the statement is introduced (I) since this is the first time students are exposed to any portion of the standard statement's learning expectations. October's learning expands the content and skills expectations:

Content

A. Number Recognition: 0–50

Skills

A1. Read orally numerals in sequence and in isolation

A2. Write numerals in a 5- to 10-number sequence starting with any given number and in isolation

Assessments

A1. Individual Performance Task (Evaluation: Teacher Ob/Checklist)

A2. 25 Item Test

Standard

A. Read and write numerals up to 100 (D)

The teacher intra-aligns the content-skills learning to the standard and indicates a develop (D) level of learning expectation since students are working toward independent mastery of the entire standard's expectation. It would not be appropriate to select introduce (I) again because a portion of the standard statement has already been introduced. Mastery (M) cannot yet be selected because the content-skills listings do not yet reflect the totality of the standard statement's expectations. Therefore, a develop (D) level of learning expectation will continue to be selected as the content-skill expectations expand over time.

In November, the skill learning is expanded while the content expectation remains the same as in October:

Content

A. Number Recognition: 0–50

Skills

A1. Read orally numerals and number words in sequence and in isolation

A2. Write numerals in a 5- to 10-number sequence starting with any given number and in isolation

A3. Write number words zero to ten in sequence and in isolation

Assessments

A1. Individual Performance Task (Evaluation: Teacher Ob/Checklist)

A2. 10 Item Test

A3. 11 Item Quiz

Standard

A. Read and write numerals up to 100 (D)

In March, the Projected Map's content and skills have expanded as follows:

Content

A. Number Recognition: 0–100

Skills

A1. Read numerals and number words in a 10- to 100-number sequence starting with any given number and in isolation

A2. Write numerals and number words in a 10- to 100-number sequence starting with any given number and in isolation

A3. Write number words zero to fifty in a 10- to 20-number sequence starting with any given number and in isolation

Assessments

A1-A3. 50 Item Test

A2. FOR 10 Item Quizzes

A3. FOR 5 Item Quizzes

Standard

A. Read and write numerals up to 100 (M)

This month the teacher selected mastery (M) when intra-aligning the learning expectations to the standard statement because the learning has reached a level of student independence and includes the entire standard statement expectation.

For this teacher's curriculum design, the learning expectations do not stop in March. While number recognition is not a focus in April, due to it being the state testing month, May's Projected Map is written as follows:

Content

A. Number Recognition: 0–125

Skills

A1. Read numerals and number words in a 10- to 100-number sequence starting with any given number and in isolation

A2. Write numerals and number words in a 10- to 100-number sequence starting with any given number and in isolation

A3. Write number words zero to one hundred in a 10- to 20-number sequence starting with any given number and in isolation

Assessments

A1-A3. 50 Item Test

A2. FOR 10 Item Quizzes

A3. FOR 5 Item Quizzes

Standard

A. Read and write numerals up to 100 (R)

The teacher has increased the content range by 25, as well as the written number words from 0 to 100. When intra-aligning the elements to the standard statement, the level of learning expectation is now reinforced (R) since the learning continuum has extended beyond the statement's expectations.

A question that is often asked at the onset of learning to write a map is "What if students are not moving along the planned-learning continuum of expectations? How is that evidenced in a map?" This is a good question, and it is one reason why mapping is often selected as a curriculum initiative. The desire of teachers and administrators is to design a collaborative curriculum that moves more students to the right in a distribution curve of academic and social success, better known as the *J Curve* (Reeves 2007). What is critical to note is that such a redistribution will not happen overnight and cannot happen unless there is a combination of a well-designed, teacher-developed curriculum; collaborative, teacher-designed assessments and immediate intervention; and collegial teacher-led action research in current and innovative pedagogical practices and strategies (Jacobs 1997, 2004b, 2006a; McTighe and Wiggins 2004; Reeves 2007; Stiggins et al. 2005; Wiggins and McTighe 2007). Therefore, at the onset of a mapping initiative, most learning organizations focus on the collective student body. As years progress, differentiation, intervention, and expansion evidence is include within elements and various features of the selected mapping system.

A reinforce (R) level of expectation can also be used to document cross-disciplinary or interdisciplinary learning. For example, a middle school science course is focusing on earth science. A particular unit's skill statement requires students to interpret tables and graphs, a mathematics standard statement. When intra-aligning the earth science content skills to science standards within the mapping system, the teacher toggles from the science standards to the mathematics standards, locates and selects the appropriate mathematics standard statement, and indicates reinforce (R).

Depending on what students must know and be able to do, a unit of study may focus on specific standard statements only one time during the school year. For example, a teacher may plan a three-week rocks-and-minerals science unit. The intra-aligned standard statements are not only introduced and developed but expected to be mastered by the end of the unit. In this case, depending on the mapping system's capabilities, the teacher will select or check either all three levels of learning expectations (I, D, M) or only one level (M). If the teacher(s) selected mastery (M) when creating a Consensus Map and finds that, even with ongoing formative assessments and interventions during the unit learning, a majority of the students did not reach independent mastery for one or more standard statements, each teacher will need to modify the level of expectation for the effected standard statement(s) from mastery (M) to develop (D) in his or her personal Diary Map.

When conducting standard statement review focuses from maps to maps or from maps to other data resources, knowing (a) what the level of expectations is for a given standard statement regarding both the planned and the operational learning, and (b) when in the school year the expectations expand or are modified aids in collegial conversation and curriculum decision making.

Visual Intra-Alignment

Since each mapping system has a unique process for documenting standard statements' intra-alignment, Figure 4.14 and all the sample map months in this book include the statements in a generic recording fashion wherein standard statements are notated in a specific column by just a numeric reference. The level of learning expectation's letter is indicated in parentheses to the right of each standard statement's numeric reference, which has been intra-aligned to the content-skills set by indicating the appropriate letter coding prior to the numeric references.

Resources

Resources in curriculum maps commonly include textbooks, materials, supplies, and Web sites that strategically aid students' learning or support teachers' or a teacher's instructional practice. Resources are usually written in a linear fashion using a double-dash prior to differentiate each listing:

Resources

--Chapters 2–3

--Video: *My Community, Our Legacy*

--Guest Speaker: Mr. Ki Yun Yoon, Mayor

--Field Trip: City Courthouse

--http://www.tia.org/marketing/tourism_ideas_unity.html
  (Unity in Community)

Most mapping systems have the capability to attach documents related to listed resources. Be aware that the systems often limit the amount of storage space allowed per teacher or school. Additional storage space is available for a minimal fee.

Hyperlinks

Hyperlinks, sometimes used to indicate uniform resource locators (URLs) or Web addresses, are one way to include online resources without using a mapping system's allotted storage space. Clicking on an included URL within a Web-based curriculum map takes readers directly to the linked destination.

Linking to a Web site's home page is not usually sufficient if the desired information is located deeper within the Web site. For example,

http://www.superkids.com *(Differentiated Addition Worksheets)*

directs map readers to the Web site's home page, but map readers will then have to guess and search to locate the actual recommended resource. Map writers must record the entire URL of the final destination. In the case of the previous URL, the actual destination should read as follows:

http://www.superkids.com/aweb/tools/math/add/ *(Differentiated Addition Worksheets)*

Figure 4.14 German I Diary Map Month Including Unit Name, Content, Skills, Summative and Formative Assessments, Standards, and Intra-Alignment Coding

Month	Content	Skills	Assessment	Standards
September	**GUTEN TAG** A. Alphabet: Letter Name, Pronunciation	A1. Recite A–Z in and out of sequence using German pronunciation A2. Pronounce and spell orally letters in translated or given German name	A1. 30 Sound Oral Pronunciation Test A2. FOR Personal Oration (Evaluation: Teacher Ob/Checklist)	A. WL.2.1 (I) WL.4.1 (I)
	B. Masculine/Feminine/Neuter Nouns: Classroom Environment	B1. Translate orally into English German names of common objects (e.g., desk, chair, door, window, pen, pencil, paper, board, light, other single object items) using proper gender: der, die, das B2. Identify orally classroom objects in German when told English name using proper gender	B1–B2. Talk With Your Neighbor Simulation (Evaluation: Teacher Ob/Checklist)	B. WL.2.4 (I)
	C. Time: Calendar, Seasons	C1. State orally 7 days (Sunday, Monday, Tuesday, Wednesday, Thursday, Friday, Saturday), 12 months (January, February, March, April, May, June, July, August, September, October, November, December), 4 seasons (Winter, Spring, Summer, Fall) in and out of sequence C2. Write 7 day names in sequence and in isolation	C1. FOR 25 Word Oral Test C2. 10 Word Quiz	C. WL.2.5 (I) WL.2.6 (I)

To capture a desired URL, take the following steps:

- Highlight the entire URL (including http://) in the browser window while on the desired resource page.
- Copy the URL (Ctrl + C on PC or Apple + C on Mac).
- Return to the map's add/edit window, and place the cursor in the desired recording space.
- Paste the URL (Ctrl + V on PC or Apple + V on Mac).
- Click Save button or feature within mapping system.

Adopted Resources

Officially adopted textbooks, teacher's guides, or other materials are typically listed first in a resource listing. If an entire chapter, unit, or kit is used, the teacher simply includes the appropriate reference number(s). If only a portion of the chapter, unit, or kit is planned or was used, the specific pages or sections are included:

Resources

--Chapter 2, pp. 23–32

--Unit 3, pp. 43–51

--Kit 2, Section 3

Notice that the above examples do not include the official title of the textbook, unit, or kit. This is because most mapping systems provide a course description component wherein this data can be notated and therefore does not need to be included in each unit or month when adopted materials are listed. If multiple adopted materials are part of the learning, each resource listing is preceded by the initials of the appropriate resource since the full titles and abbreviations are included in the course description:

Resources

--SST Chapter 9, pp. 141–160

--SBM Kit 2, Sections 2–3

If a mapping system does not include a course-description feature, the official title of an adopted textbook, unit, or kit is written in full only once when it is first included in a map.

A Consensus Map or an Essential Map only includes resources available to all who are teaching the course. For these types of collaborative planned-learning maps, some schools and districts include the term *suggested* prior to the word *resources* to indicate optional rather than compulsory usage. If a learning organization has Consensus Maps that contain resources, a teacher's Projected Map or Diary Map may include some or all of the agreed-upon resources as well as personal resources (see Figure 4.15).

Figure 4.15   Consensus Map and Diary Map Resources Comparison

Consensus Map	Diary Map
Resources --Chapter 5 --Periodic Table Chart --http://www.nyu.edu/pages/mathmol/textbook/ statesofmatter.html *(States of Matter Resource Page for Middle and High School)*	Resources --Chapter 5, pp. 186–192 --Lessons 18–19, pp. T45–T51 --Periodic Table Chart --Video: *It Does Matter!* --http://www.nyu.edu/pages/mathmol/textbook/ statesofmatter.html *(States of Matter Resource Page for Middle and High School)* --Teacher-Created Matter Packet

Intra-Alignment Coding

Some mapping systems have a specific field predesignated for resources. Other systems allow a learning organization to name or rename designated fields. In the case of the latter, it is highly recommended that an element field not be titled *Resources.* Doing so wastes valuable data-information space. Since resource listings do not take up much textual space, it is recommended that they be included within the content field (see Figure 4.16B).

Criteria

Figure 4.16A addresses resources wording, format, intra-alignment, and distinctive features.

(Text continues on page 89)

Figure 4.16A Recommended Resources Norms

	Reference Points
Wording	• Resource listings are materials that aid or enhance learning or instruction. Everyday items such as pens, pencils, and paper are not included. • Resource listings must be clear and concise. They are not meant to be explanations. If this information is desired, include it as an attached document within the mapping system. • If a teacher has created a self-generated resource, it is typically noted as *Teacher-Created* _____. Example: Resources --Chapter 20, pp. 213–221 --DVD: *What Causes Sickle Cell Anemia?* --Teacher-Created Sickle Cell PowerPoint
	• When including a textbook chapter, kit unit, or other adopted materials, these resources are listed first in a series of resource listings. • The title of the textbook does not need to be included in the listing when using a mapping system as this data can be included elsewhere in the course description. If using a table template, the full name of the textbook, kit, or other adopted materials is only mentioned one time in the first month or unit it is used. • In a Projected/Diary Map, if the listing indicates the chapter name or material reference only, this implies that the entire chapter will be or was used in instruction. If the listing includes the chapter and specific page numbers, this indicates that only a portion or portions of the chapter will be or were used during instruction. Examples: Resources --Chapter 10 --Heredity Kit 2B Resources --Chapter 10, pp. 101–107 --Heredity Kit 2B, T5-T8
Format	• Either the first word or all the words begin with a capital letter. The choice is personal preference. • A double-dash is made before each listing to differentiate each included resource. • If a mapping system does not have a designated *resources* field, the term *resources* serves as a header each time this element is included directly below a content listing in the content field. Example: *Content* A. Light Refraction: Positive, Negative Lens Resources --Chapter 10 --Prism Lab, pp. 122–124 • If the resources are identical for all of the content-skills sets, the map writer(s) may choose to list the resources one time after the first content listing and

	Reference Points
	indicate that the resources are used throughout by recording the appropriate letter coding series in front of the term *resources*. If there are additional resources for some of the content-skill listings, these specific resources are listed under the appropriate content listing(s). Example: **DATA AND STATISTICS** A. Data Organization: Mean, Median, Mode, Range A–B. Resources --Chapter 3, pp. 46-53 --Colorado Rockies Baseball Statistics B. Histograms: Accuracy Versus Inaccuracy **NUMBER COMPUTATION** C. Fractions: Equivalent Resources --Fractions Kit, Section 2 D. Fractions: Mixed Numbers, Improper Resources --Teacher-Created *Mixed-Up World* PowerPoint
Alignment	• When resources are included within the content field, they are automatically intra-aligned since they are recorded directly under the content–letter codings. • If a mapping system has a predesignated resources field, intra-alignment is visually created using appropriate content-letter coding. Example within a mapping system's predesignated resources field: A. --Multiviewpoint Simulation: *3 Days, 6 Perspectives* --Video: *Battle of Gettysburg: Tragedy or Triumph?* --http://www.gettysbg.com/battle.shtml *(Battle of Gettysburg Day-By-Day Synopsis)* B. --Chapter 10 --DVD: *November 1863: The Battle of Chattanooga*
Distinictive Features	• Be certain to capture the entire URL needed to ensure that map readers will be linked to the specific desired location within a Web site. Likewise, to aid map readers, include a simple descriptor in italics and parentheses after the URL regarding the Web site's focus. Vague URL: --http://www.owlpages.com Detailed URL: --http://www.owlpages.com/owls.php?genus=Tyto&species=alba *(Barn Owls)* • The ability to attach documents to listed resources can be beneficial to map readers. Be aware that this takes up storage space, and a mapping system usually limits this space per user account.

(Continued)

Figure 4.16A (Continued)

	Reference Points

	Examples of attached documents may include the following:
	  Resources
	    --Teacher-Created Presentations
	    --Teacher-Created Activities
	    --Teacher-Created Lecture Notes
	    --Teacher-Created FOR Assessments

Figure 4.16B German I Diary Map Month Including Unit Name, Content, Skills, Summative and Formative Assessments, Standards, Resources, and Intra-Alignment Coding

Month	Content	Skills	Assessment	Standards
September	**GUTEN TAG** A. Alphabet: Letter Name, Pronunciation Resources --*Sprechen Sie Deutsch* Chapter 1, pp. 3–7 --Alphabet Pronunciation Charts	A1. Recite A–Z in and out of sequence using German pronunciation A2. Pronounce and spell orally letters in translated or given German name	A1. 30 Sound Oral Pronunciation Test A2. FOR Personal Oration (Evaluation: Teacher Ob/Checklist)	A. WL.2.1 (I) WL.4.1 (I)
	B. Masculine/ Feminine/Neuter Nouns: Classroom Environment Resources --Chapter 2, pp. 16–21 --Object Cards	B1. Translate orally into English German names of common objects (e.g., desk, chair, door, window, pen, pencil, paper, board, light, other single object items) using proper gender: der, die, das B2. Identify orally classroom objects in German when told English name using proper gender	B1-B2. Talk With Your Neighbor Simulation (Evaluation: Teacher Ob/Checklist)	B. WL.2.4 (I)
	C. Time: Calendar, Seasons Resources --Video: *Welchen Tag Haben Wir Heute?* --Flashcard Word Set: 1 Set Per Student	C1. State orally 7 days (Sunday, Monday, Tuesday, Wednesday, Thursday, Friday, Saturday), 12 months (January, February, March, April, May, June, July, August, September, October, November, December), 4 seasons (Winter, Spring, Summer, Fall) in and out of sequence C2. Write 7 day names in sequence and in isolation	C1. FOR 25 Word Oral Test C2. 10 Word Quiz	C. WL.2.5 (I) WL.2.6 (I)

A Moment to Reflect

You have just finished reading a plethora of pages dedicated to writing five elements. Having had the privilege of being involved in training many teachers and administrators in curriculum mapping and writing quality maps, I offer the following suggestions that teachers have shared with me while trying to make sense of such a large amount of new learning.

Four Helpful Hints

1. If you feel overwhelmed by all the recommendations and requirements, don't worry; this is normal. Get the elements written, but focus on one or two elements at a time that you really want to gain confidence in writing well. This way, over time, all the elements will become succinct and provide clarity and quality for the map's readers.

2. When writing a three-part skill statement, some teachers prefer to write the measurable verb and descriptor first, and then go back and add in the appropriate target given the planned or actual assessment(s). If you choose to do this, remember that the target goes directly after the measurable verb, not after the descriptor.

3. Some teachers prefer to leave out the words *the, and, a,* or other wordiness whenever possible because it saves time when writing and reading maps. For example, instead of

- Identify visually and orally the 5 common features found on or in wind instruments: mouthpiece, resonator, holes, valves, and bell

the map reads

- Identify visually and orally 5 common features of wind instruments: mouthpiece, resonator, holes, valves, bell

4. When including evaluations for appropriate assessments, it is less stressful during the first year if you include the basic information in parentheses after the appropriate assessment names. During the second year, when revising maps, attaching evaluation information and documents based on your selected mapping system's features can be a specific focus for improving the quality of the maps.

Remember that designing curriculum and writing maps is a process; it will take time and consistent practice over a period of years to gain a comfort level such that the process begins to feel natural and not forced.

A Call for Consistency

When reading and reviewing curriculum maps, map readers in all disciplines and all grade levels must be able to interpret the data without the map writer(s) present. Therefore, it is critical that a learning organization establish norms for mapping each element. The excerpts in Figure 4.17 represent learning about matter from actual science Diary Maps in a school district that did not consider map element norms an important requisite.

Figure 4.17   Non-Normed Diary Map Excerpts

Content	Skills	Assessments
Grade 1		
Matter		
Matter can be observed, described, and classified. Matter exists as a solid, liquid, or gas and can change from one form to another. When matter changes form, no mass is gained or lost. Everything around us is matter. Solids are matter that keeps its shape.	Recognize that everything around us is matter Observe and describe the properties of solids Recognize that things can be done to solid matter to change its properties Observe and describe the behavior of solid matter when we do things to change it	Teacher Observation Activity Sheets KWL Charts Journal Writing
Grade 6		
A. Matter

B. Elements | A. Compare matter with nonmatter A. Describe the smallest unit of matter A. Distinguish between the various parts of an atom A. Explain how models of the atom are used B. Explain the meaning of atomic mass and atomic numbers B. Distinguish among isotopes of the same elements B. Classify elements of metals, nonmetals, and metalloids based on properties B. Memorize symbols of elements 1–20 | A, B. Lab Activities A, B. Worksheets A, B. Written Test |
| **Grade 9** | | |
| What is matter? How are mass and volume related? What makes things float? How can mixtures be separated? What are elements, compounds, and mixtures? What makes things move? What are some types of forces? | Understand the fundamental nature of matter Understand the relationship between mass and volume (density) Differentiate elements, compounds, and mixtures Understand how forces act on objects Identify the 4 fundamental forces Use vectors to calculate forces | Regular homework assignments Tests and quizzes Labs: matter in motion, mystery mixtures, colloids, chromatography |

If one of this district's mapping goals is to locate vertical gaps, repetitions, and absences, the current variety in wording, format, and intra-alignment practices will make it difficult or nearly impossible to do so without each map writer present to explain his or her map's specifics.

To increase consistency in mapping norms regarding wording, format, and intra-alignment, teachers just beginning to write maps appreciate visual models to aid in remembering the basics regarding what a quality map looks like visually. Figures 4.18 to 4.20 represent a map month written at three stages of readability. Figure 4.18 is a quality Projected/Diary Map; map readers do not need the map writer present to correctly interpret the map's data. All intra-aligned elements are clear and concise, and they incorporate the recommended norms.

Figure 4.19 is moving toward quality, yet it exhibits some concern. While there is some understanding of connections between content skills, assessments, and standards, there are no resources, no standard statements' level of learning expectations, and no detail regarding the intra-alignment. Which assessments measure which skills? What about evaluations for the essay assessments? Since some skill statements do not include detailed descriptors, what must students specifically do in relationship to the knowing in relationship to the assessments?

Figure 4.20 is referred to as a *laundry list* map. Map readers may glean some information, but it is difficult to do so without speculation because it lacks all of the following: (a) intra-alignment, (b) targets or detailed descriptors in the skill statements, (c) assessment definition or evaluation, and (d) resources. Map readers must depend heavily on inference, which is not in the best interest of students or teachers.

Notice the difference in the quality between Figures 4.21 and 4.22. Figure 4.21 is a map written by a teacher who was not given much direction or training in writing a quality map. Figure 4.22 is the teacher's revision after trainings based on the norms shared in this chapter.

Chapter 7 focuses on using created maps to conduct reviews regarding focuses such as gaps and repetitions. If maps are not adequately detailed, such anomalies will not be able to be found. When teachers begin conducting reviews, accurate interpretation of map data does not mean that every term included in a map must be explained. Teachers may or may not be familiar with other grade levels' or disciplines' academic terms. For example, high school teachers may not know what *Phoneme: /t/ /m/* means when reading the content field of a language arts elementary school map, and elementary school teachers may not know what *Anglo-Saxon Lyricisms* means when reading the content field of a language arts high school map. An asset to having curriculum maps is that teachers can gain a better understanding of and insight into students' step-by-step learning journey.

Course Names

When teachers begin to map, the selected mapping system company or someone in the learning organization will input the course titles offered at each grade level or within a department. Be aware that the entered course names are not finite. There may be a need for additions or revisions to the course titles. For example, if there is a course name that applies to a course that is repeated in

(Text continues on page 97)

Figure 4.18 Quality Written Map Sample Month

Month	Content	Skills	Assessment	Standards
September	**EXPOSITORY READING** A. Informational Text: Inform, Instruct, Guide, Direct, Show Resources --Chapter 10, pp. 135–152 --*The Arizona Republic* --A Variety of How-To Manuals	A1. Justify in writing 5 key purposes of informational reading using supporting examples A2. Identify in writing 3 self-determined attributes for a reader's use of informational text versus fictional text A3. Differentiate visually and in writing textual and visual details to support 5 informational purposes A4. Justify in writing hypotheses for a writer's purpose and methods in meeting audiences' textual and visual needs	A1–A2. 10 MC/ 5 Primary-Source Identification Test A1. 10 Statement Matching Quiz A3. 5 Informational Excerpts Mini-Essays (Evaluation: Rubric) A4. FOR Audience Identification Quiz (Evaluation: Rubric/Peer Review)	A. 6.3.1.0 (D) 6.3.1.1 (D) 6.3.2.1 (I) 6.3.2.3 (I)
	B. Stated or Implied Main Idea: Textual, Visual Resources --A Variety of How-To Manuals	B1. Summarize orally and in writing central idea based on chronological, sequential, or logical order B2. Locate visually and in writing directional information based on 4 organizational features: bold print, numbers, captions, keys	B1–B2. 25 Short-Answer Test B1. FOR 2-Minute Oral Presentation (Evaluation: Teacher Ob/Rubric)	B. 6.3.1.0 (D) 6.3.1.3 (D) 6.3.1.2 (I)
	FICTIONAL READING C. Historical Fiction Text: Fact Versus Fiction Resources --Excerpts From a Variety of Scholastic's *Dear America/My Name Is America* Series Titles	C1. Compare and contrast in writing similarities and differences between historical expository text and historical fiction text C2. Identify and define in writing 5 common literary devices used in diary-based reading: structure, tone, theme, point of view, characterization C3. Characterize in writing personality traits of main characters based on literary devices used by author	C1–C3. James Edmond Pease Essay (Evaluation: 6+1 Trait Rubric--Voice and Word Choice)	C. 6.2.1.0 (D) 6.2.1.2 (D) 6.2.2.5 (I)

Figure 4.19   Moving Toward Writing a Quality Map Sample Month

Month	Content	Skills	Assessment	Standards
September	A. Informational Text: Inform, Instruct, Guide, Direct, Show Resources --Textbook --Magazine --Manuals	A. State five key purposes for informational reading A. Identify three attributes for a reader's use of informational text versus fictional text A. Differentiate details to support five informational purposes A. Justify hypotheses for a writer's purpose and methods in meeting audiences' textual and visual needs	A. Matching Quiz A. MC/Primary-Source Identification Test A. Mini-Essays	A. 6.3.1.0 6.3.1.1 6.3.2.1 6.3.2.3
	B. Stated or Implied Main Idea: Textual, Visual Resources --Manuals	B. Summarize idea based on chronological, sequential, or logical order B. Locate directional information based on organizational features	B. Short-Answer Test	B. 6.3.1.0 6.3.1.3 6.3.1.2
	C. Historical Fiction Text: Fact Versus Fiction Resources --Historical Fiction Books	C. Compare and contrast similarities and differences between historical expository text and historical fiction text C. Identify and define common literary devices used in diary-based reading C. Characterize personality traits based on literary devices used by author	C. Essay	C. 6.2.1.0 6.2.1.2 6.2.2.5

Figure 4.20 Laundry List Map Sample Month

Month	Content	Skills	Assessment	Standards
September	Informational Text: Inform, Instruct, Guide, Direct, Show Stated or Implied Main Idea: Textual, Visual Historical Fiction Text: Fact Versus Fiction	State purposes for informational reading Identify attributes for a reader's use of informational text versus fictional text Differentiate details to support informational purposes Justify hypotheses for a writer's purpose and methods in meeting audiences' textual and visual needs Summarize idea based on chronological, sequential, or logical order Locate directional information based on organizational features Compare and contrast similarities and differences between historical expository text and historical fiction text Identify and define common literary devices used in diary-based reading Characterize personality traits based on literary devices used by author	Matching Quiz MC Primary-Source Test Mini-Essays Short-Answer Test James Edmond Pease Essay	6.3.1.0 6.3.1.1 6.3.2.1 6.3.2.3 6.3.1.0 6.3.1.3 6.3.1.2 6.2.1.0 6.2.1.2 6.2.2.5

Figure 4.21 Intermediate Science Map Month Before Revision

Month	Content	Skills	Assessment	Standards
November	**HUMAN BODY**			
	A. Cardiovascular/Circulatory	A. Explain system functions	A–B. Written Test	A.
		A. Compare and contrast types of blood vessels	A. Notes Quiz	5.2.3
		A. Evaluate bulk flow process	A. Poster	5.2.4
			A. Pressure Lab	
	B. Respiratory	B. Explain respiration process	B. Terms Quiz	B.
		B. Analyze relationship between respiratory and cardiovascular/circulatory systems	B. Lung Capacity Lab	5.2.3
			B. Graphic Organizer/Summary Paragraph	5.2.5

Figure 4.22 Intermediate Science Map Month After Revision

Month	Content	Skills	Assessment	Standards
November	**SYSTEMS: HUMAN BODY** A. Closed System: Cardiovascular/Circulatory Resources --Chapter 7, pp. 145–159 --http://yucky.discovery.com/flash/body/pg000131.html (*Cardiovascular Fun Factoids*)	A1. Explain visually and in writing 2 main functions: deliver nutrients and oxygen to cells far removed from source of supply; to remove and transport wastes from immediate area of cells to organs designed to eliminate them from body A2. Compare and contrast visually and in writing 4 types of blood vessels: arteries (carry blood away from heart), veins (carry blood to heart), capillaries (from arteries to veins), sinusoids (similar to function of capillaries/found in liver, spleen, bone marrow) A3. Evaluate visually and in writing bulk flow process (movement of a fluid and its contents) that occurs in response to a pressure gradient; function of heart is to raise pressure of blood contained within it so blood will flow from heart to periphery (since bulk flow occurs from high to lower pressure)	A1-B2. 30 MC/Label/Short-Answer Test A1-A3. 10 Item Note-Taking Quiz A1. Circulation Poster/Summary Statement (Evaluation: Rubric) A2. FOR Vessels Venn Diagram (Evaluation: Peer Discussion/Checklist) A3. Pressure Gradient Lab (Evaluation: Experiment Journal/ Teacher Ob/Checklist)	A. 5.2.3 (D) 5.2.4 (I)
	B. Respiratory: Functions and Comparisons Resources --Chapter 6, pp. 131–140 --Vocabulary Terms: *windpipe, esophagus, air sac, capillaries, bronchioles, mucus, cilia*	B1. Explain visually and in writing 7-step respiration process, including function of mouth, nose, trachea, chest cavity, bronchi, bronchial tubes, lungs, alveoli, diaphragm B2. Differentiate in writing 3 main stages of respiration: exchange of gases within lungs' large capillaries (external respiration), internal respiration exchange of gases between cells and blood, cellular respiration's metabolic activity within cells B3. Analyze in writing relationship between respiratory and cardiovascular/circulatory systems	B1-B2. FOR 20 Term How-We-Breath Quiz B1-B2. Lung Capacity Lab (Evaluation: Journal Entry/Rubric/Checklist) B3. Double Bubble Map/ Summary Paragraph (Evaluation: Rubric)	B. 5.2.3 (D) 5.2.5 (I)

two semesters with different groups of students in each semester, it is recommended that the course title be revised so that there are three separate courses (e.g., Statistics, Statistics Semester 1, Statistics Semester 2). The reason for having three courses is that the learning may vary, even slightly, during the two semesters. Variables may include inclement weather, holidays, or student capabilities. A teacher of this course can use the mapping system to an advantage by copying the first semester's Diary Map into the second semester's map account and using the now Projected Map for planning. When reviewing the map as each month passes to ensure accuracy of the current month's map data, the teacher may or may not need to edit the existing map information as it becomes a Diary Map of the second semester course. One course title is not designated by semester because it will be the course title selected when designing a Consensus Map or Essential Map. For either of these collaborative planned-learning maps, the learning expectations for the entire course will be housed within the first semester to indicate that it is, in fact, a semester-long course. If a new teacher is hired mid-year, he or she will copy the created Consensus Map into his or her Statistics Semester 2 course map to begin the process of projected and diary mapping.

There may be some teachers who prefer not to teach using individual discipline focuses. For example, teachers in an elementary grade level may prefer to design their curriculum thematically. If all the courses in the system are titled by specific discipline, these teachers may find it convoluted to try to record the learning expectations in four separate maps rather than one map since the assessments measure multiple-discipline learning. In this case, a new course title can be created in the mapping system to accurately reflect the student learning. For example, a course name may be Grade 2 Interdisciplinary Learning or Grade 2 Thematic Units. A sample map included in Chapter 8 (Figure 8.2) demonstrates this mapping concept. Teachers and support staff often choose to map learning beyond conventional subjects or disciplines. I have seen schools that embrace the Character Counts! youth-ethics model create course names that reflect this initiative (e.g., Grade 7—6 Pillars of Character) and use the six core ethical values as unit names within the course map.

Remember that the course names within the selected mapping system need to accurately reflect the offered courses—academic, social, or otherwise—so that all teachers can successfully design and write curriculum maps that provide evidence of the students' learning world.

CONCLUSION

Establishing curriculum mapping in a learning organization is founded on the principle that all teachers at all grade levels and in all disciplines have instant access to the planned and operational curriculum to aid in ongoing curriculum decision making. In the next series of chapters, you will be given specific information about the process of creating the various types of maps. Depending on your learning organization's short- and long-range goals, these chapters can provide insight into the selection process for choosing the type of map(s) to begin writing when implementing the mapping process.

REVIEW QUESTIONS

This chapter has an immense amount of information for writing the five common initial elements. While it may seem overwhelming at first, after studying sample map months and actually writing maps, the how-tos do begin to fall into place. The following review questions focus on the main points within the chapter. Discuss your responses with a partner or in a small group.

1. Write or present orally a short summary regarding each element's definition and mapping norms, as well as how the elements are related through the intra-alignment of content, skills, assessments, standards, and resources. (You may want to include unit name in your definition, norms, and intra-alignment discussions.)

2. A quality map is one that does not need the map writer(s) present to correctly interpret the map data. When trying to remember each element's wording, format, intra-alignment, and distinctive features, what stands out as critical regarding each element's norms?

3. Study Figures 4.18–4.20. How do these three examples visually express the necessity for a map to be written with clarity to ensure map readers' ability to correctly interpret a map's data?

Descriptive or Not Descriptive? That Is the Question!

Math Focus

Read the content listings in the left column. Determine if each one is a quality recording that provides clarity for map readers or is in need of revision. Rate each listing in the middle column. If the listing warrants revision, write potential revision in the last column.

Content Statement *Key Noun/Noun Phrase:* *Descriptor*	Provides Clarity? *Write Yes, Almost, or No.* *Explain Reasoning.*	Revised Quality Content Listing *How do you recommend the* *content listing be revised to ensure* *clarity regarding specific knowing?*
Addition/Subtraction: 1 or 2 Digits With Regrouping		
Number Set		
Tell Time		
2-Dimensional Shapes: Square, Rectangle, Triangle, Circle		
Money: 1¢ to $1.00		
Patterns: No More Than Three Attributes		
Measuring		
2-D Shapes Transformation: Reflections, Rotations, Translations		

Descriptive or Not Descriptive? That Is the Question!

Math Focus Answer Key

Content Statement *Key Noun/Noun Phrase:* *Descriptor*	Provides Clarity? *Write Yes, Almost, or No.* *Explain Reasoning.*	Revised Quality Content Listing *How do you recommend the* *content listing be revised to ensure* *clarity regarding specific knowing?*
Addition/Subtraction: 1 or 2 Digits With Regrouping	*Yes* Quality Noun: Descriptor	
Number Sets	*No* There is no descriptor	Number Sets: 0–10
Tell Time	*No* Should not be a verb; no descriptor	Time: Hour, ½ Hour
2-Dimensional Shapes: Square, Rectangle, Triangle, Circle	*Yes* Quality Noun: Descriptor	
Money: 1¢ to $1.00	*Almost* Possibly include monetary forms	Money: Penny, Nickel, Dime, Quarter / 1¢ to $1.00
Patterns: No More Than Three Attributes	*Almost* Three should be a numeral not a number word	Patterns: No More Than 3 Attributes
Measuring	*No* Should not be a verb; no descriptor	U.S. Linear Units: Inch, Foot, Yard
2-D Shapes Transformation: Reflections, Rotations, Translations	*Yes* Quality Noun: Descriptor	

Descriptive or Not Descriptive? That is the Question!

Language Arts Focus

Read the content listings in the left column. Determine if each one is a quality recording that provides clarity for map readers or is in need of revision. Rate each listing in the middle column. If the listing warrants revision, write potential revision in the last column.

Content Statement *Key Noun/Noun Phrase:* *Descriptor*	Provides Clarity? *Write Yes, Almost, or No.* *Explain Reasoning.*	Revised Quality Content Listing *How do you recommend the* *content listing be revised to ensure* *clarity regarding specific knowing?*
Main Idea: Summary and Support/4–6 Events		
Nonfiction Text: Informational		
Oral Presenting		
Indefinite Pronouns: Agreement With Antecedents and Verbs		
Author's Point of View		
High-Frequency Vocabulary: 5 New Words		
Character Conflict		
Revising		
Composition: Essay		

Descriptive or Not Descriptive? That Is the Question!

Language Arts Focus Answer Key

Content Statement *Key Noun/Noun Phrase:* *Descriptor*	Provides Clarity? *Write Yes, Almost, or No.* *Explain Reasoning.*	Revised Quality Content Listing *How do you recommend the* *content listing be revised to ensure* *clarity regarding specific knowing?*
Main Idea: Summary and Support/4–6 Events	*Yes* Quality Noun: Descriptor	
Nonfiction Text: Informational	*Yes or Almost* Could have a stronger clarifying descriptor	Nonfiction Text: Informational/5–7 Step Instructions
Oral Presenting	*No* Should not be a verb; no descriptor	Oral Presentation: Tone, Rate
Indefinite Pronouns: Agreement With Antecedents and Verbs	*Yes* Quality Noun: Descriptor	
Author's Point of View	*Almost* Needs a descriptor	Author's Point of View: Bias
High-Frequency Vocabulary: 5 New Words	*Almost* What are the five new words? Five words are not too many to include.	High-Frequency Vocabulary: Another, Through, Classify, Everything, Valuable
Character Conflict	*Almost* Needs descriptor	Character Conflict: Main, Support Characters
Revising	*No* Should not be a verb; no descriptor	Revision: Sentence Fluency
Composition: Essay	*Almost* Could use a stronger clarifying descriptor since the descriptor can change the learning focus	Composition: 5-Paragraph Essay Fictional Composition: Comparative Essay Composition: Essay Preparation/Roman Numeral Outline

Skill Versus Activity

Math Focus: Primary Grades

A skill is what students must be able to do. An activity provides practice concerning a particular skill or skill set.

1. Cut apart the statement boxes.

2. Categorize each statement as a **skill** or an **activity**. The initial verb in each statement may aid you in determining the correct category.

3. Find each skill's matching activity and place the two corresponding statements side by side.

Hint: Each skill matches a specific activity. There is a total of six corresponding sets.

Practice times tables to 12 × 12	Sequence in writing order for reading vertical bar graph: bottom up, side in	Review rule for reading bar graph	Create manipulatively arrays up to 4 × 4
State in writing times using analog and digital faces	Combine in writing polygon shapes to create common objects	Memorize multiplication facts	Sing "What Is Missing?" song
Draw illustrations of own home using various shapes	Put pattern blocks in arrays	Look at watch times	Solve equations with 1 variable letter/symbol representation (e.g., 12 = n × 4)

Skill Versus Activity

Math Focus: Primary Grades Answer Key

Skills	Activities
Memorize multiplication facts	Practice times tables to 12×12
Solve equations with 1 variable letter/symbol representation (e.g., $12 = n \times 4$)	Sing "What Is Missing?" song
Sequence in writing order for reading vertical bar graph: bottom up, side in	Review rule for reading bar graph
Create manipulatively arrays up to 4×4	Put pattern blocks in arrays
State in writing times using analog and digital faces	Look at watch times
Combine in writing polygon shapes to create common objects	Draw illustrations of own home using various shapes

The measurable verb used at the onset of a skill statement is critical for accurately informing map readers, without the map writer(s) present, what students are expected to be able to do. Equally important is including an appropriate target and descriptor. Since the focus of this exercise is mathematics, the verb *solve* infers in writing unless otherwise noted as a target. The verb *memorize* infers mentally and therefore does not need a target.

Skill Versus Activity

Various-Discipline Focus: Upper Grades

A skill is what students must be able to do. An activity provides practice concerning a particular skill or skill set.

1. Cut apart the statement boxes.

2. Categorize each statement as a **skill** or an **activity**. The initial verb in each statement may aid you in determining the correct category.

3. Find each skill's matching activity and place the two corresponding statements side by side.

Hint: Each skill matches a specific activity. There is a total of six corresponding sets.

Look at artwork to see if the pieces incorporate religious icons	Evaluate orally and in writing technological developments that have influenced how humans work with genetically engineered crops	Research using the Internet the president's political arenas (state, national, international) in teams of 3	Keep a daily personal fitness journal for 1 month
Practice rotations using polygons	Describe visually and in writing examples of recession in United States history	Interview in person, by phone, or via e-mail 3 biochemists using personal, pregenerated questions	Draw transformational figures using rigid body movement while keeping point fixed in 2-D plane
Make a chart board display of ebb and flow of U.S. economic factors for 20th century and onset of 21st century	Self-evaluate in writing personal physical activities that promote lifelong involvement, well-being	Relate visually wooden artworks to religious beliefs in 2 geographic regions: Africa, Asia	Analyze in writing similarities and differences in political contributions of 3 presidents: Washington, Lincoln, Roosevelt

Skill Versus Activity

Various-Discipline Focus: Upper Grades Answer Key

Skills	Activities
Relate visually wooden artworks to religious beliefs in 2 geographic regions: Africa, Asia	Look at artwork to see if the pieces incorporate religious icons
Evaluate orally and in writing technological developments that have influenced how humans pregenerated work with genetically engineered crops	Interview in person, by phone, or via e-mail 3 biochemists using personal, questions
Analyze in writing similarities and differences in political contributions of 3 presidents: Washington, Lincoln, Roosevelt	Research using the Internet the president's political arenas (state, national, international) in teams of 3
Self-evaluate in writing personal physical activities that promote lifelong involvement, well-being	Keep a daily personal fitness journal for 1 month
Draw transformational figures using rigid body movement while keeping point fixed in 2-D plane	Practice rotations using polygons
Describe visually and in writing examples of recession in United States history	Make a chart board display of ebb and flow factors of U.S. economic for 20th century and onset of 21st century

The measurable verb used at the onset of a skill statement is critical for accurately informing map readers, without the map writer(s) present, what students are expected to be able to do. Equally important is including an appropriate target and descriptor. Occasionally, a target is not necessary. For example, in mathematics the verb *draw* infers in writing and therefore does not need a target.

Assessment Versus Evaluation

An assessment is a product or performance. An evaluation is the criteria used and judgment made for the product or performance.

If map readers cannot determine an assessment's evaluation criteria based on the assessment name, evaluation information must be included.

1. Cut apart the statement boxes.

2. Categorize each statement as an **assessment name** or an **evaluation**.

3. Match the assessment name with its appropriate evaluation.

Note: There are eight assessments matching eight evaluations.

20 Item Quiz	Thomas Jefferson Essay	African Mask	25 MC Test
Basketball Basic Plays Checklist	Penny Hardness Lab	Self-Evaluation: Audio Recording/Rubric	ORF Diagnostic Guidelines
Musical Scales Performance Task	No Evaluation Data Needed	Peer Review/Geometric Checklist	No Evaluation Data Needed
Biography Writing Rubric	Oral Reading Fluency Test	5-Member Teams Performance Task	Teacher Ob/Procedure Checklist/Findings Report

Assessment Versus Evaluation

Answer Key

Assessment Name	Evaluation
20 Item Quiz	No Evaluation Data Needed
25 MC Test	No Evaluation Data Needed
Thomas Jefferson Essay	Biography Writing Rubric
Penny Hardness Lab	Teacher Ob/Procedure Checklist/ Findings Report
Oral Reading Fluency Test	ORF Diagnostic Guidelines
African Mask	Peer Review/Geometric Checklist
5-Member Teams Performance Task	Basketball Basic Plays Checklist
Musical Scales Performance Task	Self-Evaluation: Audio Recording/Rubric

When including evaluations in a map and not yet using a mapping system's attachment or inclusion features, write the assessment name followed by a brief evaluation summary in parentheses.

Examples:

Thomas Jefferson Essay (Evaluation: Biography Writing Rubric)

Solo and Duet Performance (Evaluation: Teacher Ob/Checklist)

5-Member Team Debate (Evaluation: Peer Review/Rubric Matrix)

3 Semiregular Tessellation Configurations (Evaluation: Teacher Ob/Checklist)

Dead-Lift Performance Tasks (Evaluation: Teacher-Student Reflection/Personal Goal Setting)

What Should We Know Before Creating Diary Maps or Projected Maps?

*Reality is not the external scene, but the life that is
lived in it. Reality is things as they are.*

—Wallace Stevens

Diary Maps and Projected Maps are personal, reflective narratives. They provide primary source evidence of an individual teacher's student-learning environment, a specialist's surroundings, or an administrator's workplace. Maps relating to administrators and professional development are addressed in Chapter 11. This chapter focuses specifically on what needs to be considered for teachers to personally map curriculum.

POINTS TO PONDER

A Diary Map documents the learning that has actually happened, whereas a Projected Map documents what has been planned. As mentioned previously, the two maps are actually the same document differentiated by real time. If it is currently February, all previously recorded months are called the Diary Map. The current and future recorded months are called the Projected Map (see Figure 5.1).

Figure 5.1   Diary Map and Projected Map Differentiation

Sept	Oct	Nov	Dec	Jan	Feb	Mar	Apr	May	June
Diary Map					**Projected Map**				

When the school year ends, all months are referred to as the Diary Map. When the map is rolled over to the next school year, all the months are once again referred to as the Projected Map since the months have not yet happened again in real calendar time. As each month passes, the teacher will again examine the map data and, if necessary, modify the information to accurately reflect the current year's operational curriculum. Month by month the Projected Map will once again become a Diary Map.

As Jacobs (1997) notes, "the point is not to teach to the months, but to use the months as a common reference to plot the classroom curriculum" (p. 9). Some mapping systems require teachers to record learning by individual months. Others allow teachers to create a unit of study that can live in a portion of a month, a full month, or overlapping months.

A Projected or Diary Map is a personal map written individually by a teacher to reflect his or her learning environment. Rarely do two or more teachers literally teach the same students the same curriculum at the same time in the same environment. Here are two instances I have encountered of this atypical instructional model:

- Two teachers simultaneously coteaching a Kindergarten class of 40 students.
- Two teachers simultaneously teaching a high school physical education class of 70 freshman students in one very large gymnasium.

Both examples are different than two or more teachers documenting agreed-upon planned learning and then going into separate environments to instruct. This type of collaboration is common and is appropriately documented in a Consensus Map.

Accurate Reflections of Operational Learning

Since Diary Maps accurately reflect the current year's operational learning, there are no guarantees that last school year's Diary Map entries will be a perfect match to the next school year's operational learning. Diary Map revision may be necessary due to something as simple as losing days of school because of weather conditions or something more complex, such as curriculum shifts based on conducted mapping reviews, breakthroughs in discipline-specific knowledge, technological advancements regarding assessments or instruction, new resources, or current-year class configuration.

If each teacher does not personally read and always consider the potential need to monthly revise or refine Projected Map or Diary Map data, the operational curriculum will soon become antiquated and the maps will no longer accurately reflect the current learning.

Consensus Map to Diary Map

If teachers have designed a collaborative Consensus Map that serves as the foundation for a course's planned learning, each teacher's personal Projected/Diary Map will contain the data found in the Consensus Map, but should not be a carbon copy. Each teacher's personal map should always have more detail and data than a collaborative planned learning map.

Using one of the mapping system's report features, three teachers comparatively reviewed one another's Diary Maps in relation to their collaborative Consensus Map. Based on the additional data in each other's Diary Map, they discovered the following:

- One teacher used resources the other two had not.
- Two teachers included two different additional aligned skills in the agreed-upon content-skills sets.
- One teacher included an additional aligned content-skills-assessment set.
- All three teachers had variations in the assessments and evaluations used besides the one agreed-upon SAME 25 MC Test.

This informal Consensus Map–Diary Maps comparison review led the teachers into a deep discussion regarding current and future learning expectations and specific pedagogical practices to aid them in reaching all of their students.

Intimate Reflections

Diary Maps and Projected Maps are intimate reflections that must correctly reflect the current year's student population. Therefore, the uniqueness of a teacher's current class configuration may affect the personal planned and operational curriculum.

Four teachers had been planning grade-level learning informally for the past five years. When mapping was introduced, they formally designed a mathematics Consensus Map and recorded it in the mapping system. They were anxious to use the map as the base for the coming school year's instructional learning. At the onset of the new school year, each teacher's roster consisted of 25 students:

- Teacher A received a 100% average learner student population.
- Teacher B received a 70% above-average to gifted learner and 30% average learner student population.
- Teacher C received a 40% English, 30% Spanish, 20% Asian, and 10% African first-language learner student population.

(Continued)

(Continued)

> • Teacher D received a 50% average, 30% low, and 20% fully included, special-education learner student population.
>
> It is unlikely that all four teachers' students will have the exact same learning experience. As the Consensus Map months are replicated into each teacher's personal account, authentic variation regarding Projected Map and Diary Map evidence of the planned and operational learning can be expected.
>
> At the onset of the following school year, the next grade-level teachers will appreciate having the personal documentation of what truly took place in each classroom when compared to the collaborative grade-level planned learning expectations.
>
> For the next school year, these three teachers may well have different class configurations. Because of the natural ebb and flow of learner abilities that each teacher receives, from year to year the Consensus Map may change very little or not at all, but Projected Maps and Diary Maps must always be open to necessary revisions that accurately reflect the current learners' operational curriculum.

It is important to note that each year a teacher does not literally rewrite the entire Projected/Diary Map. The previous year's Diary Maps are rolled over using the selected mapping system's features and become the next school year's Projected Maps. As the year unfolds, the maps are edited, if necessary, to reflect the current school year's learning.

Professional Courtesy: Establishing a Due Date

Most mapping systems provide map readers with the date when a map was last updated. This is important because it conveys to map readers whether a map's data can be considered accurate and reliable given the current month of the school year. Therefore, it is important for a learning organization to establish a monthly due date for the ongoing task of revisiting Projected Maps and Diary Maps recorded within a mapping system. Most schools and districts select a specific day, often the seventh day of the following month. For example, September's Diary Maps are due by October 7, October's Diary Maps are due by November 7, November's Diary Maps are due by December 7, and so on.

A due date is not intended to be a burden or indicative of possible punishment. It is a matter of professionalism. Maps that properly reflect the previous months' operational learning, not only for the current year but for the archived years as well, are critical for conducting curriculum reviews since the map writer(s) may not be present for the review, and teachers must be able to make effective decisions based on the map's data.

Student-Designed Learning

If a learning organization offers student-designed courses or units of study, the need for monthly operational curriculum documentation is paramount. Teachers need access to the students' operational and planned learning. Using this data to evaluate trends and patterns in the student-generated learning aides in curriculum decision making that is beneficial to both students and teachers.

Some learning organizations are now asking students to create personal Diary Map portfolios to aid in curriculum conversations regarding what is truly learned versus what teachers perceive is being learned. This is an excellent approach for enhancing the authenticity of the operational learning documentation.

Learning to Write a Personal Map: A Cautionary Note

If no Consensus Map exists to serve as the basis for a Projected or Diary Map, when teachers begin to record personal map data, each teacher's map may have similarities, but should have differences as well. When teachers are new to mapping and are trying to internalize how to write the map elements, carbon-copy Projected or Diary Maps raise a red flag. If all the maps are textually identical, a misunderstanding regarding individual mapping may be occurring. Here are four common misunderstandings:

- Teachers sit in close proximity and collectively discuss what they think each intra-aligned element should say, then individually write the agreed-upon text in each individual map.
- One teacher creates an individual map, and other teachers copy it and consider the task done.
- Teachers collectively search for what they perceive to be a quality map using the mapping system's worldwide search feature, replicate a map they think works into each teacher's map account, and make no individual changes to the copied map's elements.
- Each teacher copies verbatim the content, skills, and assessments from a previous curriculum document or textbook.

None of these actions expresses the intent and purpose of projected mapping or diary mapping. Everyone must realize upfront that these maps are meant to reflect students' current learning environment under a specific teacher's tutelage.

When learning to write the map elements for a personal map, there is nothing wrong with meeting in a small group and working side by side as long as the teachers in the small group do not teach the same grade level or course. Teachers can then help one another with quality wording, format, and intra-alignment without copying each other's map entries.

IMPLEMENTATION CONSIDERATIONS

Before teachers are asked to begin mapping, the Curriculum Mapping Cabinet or persons responsible for the initiative should predetermine a specific discipline as the first districtwide vertical focus. If only one school is initiating curriculum mapping, a school-site vertical focus should likewise be selected. Most learning organizations make this decision based on current data, including local or state test results or an appraisal of the current academic climate and culture. As mentioned previously, if there is flexibility in choice, mathematics is recommended as the first subject to map. Whatever discipline is chosen, however, those not teaching the discipline still map, since all disciplines will have a turn in the curriculum spotlight.

Teachers are often asked to start the learning process by recording a Diary Map in the selected mapping system. As mentioned in Chapter 2, if this is the map choice, during the first year of mapping each teacher should be responsible for mapping one grade-level discipline (elementary), one grade-level or course period (middle school, high school), one grade-level discipline or course (specialists), or one or two specific students or one pullout period (special education).

Chapter 4 revealed that there is much to be aware of and to remember when writing intra-aligned content, skills, assessments/evaluations, standards, and resources. It is therefore prudent to consider options for how this learning task and process may take place.

Recording Elements Incrementally

Some learning organizations embrace the *one step at a time* philosophy. Before writing a map within the mapping system, teachers are provided training on the following topics:

- reasons why curriculum mapping was selected as an initiative
- a general overview of curriculum-mapping concepts
- insights into the various types of maps
- the process used for selecting the chosen mapping system
- the learning organization's long- and short-term mapping goals

This informational training usually takes place toward the end of a school year or during the first month of a new school year. The next step is to train teachers to write and record one or two elements per month until all five common initial elements are incorporated. Many find that using an incremental process gives each teacher time to cognitively comprehend, apply, synthesize, and internalize each element's form and function. Figure 5.2 outlines a plausible timeline for an incremental element-introduction process.

During the trainings, teachers are encouraged to raise questions and concerns regarding the dual process of writing a quality map and recording it in a mapping system. Some choose to conduct training sessions in large-group settings, while others prefer small-group gatherings. Some prefer meeting in computer labs, while others prefer meeting with mobile laptops. When using an element-by-element learning process, it usually takes approximately half a school year to reach the point of incorporating all five elements.

Some will find writing and recording the elements easy. Others will have difficulty and will need varying levels of assistance to build personal confidence. Because of this, it is recommended that a team of trainers (e.g., Curriculum Mapping Coordinator, Cadre, Cabinet, and/or Council members) be in attendance to aid those who need extra assistance.

Figure 5.2 Diary Map Element Implementation Timeline

	Map Elements	Training Focuses	Monthly Recording Expectations
Mid-September	Unit Name	Brief overview or reminder for establishing common mapping wording, format, and intra-alignment	Teacher logs in to mapping system and personalizes mapping account information (e.g., teacher identification, password, e-mail address).
	Content	Hands-on introduction to selected mapping system	Teacher selects appropriate Diary Map course title and records unit name(s) and content for month of September. This month's recording is due in mapping system by October 7.
		Unit name: Wording, format	
		Content: Wording, format, intra-alignment coding	
Mid-October	Unit Name	Open discussion and review of unit name and content listings while viewing personal Diary Map for September.	Teacher includes unit name(s) and intra-aligned content-skills-resources for month of October. This month's recording is due in mapping system by November 7.
	Content		
	Skills	Skills: Wording, format, intra-alignment coding	
	Resources	Resources: Wording, format, intra-alignment coding	
Mid-November	Unit Name	Open discussion and review of unit name, content, skill, and resource listings while viewing personal Diary Map for October.	Teacher includes unit name(s) and intra-aligned content-skills-resources-assessments-evaluations for month of November. This month's recording is due in mapping system by December 7.
	Content		
	Skills	Assessments/evaluations: Wording, format, intra-alignment coding	
	Resources		
	Assessments		
	Evaluations		

(Continued)

115

Figure 5.2 (Continued)

	Map Elements	Training Focuses	Monthly Recording Expectations
Mid-December	Unit Name Content Skills	Open discussion and review of unit name, content, skill, resource, assessment, and evaluation listings while viewing personal Diary Map for November.	Teacher includes all elements for month of December. This month's recording is due in mapping system by January 7.
	Resources Assessments	Standards intra-alignment: How-tos may vary slightly depending on mapping system used.	Teachers are informed that they will be placed in preplanned, vertical, mixed-group review teams to conduct an initial read-through in mid-January.
	Evaluations Standards	Preliminary explanation of both purpose and process for conducting an initial read-through review.	(Preplanning and procedural directions can be found in the Facilitator Explanation and How-To Guide at the end of this chapter.)
Mid-January	Initial Read-Through	Vertical, mixed-group teams meet to collaboratively discuss their individual review findings for each small-group member's December Diary Map regarding quality mapping of all map elements' wording, format, and intra-alignment.	The initial read-through review is conducted after January 7 using December's Diary Map.

Recording Elements All at Once

Some learning organizations do not want to wait until mid-year to have all five elements included in a Diary Map. A second option is to have each teacher include all elements from the onset of diary mapping. If this is the selected method, make certain that teachers are well trained concerning each element and have a strong, independent understanding of each element's wording, format, and intra-alignment before mapping begins. Having to map all the elements at once with little or no training can be emotionally overwhelming for some teachers. Teachers need adequate time to reflect on their current mental models regarding each element. If possible, allow teachers time to explore the concept of each element independently and collectively by providing training in the school year prior to the official mapping school year that will require teachers to diary map all five elements simultaneously.

Conducting an Initial Read-Through

Regardless of whether teachers are asked to map the elements over a period of a few months or all at once, as soon as all five elements have been included for one month, it is recommended that teachers be given formal feedback regarding map quality. One way to accomplish this is by having teachers participate in a review process known as an *initial read-through.*

This process aids in internalizing two important mapping concepts. The first is that no type of map, including a Diary Map, is meant solely for personal use. This may be a difficult concept to grasp if teachers have an *island teaching* frame of mind. When teachers focus so intently on the discipline(s) they teach, they sometimes lose sight of the need for horizontal or vertical articulation. Mapping embraces *continent teaching* wherein there is appreciation for and connection between grade levels and disciplines. Maps are meant to be read and reviewed by teachers throughout a learning organization and used as a hub of data that represents the interplay of the learning organization's curriculum (Jacobs 2004b).

The second concept relates to the need for all teachers in the learning organization to speak the same mapping language. Establishing wording, format, and intra-alignment norms is strategic and purposeful. Beyond the need for map readers to be able to read and interpret any map, clarity and consistency improve the use of a mapping system's search and report features, which cannot function well if there is no consistency.

The initial read-through review takes preplanning and has specific implementation protocols. Detailed explanations, procedural recommendations, and participant handouts can be found in the facilitator's how-to guide at the end of this chapter. After conducting an initial read-through, teachers independently continue diary mapping monthly while (a) continuing to monitor themselves regarding quality map element entries, (b) beginning to meet and discuss curriculum issues that mapping the elements has already begun to bring to the surface, and (c) learning procedural steps for using a mapping system's search and report features.

Recording Projected Maps

A third initial map-writing option is to start with each teacher writing a Projected Map. Each teacher records all five elements for every month of the coming school year prior to instruction. Please be aware that this option takes time for each teacher to accomplish. It cannot happen in one hour here and one hour there. As with diary mapping, each teacher must make sense of each map element and how the elements relate to one another, as well as record the elements within a map in a mapping system.

Some learning organizations choose to provide three- or four-day summer workshops to allow adequate time for teachers to write Projected Maps. The first day or two is spent training teachers extensively on the wording, format, and intra-alignment of each element and how to log in to the selected mapping system and become familiar with its basic features. The remaining days are allotted for each teacher to create a personal Projected Map. Teachers are supported throughout the process via small-group gatherings or one-on-one mentoring led by Curriculum Mapping Cabinet or Council members or others who have experience in writing the elements and creating Projected Maps.

During the afternoon of the second or third day, the teachers participate in a formal initial read-through review so that they can receive formal feedback regarding the quality of the recorded elements. The remainder of the workshop time is dedicated to each teacher entering or revising the Projected Map data. Some teachers who catch on quickly may even be able to record a second Projected Map for another course or discipline. When the school year begins, each teacher revisits and, when necessary, modifies the Projected Map monthly to reflect the operational learning. If providing summer work days is not possible, an alternative may be to provide early-release or late-start days dedicated to the task of creating Projected Maps.

If time is a critical concern and providing time during the school year or summer is difficult, teachers may be asked to record a Projected Map for the first grading period and continue to add projected months with the passage of each grading period. While doing this, though, teachers must in tandem be ready to revisit months that have passed in real time to reflect the operational learning as Diary Map months.

What About the Second Year and Beyond?

Given that mapping has just begun and teachers have been individually mapping for one school year, a question often asked toward the end of the school year is "What are we going to map in the second year?"

The first year should be recognized as an introductory year dedicated to learning how to write a quality map and record a map within the mapping system. From experience, many teachers feel the first-year maps are not up to a desired level of quality since the learning curve for writing the map elements is quite high. I have found that when teachers contemplate what to map the second year, they have a tendency to choose one of three options:

1. Each teacher rolls over his or her current year's Diary Map into the next school year within the mapping system. As each month passes, each teacher

edits the now Projected Map by adding missing elements or improving the quality of existing elements to accurately reflect the current year's operational learning.

2. Teachers choose Option 1 *and* write a second discipline or course's Projected Map within the mapping system, including all five elements from the onset of recording the personal planned learning map. As the school year unfolds, both Projected Maps are edited monthly and become Diary Maps reflecting the operational learning for the current school year.

3. Teachers reflect on the learning process of writing and recording the five elements in a personal map as a purposeful cognitive-process precursor to working in collaboration to design Consensus Maps using protocols including breaking apart the standards (Chapter 9) and reviewing existing Projected/Diary Maps. Critical to this choice is the understanding that the previous year's Diary Maps may, or may not, be used as Projected Maps at the onset of the school year. Each teacher's personal map may need to be slightly or dramatically revised after the collaborative Consensus Maps become the foundation of the students' learning expectations.

It is important that the teachers be the leaders in this decision-making process regarding what to map in the second year. Their input can be presented to the Curriculum Mapping Councils and Cabinet for consideration. Remember, there is no single correct option. The choice must be based on the needs of the teachers as learners and how the decision will positively impact the goal of articulating and improving student learning.

Private Versus Public

Some perceive that Projected Map and Diary Map data should be private and not viewable by others. It is important to remember, however, that curriculum mapping is about full disclosure. Kallick and Wilson (2004) point out that "what is implied is that new knowledge about teaching and learning is created by bringing what has previously been tacit to an individual to a more explicit public dialogue" (p. 83).

All maps are meant to be accessible to all teachers. Most systems provide a screening filter that permits students, parents, and the community to view only Consensus Maps and Essential Maps by using a guest pass or code. This makes sense because these collaborative maps are meant to be a public record of the agreed-upon planned learning for a learning organization.

CONCLUSION

As educators, we are only as effective as what we know. If we have no working knowledge of what students studied in previous years, how can we build on their learning? If we have no insight into the curriculum in later grades, how can we prepare learners for future classes? Reading and examining curriculum maps enable us to create a database for making important decisions (Jacobs 1997, 17).

It is unprecedented that teachers can easily log in to a mapping system at any time and from any place to see what the planned or operational learning is in any classroom in the same school, another school, or throughout the learning organization. Throughout the implementation of curriculum mapping, everyone must be constantly reminded that curriculum mapping is not about reaching an end. Curriculum mapping is about embracing the students' operational and planned learning journey and using knowledge of this ongoing process to make collegial decisions about what is in the students' best interests. Be sure to celebrate the small steps and little changes as teachers and administrators learn to systemically change how the curriculum and related decisions are made based on evidence and collective agreement.

While many learning organizations choose to begin with individual mapping, others choose the option of having teachers start with collaborative mapping. If this is the choice of the learning organization, it is still recommended that all teachers first learn to individually write all the elements within a personal map for at least a few months to internalize the writing processes and procedures.

SAMPLE PROJECTED/DIARY MAPS

Figures 5.3 through 5.8 display individual teachers' documentation. While the maps may not represent your discipline or grade level, they provide visual examples of the incorporation of the common initial map elements' recommended wording, format, and intra-alignment. Since differentiation of these two map types is only based on real time, both are written in the same manner and include the same level of detail.

(Text continues on page 129)

Figure 5.3   Primary Mathematics Projected/Diary Map Month

Month	Content	Skills	Assessment	Standards
November	**DATA ANALYSIS** A. Graphs: Bar, Table, Tally, Picto Resources --Chapter 2 --Vocabulary: *sort, re-sort, as many as, more, fewer, equal to, sorting rule* B. Probability: 2 Variables Resources -Plastic Probability Beans --Teacher-Created Worksheets --Vocabulary: *certain, impossible, possible, total, prediction, revision, conclusion* **MEASUREMENT** C. U.S. Standard Length: Inches Resources --Chapter 3, pp. 30–35 --Vocabulary: *inch, inches, symbol, ruler, measure, length, longer, shorter, about*	A1. Classify in writing given data not to exceed 10 items per subset A2. Interpret in writing multiple graph-data comparisons using appropriate vocabulary terms B1. Conduct manipulatively simple experiments of no more than 10 trials B2. Record in writing data result from each trial B3. Interpret orally and in writing recorded results based on predictions, revisions, conclusions C1. Align visually and manipulatively proper endpoint of ruler to object C2. Measure manipulatively a length not to exceed 12 inches C3. Record in writing measured object to nearest inch using word inch, inches, or symbol" C4. Measure visually and record in writing length of illustrated representations of ruler/object	A1-A2. FOR Thanksgiving Graphs (Evaluation:Teacher Ob/Checklist) A1-A2. 5 Graph Problems Test B1-B2. FOR Small-Group Experiments (Evaluation:Teacher Ob/Feedback Form) B3. Personal Results Performance Task (Evaluation:Teacher Ob/Checklist) C1-C3. Ruler Measurement Performance Task (Evaluation:Teacher Ob/Checklist) C4. 10 Item Test	A. M1.05 (D) M1.05.01 (D) M1.05.02 (D) B. M1.05 (D) M1.05.02 (D) M1.05.03 (I) C. M1.03 (D) M1.03.01 (I)

Figure 5.4 Primary Reading Projected/Diary Map Month

Month	Content	Skills	Assessment	Standards
November	**COMPREHENSION**			
	A. Cause and Effect: Explicit/Implicit Evidence	A1. Support in writing how event or series of events impact a character's life using 3 to 5 explicit evidences	A1-A2. 4 Paragraph Response (Evaluation: ISAT/6-Trait Rubric)	A.
	Resources	A2. Summarize in writing implicit main idea of a reading passage using 3 textual supports and 2 text-to-self connections	A1. Cause/Effect Event T-Chart (Evaluation: Teacher Ob/ Checklist)	3.1.3.14 (D)
	--*Alejandro's Gift*			3.1.3.15 (D)
	--*The Armadillo From Amarillo*			3.1.3.17 (D)
	--Cause/Effect Evidence T-Chart using explanation terms: *so, because, therefore, as a result*			3.1.3.18 (D)
	VOCABULARY DEVELOPMENT			
	B. Words in Isolation: Prefixes: bi-, ex-, geo-, il-, non-, pre-, tri- /Suffixes: able, -al, -ance, -ish	B1. Define in writing single or multiple meaning for each prefix or suffix	B1-B3. 20 Word Matching/ Dictation Quiz	B.
		B2. Identify in writing word meaning using word structure: base + affix		3.1.4.01 (D)
		B3. Generate in writing new word meaning by changing affix		
	C. Words in Context: Multiple Sentences	C1. Determine in writing appropriate word to complete sentence using explicit contextual clues	C1. 20 Item MC/Cloze Test	C.
	Resources			3.1.4.04 (D)
	--Cloze Worksheets			3.1.4.05 (D)
	FLUENCY			
	D. Poetry: Enjambment Poems	D1. Differentiate aurally end-stop lines (lines that end with punctuation) and enjamb lines (lines that break with no punctuation and continue reading in same breath)	D1-D2. FOR Self-Selection Poem Readings (Evaluation: Audio Recording/Self-Critique)	D.
	Resources	D2. Read orally 5- to 10-line enjamb poems	D3. FOR Self-Selected Theme Unrhymed Poem (Evaluation: Peer Review/Checklist/Feedback)	3.C.2a (D)
	--*Playing With Poetry*	D3. Compose in writing 5- to 10-line enjamb poem		3.2.A.2c (I)

Figure 5.5   Intermediate Science Projected/Diary Map Month

Month	Content	Skills	Assessment	Standards
January	**SIMPLE CHEMISTRY** A. Chemical Reactions: Acids/Bases Resources --pH Log Scale --http://chemistry.about.com/od/acidsbases/Acids_Bases_and_pH.htm (*Acids and Bases*)	A1. Define in writing acidity, alkalinity, pH A2. Explain in writing examples of properties of acids (change litmus from blue to red) A3. Explain in writing properties of bases (does not change color of litmus; can turn red litmus back to blue) A4. Categorize in writing common items as acids or bases based on property attributes (e.g., Acids: citrus acid in fruits, ascorbic acid in vitamin C, carbonic acid in soft drinks/Bases: detergents, soaps, lye, household ammonia) A5. Differentiate visually and in writing strong/weak bases in common natural/man-made products using litmus test/pH scale A6. Determine in writing pH based on given data using pH scale	A1-A4. 25 Item (MC/FinB/Short-Answer) Quiz A5-A6. Red Cabbage pH Indicator Lab (Evaluation: Teacher Ob/Grading Scale) A5-A6. Apple Browning Lab (Evaluation: Teacher Ob/Grading Scale) A6. 5 Problem pH Liquids Quiz	A. S7.2.1 (D) S7.2.2 (I) S7.2.3 (I) M7.4.1 (R) M7.6.3 (R)

Figure 5.6 Middle School Physical Education Projected/Diary Map Month

Month	Content	Skills	Assessment	Standards
September	**FITNESS TESTING** A. President's Challenge: Fitness Test Resources --http://www.presidentschallenge.org/educators/program_details/physical_fitness_test.aspx (*President's Challenge Guidelines*) --Wood Blocks --Yardsticks --Pull-Up Bars --Running Track --Physical Fitness Awards --Fitness Portfolios **TEAM SPORTS** B. Soccer: Fundamentals Resources --Soccer Basics Handbook --Orange Cones	A1. Determine kinesthetically and in writing best score/time by participating in 5 events: --Shuttle Run (agility) --V-Sit or Sit and Reach (abdominal strength) --Pull-Ups or Flex Arm Hang (upper body strength) --Curl-Ups or Partial Curl-Ups (upper body strength) --Mile/Walk Run (endurance) A2. Calculate kinesthetically and orally resting heart rate B1. Memorize 12 soccer rules B2. Differentiate visually and orally front/back field positions B3. Maneuver ball using right and left foot in weave pattern	A1. Fitness Skills Test (Evaluation: Presidential/National/Participant Guidelines) A1. Individual Annual Improvement Chart (Evaluation: Self-Critique) A2. Pre-Event/Post-Event Performance Task (Evaluation: Teacher Ob/Student Self-Check) B1. 25 FinB Quiz B2-B6. Drill-Skill Performances (Evaluation:Teacher Ob/Checklists)	A. 6.9.1.1 (D) 6.9.1.2 (D) M6.3.2 (R) B. 6.5.4.1 (D) 6.5.4.2 (I) 6.5.4.3 (I)

Month	Content	Skills	Assessment	Standards
		B4. Pass ball using 2- to 3-person passing sequence	B7. Team Scrimmages (Evaluation: Video/ Behavior Peer Review)	
		B5. Evaluate kinesthetically best goalie tactics for scoring		
		B6. Place and execute goal shots		
		B7. Display visually and orally good sportsmanship conduct while playing		
	C. Flag Football	C1. Memorize 12 basic flag football rules	C1. 25 MC Quiz	C.
	Resources	C2. Recognize visually and orally 4 positions/purposes of players on playing field: quarterback, center, receiver, blocker	C2-C7. FOR Team Play Performance Checks (Evaluation: Teacher Ob/ Checklists)	6.4.1.1 (D)
	--Flag Football Handbook	C3. Throw football to moving receiver at varying lengths of distance (e.g., 10 yards, 20 yards, 30 yards)		6.4.1.2 (D)
	--Red/Yellow Flags	C4. Catch football using window technique at varying lengths of distance (e.g., 10 yards, 20 yards, 30 yards) from thrower		6.4.1.4 (D)
	--Orange Cones	C5. Run with football using proper hold technique (grip and tuck while in traffic)		
		C6. Determine orally offense/defense strategies when participating in a game		
		C7. Display visually and orally good sportsmanship conduct when playing		

125

Figure 5.7   Middle School Computer Keyboarding and Processing I Projected/Diary Map Month

Month	Content	Skills	Assessment	Standards
August	**KEY FUNDAMENTALS** A. Work Area: Arrangement Placement Resources --Lesson 1, p. R2 (4-Step Guide) --Keying Copy	A1. Arrange kinesthetically work area using 4-step guide: alphanumeric (main) keyboard directly in front of chair; front edge of keyboard even with edge of table or desk; monitor placed for easy viewing; disk drives placed for easy access and disk within easy reach (unless using a network); book behind or at side of keyboard; top raised for easy reading	A1–D1. FOR Daily Area/Technique Checks (Evaluation: Teacher Ob/ Checklists)	A. KP1.1 (I)
	B. Keying Position: Body Placement Resources --Lesson 1, p. R2 (5-Step Guide)	B1. Position kinesthetically body at computer terminal using 5-step guide: fingers curved and upright over home keys; wrists low, but not touching keyboard; forearms parallel to slant of keyboard; body erect, sitting back in chair; feet on floor for balance		B. KP1.2.1 (I)
	C. Home-Key Position: Finger Placement Resources --Lesson 1, p. R3	C1. Position kinesthetically fingers on keyboard using home row as a guide		C. KP1.2.2 (I)
	D. Technique: Keyboard Keys Resources --Lessons 1–5, pp. R3-R13 --Microsoft Word Software --Microtype Pro Software	D1. Key manually lines using correct techniques: striking each key with light tap at tip of finger; snapping fingertip toward palm of hand (keys: j, k, l, semicolon, a, s, d, f, h, e, i, r, o, t, n, g)	D1. 24 Keyboarding Applications Finger Reaches (Evaluation: Teacher Ob/Accuracy Chart)	D. KP1.2.3 (I)

Month	Content	Skills	Assessment	Standards
	E. Document Terminology: Paper Size, Horizontal/Vertical Alignment, Paper Lines, Punctuation Spacing, Line Spacing Resources --Department-Created Handout	E1. Identify in writing standard paper size used in most workplaces E2. Identify in writing document alignments for most workplace environments E3. Identify in writing standard paper lines E4. Identify in writing correct spacing for punctuation E5. Identify in writing line-spacing abbreviations: ss, ds, ts, qs	E1-E5. 50 Item FinB/Label/Short-Answer Quiz	E. KPI.4.1 (I)
	MICROSOFT WORD SOFTWARE F. General Information: Document Open/Save/Close Resources --Microsoft Word Software Help Menu	F1. Identify visually and orally open, save, close icons on toolbar F2. Execute electronically 3 actions to create/save document	F1. FOR Performance Check (Evaluation: Teacher Ob/ Checklist/Feedback) F2. Document Creation (Evaluation: Teacher Ob/ Checklist)	F. KPI.3.1 (I)

Figure 5.8 High School Visual and Performing Arts: Semester 2 Projected/Diary Map Month

Month	Content	Skills	Assessment	Standards
January	**PERSONAL CONNECTIONS: VISUAL ARTS**			
	A. The "Art" of Communication: Personal Position Resources --Student-Selected Visual Art Samples	A1. Defend orally personal stance while communicating responses to visual art using domain-specific language A2. Speak in qualitative terms when responding to works of art	A1–A2. FOR Rotating Small-Group Discussions (Evaluation: Teacher Ob/ Anecdotal Records)	A. VA2.1.401 (D) VA2.1.402 (D) VA2.1.403 (D) ELA S2.1.3 (R)
	B. Sculpture: Compositional Techniques Resources --Art Period of Personal Interest Web-Based Research --Wet/Dry Clay	B1. Define visually and orally 3 self-selected rules of proportion, form, shape using personal-choice examples B2. Sketch personal idea concept for planned freeform sculpture B3. Construct clay-based work of art in response to stylized characteristics observed in visual arts from self-selected culture/era	B1. Art Portfolio (Evaluation: Teacher Ob/Rubric) B2–B3. Freeform Sculpture (Evaluation: Rubric/ Peer Review)	B. VA1.1.303 (R) VA1.2.301 (R) VA1.3.301 (R)
	C. Cultural Influence on the Arts: A Historical Perspective Resources --Across Indian Lands DVD --Exploring Cultural Traditions: Art of Japan Book --Fantastic Figures, Oaxacan Ceramic Folk Art DVD --Student-Selected Internet Sites	C1. Compare and contrast orally and in writing works of art that communicate significant cultural meanings based on designated era C2. Research electronically and write position paper: theme of thesis statement--how exposure to various cultures and styles influences individuals' feelings toward art forms and artworks	C1–C2. Arts/Culture Position Paper (Evaluation: Arts Rubric/Language Arts Rubric) C1. FOR Large-Group Discussions (Evaluation: Peer Critique/Rubric)	C. VA2.3.301 (D) VA2.3.302 (D) VA3.3.203 (D) VA3.5.302 (D) ELA W1.2.1 (R) ELA R2.3.2 (R)
	D. Artistic Ideas: Expressions/ Interpretations Resources --Student-Selected Mixed-Medium Art Samples	D1. Defend orally personal stance reflecting on nature of defining "What is art?"/"What is beauty?" D2. Appraise visually and orally works of art and art elements designed to imitate systems in nature	D1. Art-Versus-Beauty Debate (Evaluation: Peer Review/Debate Guidelines) D2. Gallery Walk 2-Minute Presentation (Evaluation: Peer Review/Rubric)	D. VA3.1.301 (D) VA3.1.303 (D) VA3.5.303 (D) ELA S2.1.3 (R)

REVIEW QUESTIONS

Depending on your Projected Map and Diary Map prior knowledge, this chapter may have provided affirmation, modification, or revelation. Use the following fill-in-the-blank sentences to spark collegial dialogue. When ready, discuss your thoughts with a partner or in a small group.

1. Of the following statements, select the one that best represents your current feelings:

    A. I believe the main purpose for having each teacher start by creating a Diary Map is _____. I currently see this choice as being a _____ choice for the onset of our initiative because _____.

    B. I believe the main purpose for having each teacher start by creating a Projected Map is _____. I currently see this choice as being a _____ choice for the onset of our initiative because _____.

    C. I am not yet certain which is the best type of map to have teachers begin mapping. I want to read the remaining chapters before concluding what would be the best type. The reason I feel this way is

    _____.

2. Regarding training and facilitating learning, I currently think that _____ (name of person or persons) is/are the right choice for being responsible for the initial task of training teachers to become independent and confident in writing a quality map and recording the map within the mapping system. I also suggest that _____ (name of person or persons) is/are the right choice for follow-up and ongoing training support. I selected this person/persons for the following reasons:

    _____.

CONDUCTING AN INITIAL READ-THROUGH: FACILITATOR EXPLANATION AND HOW-TO GUIDE

Overview

The initial read-through provides teachers with an opportunity for self-evaluation as a map writer and provides a collaborative perspective of how map readers interpret what has been recorded by the map writer. For the read-through process to be most effective, teachers must first have training, support, and practice in writing and intra-aligning the map elements. There are four specific goals for conducting an initial read-through:

1. To provide a beginning map writer with the experience of others reading his or her map without being present to explain the recorded data. Consistency in one's ability to write map data using each element's wording, format, and intra-alignment norms will be peer-evaluated by map readers.

2. To provide a beginning map writer with a common mapping review protocol of first individually reading and reviewing the focused-on data before attending a meeting and collaboratively discussing personal findings immediately when the meeting begins.

3. To provide a beginning map writer with the concept of collegial collaboration, for both personal and collective learning and growth since everyone participating gains insight into one another's current understanding and mental models of what constitutes a quality map.

4. To provide a beginning map writer with immediate, positive, and encouraging feedback concerning each element's wording, format, and intra-alignment so that the learning organization can establish consistency and clarity in writing quality maps.

An initial read-through review is conducted by dividing the participating faculty members into small, preplanned teams within individual school sites. All schools within a district may choose to conduct the initial read-through on the same day, or each school may designate its own day and time.

Preplanning is imperative for a successful read-through. There are strategic behind-the-scenes preparations. Those who are designated as initial read-through facilitators will want to familiarize themselves with both this document and the Team Member Explanation and How-To Guide (which immediately follows this guide). This secondary document is similar to the information provided here, but it does not contain the preplanning information.

After conducting the initial read-through small-group meetings, the small-group teams debrief on their own, or all persons participating in the initial read-through review gather as one group for a debriefing time. The Initial Read-Through Card Shuffle Debrief activity may spark conversation and encourage the sharing of personal insights and benefits of participating in the initial read-through process.

Initial Read-Through Card Shuffle Debrief Preparation

To prepare for the Card Shuffle Debrief:

- Reproduce the Initial Read-Through Card Shuffle Debrief sheet (found on the last page of this chapter) on either cardstock or ordinary paper. Note: Each participant will need one set of four cards and a directions slip.
- Cut apart each copy of the four playing cards into four individual cards and a direction strip; fold direction strip in half.
- Place the five pieces in a small, self-sealing plastic bag, or paper clip each set; repeat for remaining sets.

Each participant receives one set of cards. Direct everyone to separate the set of cards, read the direction strip, and personally stack the statement cards as the directions request.

When a designated person signals to flip over the first card, each person reveals his or her top-ranked card. Everyone reads each card to see the similarities and differences in choice. Open conversation ensues regarding the various perceptions of how conducting the review impacted each participant personally. The people who chose the playing-card symbol that appears most frequently begin conversation about what the card's personal statement means. When discussion wanes, those responsible for laying the remaining cards on the table have a turn sharing why their cards were chosen. For example, a team of five teachers lays down three hearts, two spades, and one club. Those laying down the heart cards begin the discussion. After the people with the leading suit have shared, the remaining suits' card owners discuss why they selected their card choices. When it feels natural to do so, participants reveal the next card until all cards are revealed and discussion draws to a close.

Preplanning and Preparation

The following time frame includes both preparation and implementation components. The first three asterisked statements indicate facilitator or facilitators and, if appropriate, team leaders' responsibilities.

- *Forming preplanned, small-group teams—15 minutes
- *Explanation of purpose, procedures, and expectations to teachers—15 minutes
- *Collection, collation, and distribution of initial read-through packets—10–15 minutes *per team*
- Individual preread and review process of team's initial read-through packet—25–30 minutes
- Participation in the initial read-through small-group team and large-group debrief meetings—60–90 minutes

Forming Preplanned, Small-Group Teams

Divide participants into predetermined small-group teams based on the following criteria:

- Assign no less than three and no more than six members per team.
- Include a variety of grade levels and discipline areas per team; vertical, mixed groups are preferred (e.g., Grade 2 Math, Grade 5 Math, Grade 6 Science, Art, Special Education / U.S. History teacher, Algebra II teacher, Introduction to Computer Science teacher, Grade 11 Art teacher). Note: If in an elementary school wherein the majority of teachers are mapping the same discipline, each small-group team should have teachers from different grade levels on a team (e.g., Grade 1 Math, Grade 4 Math, Grade 5 Math, Grade 2 Art, Grade K Physical Education).
- Break up cliques and naysayers.
- Consider the emotional dynamics of each planned team's members.
- If possible, predesignate one person on each team to be the team leader. If a Curriculum Mapping Council has been established at each school site, its members are often designated as team leaders. Preferably, a team leader is someone who has had adequate training in quality mapping and the mapping process.

Explanation of Purpose, Process, and Expectations to Teachers

There are two phases to conducting an initial read-through meeting:

- **Phase One:** Individually and privately, team members read and review their small-group team's collection of maps and record commentaries before meeting as a small group.
- **Phase Two:** The predesignated, small-group teams meet for collaborative dialogue based on the maps and accompanying commentaries.

Before Phase One begins, the facilitator or facilitators need to share with the entire faculty: (a) the four goals for conducting an initial read-through, (b) the two phases of conducting the initial read-through, (c) the reminder that quality is based on map readers' ability to correctly interpret a map's data without the map writer present, and (d) a reminder of each element's wording, format, and intra-alignment norms.

Collection, Collation, and Distribution of Initial Read-Through Packets

Each member of a small-group team will receive an initial read-through packet. The packet preparation explanation below assumes that a team leader has been designated for each small-group team. If there are no predesignated team leaders, the packets will need to be collected, collated, and distributed by the facilitator or facilitators.

- Teachers are informed via an e-mail or mailbox reminder slip of the due date for having the designated month's map completed in the mapping system. An important point to also make in the reminder notice is that each teacher in the small group is responsible for informing his or her team leader in writing (e-mail or note) of the course name (and depending on the mapping system used, unit name) to be printed out.

- On or soon after the predetermined date, the team leader prints out one copy of each team member's designated map month (or unit) using the mapping system's predetermined print-map feature. Note: The team leader must also print out his or her map month. Important Note: An alternative to having the team leader print out the map month samples for his or her team members is to ask each team member to print out his or her own copy. This can be problematic since each mapping system has more than one view for printing out a map month. Therefore, if choosing this alternative, be specific regarding the desired map view and provide step-by-step directions for how to print the desired view.
- The team leader first collates the map month printouts into one pile. On top of this pile, the team leader places a copy of the Initial Read-Through: Collaborating to Create Quality Maps as the cover sheet (cover sheet can be found after the Team Member Explanation and How-To Guide at the end of this chapter and consists of two pages). Using a copy machine, the team leader makes a single-sided, stapled packet consisting of the cover sheets and the collective maps—one copied set for each team member.
- The team leader delivers a prepared initial read-through packet and a separate copy of the Conducting an Initial Read-Through: Team Member Explanation and How-To Guide (which can be found later in the chapter, after this guide) to each member in person or by placing the documents in each team member's mailbox.

  o *Optional:* If the school or district has been using a recording-the-elements reminder sheet as a resource, a copy of this may be included with the two previously mentioned documents in case the original reminder sheet may have been misplaced.
  o *Optional:* The team leader provides each member with two colors of highlighters to be used during Phase One's prereading and reviewing process.

Individual Preread and Review of Team's Initial Read-Through Packet

Phase One

To conduct the individual prereading review, each team member needs the prepared initial read-through packet, the Conducting an Initial Read-Through: Team Member Explanation and How-To Guide, and two colors of highlighters:

- One color is for highlighting positives found in each map. The other color is for highlighting concerns or needed clarifications:

  o *Positives* are examples in which the map writer's elemental wording, format, or intra-alignment is properly incorporated. Positives are noted directly on the maps using the highlighter as well as noted using a pen or pencil textually on the cover sheet. Specific examples are critical to the review process when the team members begin to verbally share their thoughts about each map during Phase Two. For example, "You did a nice job with your content listings," is not specific. But this is: "Your first content listing, Informational Text: Current Event Magazines, is descriptive since *current event magazines* tells me the exact type of informational text the students must know for the unit of study."

  o *Concerns* represent instances in which the map writer's elemental wording, format, or intra-alignment appears to be incorporated improperly or missing entirely. Concerns are highlighted on the map, and specific comments are noted textually on the cover sheet.

  o *Needed clarifications* are textual and/or visual puzzlements in which a map reader cannot easily figure out what the map writer is trying to convey. These needed clarifications are highlighted as well as noted on the cover sheet.

During the preliminary reading, the first three columns of the cover sheet are completed. During the small-group team meeting, the last column is filled in as part of the meeting process.

Phase Two

If the faculty is first meeting as an entire group before separating into small groups, this is an appropriate time to model small-group meeting expectations. Many schools create and present an expectation presentation. The central theme of the collaboration's hallmark is that all participants be kind and respectful of one another's feelings and earnestly focus on the task of providing beneficial feedback that encourages everyone to write quality maps. For example, Lakeville Public Schools created a *Conducting the Initial Read-Through* DVD (available at the Resources section of www.CurriculumMapping101.com), which presents a simulation that conveys not only the desired collaborative behavior but also the potential misbehaviors that may be exhibited during a small-group meeting.

When ready to begin, small-group team members should sit in a cooperative-style arrangement (e.g., around a circular or rectangular table). One person needs to be designated as the official timekeeper. Because everyone deserves equal time, plan on approximately 5–10 minutes per map writer. A second person needs to be designated as the parking lot attendant. This person's role is to stop any conversation that strays from the purpose and goals of the initial read-through. For example, if a conversation begins about "not enough time is being given to us to map," the parking lot attendant literally calls out, "Parking lot!" This person then makes note of the mentioned concern(s). The small-group leader immediately refocuses the group on the task at hand and continues the discussion about the wording, format, and intra-alignment of the selected map. At the end of the meeting, the parking lot attendant's notes may be addressed immediately or can be included in a future large-group or small-group meeting. The parking lot attendant also makes note of any questions that the team members or team leader cannot answer regarding wording, format, and intra-alignment norms. When meeting as a large group, the questions can be addressed by the facilitator or facilitators.

The designated team leader is provided feedback about his or her map first. (If no team leader has been designated, the team will have to select someone.) All team members retrieve this member's map and cover sheet notes from their packets and begin the collaboration by sharing positives about the map's quality. After everyone shares a specific positive comment, the focus shifts to concerns or needed clarifications. It is recommended that the full allotted time be spent on each person's map. In other words, do not rush through each map. A critical feature of the read-through process is the conversation sparked by reviewing each map.

When the allotted time is almost up and before moving on to the next team member, everyone records a personal, reflective comment in the last column's cell on his or her personal cover sheet that corresponds with this team member's map. In addition to commenting on other writers' maps, each person makes a comment regarding what he or she has learned when his or her own map is in focus.

The following conversation features a four-member, small-group team. Barbara, the team leader, is the first to request input from the group.

Barbara: I'll go first.

Everyone retrieves Barbara's map from within the packet. Team members prepare to share using highlighted notations and summary comments.

Beth: You used a capital letter at the beginning of each word for all of the content listings.

Barbara: Thank you.

Nancy: All of the skill statements start with a measurable verb, and you included targets. For example: Differentiate in writing special and general relativity.

Barbara: Thank you.

Andrea: I noticed that when an assessment name did not provide enough information, you included the evaluation summary such as Energy Lab (Evaluation: Checklist/Journal Entry Rubric).

Barbara: Thank you.

Lisa: It was easy to follow your intra-alignment because you used the letter–number coding. *(Points to specific areas in Barbara's map.)* I know that this content is aligned to these three skills, these two assessments, and these standards. No guesswork here.

Barbara: Thank you.

Important Note: The hardest aspect of this phase of the sharing process is for the map writer to not provide personal thoughts or comments as each person shares a positive. Notice that Barbara simply said "Thank you" each time she was given a compliment. While this may seem trite, it is not. The initial read-through's key purpose is to encourage collaboration and trust. During the positive sharing time, the map writer simply says "Thank you" or nods in acknowledgment. When sharing concerns or needed clarifications, however, the map writer is allowed and encouraged to share personal thoughts and comments based on the team members' comments.

Barbara: Does anyone have any concerns or needed clarifications about what I wrote?

(Continued)

(Continued)

The floor is open. Team members respectfully share personal notations. It is recommended that if a team member has more than one comment to share, he or she shares only one to begin with so that other team members can also actively participate. Since this is a time to provide constructive feedback, it is important that the map writer not feel defensive or put on the spot.

Andrea: I noticed you did not include any resources. Is there a reason you left them out?

Barbara: Honestly, no. I know that I forgot to add them. I just figured I could add them later. Obviously with you noticing they were not there, it tells me I need to add them in, for certain, when I am writing my next month's map.

Nancy: I was a little confused by the last content–skill set. The wording is just about identical for the content and the skill. The descriptor for the content is in the same wording as the skill statement.

Barbara: *(Pauses as she reads the map entry.)* I see what you mean. I know what I was thinking. I just didn't get it on the map! I can revise the skill statement's descriptor so that it lists the various types of energy pertaining to the three categories I included in the content listing. . . . This really is helping me. Is there anything else anyone noticed?

When the open-floor discussion concerning Barbara's map naturally comes to a close (or a designated time limit is reached), all team members share a final compliment regarding Barbara's willingness to be open to the team's comments.

Before moving on to Nancy's map, each member, including Barbara, writes a self-reflection note concerning the discussion of Barbara's map in the last column's cell that corresponds with Barbara's map. The sharing cycle of specific positives, open-floor concerns or needed clarifications, and recording final thoughts in the last column is repeated until the remaining team members have each had a turn.

Conclusion

After everyone has received feedback, conclude the initial read-through small-group or large-group meeting by conducting the Initial Read-Through Card Shuffle Debrief or other type of closure activity.

Allow time for questions to be asked and answered by the facilitator(s) that the small-group teams may not have been able to answer on their own. A question that often comes up during the debriefing time is "Do we have to go back and revise the already passed month(s) we recorded so that they are of better quality?" The answer needs to be based on where teachers are in the map-writing process. If the initial read-through is conducted after teachers have mapped all the elements at once for one or two months, revising the months will aid in synthesizing the learning from the initial read-through. If the teachers have mapped one or two elements per month, some teachers prefer to revise previous months' existing elements, whereas others prefer to simply move forward and focus on mapping the upcoming months writing all five elements. If the read-through is part of a Projected Map summer workshop, element revision in all the months is part of the workshop process.

Plan to conclude the review process with a celebration. Food always works well! Creative ideas I have seen include giving everyone a miniature empty chair to remember that doing what is in the students' best interest includes learning to write quality maps; handing out compact mirrors to reflect on the fact that teachers are learners, too; and handing out a school bus pin or tie tack representing the commitment of getting on the bus and moving forward to reach the goal of a vertical, teacher-designed, dynamic curriculum.

An Optional Second Round

Most teachers still want and appreciate additional feedback after recording the next month's map. Conducting a second initial read-through round focuses on the same goals, but is accomplished using 21st-century technology. The entire process is accomplished via cyberspace using the mapping system and e-mail.

Procedure

The second round is an excellent opportunity for teachers to be placed in small-group teams that consist of teachers throughout the district since no one has to actually meet in person. This is accomplished by creating new small-group teams using the same criteria as for the original initial read-through, but with a twist.

1. Choose a team leader for each new small group that is formed. Each team leader acts as a communicator and liaison for his or her small group's team members and provides the following information to members via e-mail:

   - who is in the small-group team, including the team leader
   - the due date for completion of the designated month's map in the mapping system
   - a reminder that each member needs to personally e-mail the other team members with the course name (and depending on the mapping system, the unit name) of the map to be reviewed
   - the ending date for individually contacting each team member via e-mail to share positives and concerns or needed clarifications about his or her reviewed map

2. After the ending date of the second-round experience, a read-through facilitator or facilitators conduct an online or e-mail survey asking all participants to comment on what they learned from participating in the second read-through as well as what professional development or additional

support they need or desire. After receiving the completed surveys, the facilitator or facilitators share via e-mail the collective survey results.

3. Celebrate the end of the second round, too. One way may be to ask a local business to donate free passes or a special coupon for all second-round initial read-through participants—sent via e-mail to convey the message that much of the mapping process can be conducted online.

Closure

Please be aware that the initial read-through process is designed to focus only on quality map element-writing norms. The initial read-through is not meant to be officially conducted more than two times, whether the second time takes place via cyberspace or in person. This provides ample opportunity for teachers to collaboratively focus on the mechanics of writing a quality map.

If a learning organization gets stuck in a rut of just focusing on writing a quality map, there is a high probability that momentum for teachers seeing the full value of mapping will be lost. Teachers must start using the maps via the mapping system's search and report features to conduct curriculum reviews. This enables and enhances collegial conversations focused on improving student learning and instruction.

CONDUCTING AN INITIAL READ-THROUGH: TEAM MEMBER EXPLANATION AND HOW-TO GUIDE

Phase One

To conduct the individual prereading review, you will need this handout, the initial read-through map packet, two colors of highlighters, and a pen or pencil.

- One color is for highlighting positives found in each map. The other color is for highlighting concerns or needed clarifications:

    o *Positives* are examples in which the map writer's elemental wording, format, or intra-alignment is properly incorporated. Positives are noted directly on the maps using the highlighter as well as noted using a pen or pencil textually on the cover sheet. Specific examples are critical to the review process when the team members begin to verbally share their thoughts about each map during Phase Two. For example, "You did a nice job with your content listings," is not specific. But this is: "Your first content listing, Informational Text: Current Event Magazines, is descriptive since *current event magazines* tells me the exact type of informational text the students must know for the unit of study."

    o *Concerns* represent instances in which the map writer's elemental wording, format, or intra-alignment appears to be incorporated improperly or missing entirely. Concerns are highlighted on the map, and specific comments are noted textually on the cover sheet.

    o *Needed clarifications* are textual and/or visual puzzlements in which a map reader cannot easily figure out what the map writer is trying to convey. These needed clarifications are highlighted as well as noted on the cover sheet.

During the preliminary reading, you will fill in the first three columns of the cover sheet of your map packet. During your small-group team meeting, you will fill in the last column as part of the meeting process.

Phase Two

When your small group meets, sit in a cooperative-style arrangement (e.g., around a circular or rectangular table), and designate someone to be the official timekeeper. Because everyone deserves equal time, plan on approximately 5–10 minutes per map writer. A second person needs be designated as the parking lot attendant. This person's role is to stop any conversation that strays from the purpose and goals of the initial read-through. For example, if a conversation begins about "not enough time is being given to us to map," the parking lot attendant literally calls out, "Parking lot!" This person then makes note of the mentioned concern(s). The small-group leader immediately refocuses the group on the task at hand and continues the discussion about the wording, format, and intra-alignment of the selected map. At the end of the meeting, the parking lot attendant's notes may be addressed immediately or can be included in a future large-group or small-group meeting. The parking lot attendant also makes note of any questions that the team members or team leader cannot answer regarding wording, format, and intra-alignment norms. When meeting again as a large group, the questions can be addressed by the facilitator or facilitators.

The designated team leader will be provided feedback about his or her map first. (If there is no team leader, select someone to be first.) All team members retrieve this member's map and cover sheet notes from their packets and begin the collaboration by sharing positives about the map's quality. After everyone shares a specific positive comment, the focus shifts to concerns or needed clarifications. It is recommended that the full allotted time be spent on each person's map. In other words, do not rush through each map. A critical feature of the read-through process is the conversation sparked by reviewing each map.

When the allotted time is almost up and before moving on to the next team member, everyone records a personal, reflective comment in the last column's cell on his or her own cover sheet that corresponds with this team member's map. In addition to commenting on other writers' maps, each person makes a comment regarding what he or she has learned when his or her own map is in focus.

The following conversation features a four-member, small-group team. Barbara, the team leader, is the first to request input from the group.

Barbara: I'll go first.

Everyone retrieves Barbara's map from within the packet. Team members prepare to share using highlighted notations and summary comments.

Beth: You used a capital letter at the beginning of each word for all of the content listings.

Barbara: Thank you.

Nancy: All of the skill statements start with a measurable verb, and you included targets. For example: Differentiate in writing special and general relativity.

Barbara: Thank you.

Andrea: I noticed that when an assessment name did not provide enough information, you included the evaluation summary such as Energy Lab (Evaluation: Checklist/Journal Entry Rubric).

Barbara: Thank you.

Lisa: It was easy to follow your intra-alignment because you used the letter–number coding. *(Points to specific areas in Barbara's map.)* I know that this content is aligned to these three skills, these two assessments, and these standards. No guesswork here.

Barbara: Thank you.

Important Note: The hardest aspect of this phase of the sharing process is for the map writer to not provide personal thoughts or comments as each person shares a positive. Notice that Barbara simply said "Thank you" each time she was given a compliment. While this may seem trite, it is not. The initial read-through's key purpose is to encourage collaboration and trust. During the positive sharing, the map writer simply says "Thank you" or nods in acknowledgment. When sharing concerns or needed clarifications, however, the map writer is allowed and encouraged to share personal thoughts and comments based on the team members' comments.

Barbara: Does anyone have any concerns or needed clarifications about what I wrote?

The floor is open. Team members respectfully share personal notations. It is recommended that if a team member has more than one comment to share, he or she shares only one to begin with so that other team members can also actively participate. Since this is a time to provide constructive feedback, it is important that the map writer not feel defensive or put on the spot.

Andrea: I noticed you did not include any resources. Is there a reason you left them out?

Barbara: Honestly, no. I know that I forgot to add them. I just figured I could add them later. Obviously with you noticing they were not there, it tells me I need to add them in, for certain, when I am writing my next month's map.

Nancy: I was a little confused by the last content–skill set. The wording is just about identical for the content and the skill. The descriptor for the content is in the same wording as the skill statement.

Barbara: *(Pauses as she reads the map entry.)* I see what you mean. I know what I was thinking. I just didn't get it on the map! I can revise the skill statement's descriptor so that it lists the various types of energy pertaining to the three categories I included in the content listing. . . . This really is helping me. Is there anything else anyone noticed?

When the open-floor discussion concerning Barbara's map naturally comes to a close (or a designated time limit is reached) all team members share a final compliment regarding Barbara's willingness to be open to the team's comments.

Before moving on to Nancy's map, each member, including Barbara, writes a self-reflection note concerning the discussion of Barbara's map in the last column's cell that corresponds with Barbara's map. The sharing cycle of specific positives, open-floor concerns or needed clarifications, and recording final thoughts in the last column is repeated until the remaining team members have each had a turn.

Conclusion

After everyone has been provided feedback, conclude your initial read-through meeting by conducting a debriefing time. An activity may already be planned by your small-group leader or large-group facilitator.

INITIAL READ-THROUGH: COLLABORATING TO CREATE QUALITY MAPS

Please read your small-group team's set of maps individually before your designated meeting time. The initial read-through focuses specifically on the quality of each element's wording, format, and intra-alignment. A map's data must provide clarity for map readers regardless of grade level, discipline, or course context.

Map Writer/ Course Title	Positive Notes About This Map	Concerns and Needed Clarifications About This Map	How Has Discussing This Map Helped Clarify What Is Needed to Write a Quality Map?

INITIAL READ-THROUGH: COLLABORATING TO CREATE QUALITY MAPS (Continued)

Please read your small-group team's set of maps individually before your designated meeting time. The initial read-through focuses specifically on the quality of each element's wording, format, and intra-alignment. A map's data must provide clarity for map readers regardless of grade level, discipline, or course context.

Map Writer/ Course Title	Positive Notes About This Map	Concerns and Needed Clarifications About This Map	How Has Discussing This Map Helped Clarify What Is Needed to Write a Quality Map?

INITIAL READ-THROUGH
CARD SHUFFLE DEBRIEF

Directions: Personally rank the statements by stacking the four cards: the top card represents the most important comment regarding your personal initial read-through experience; the bottom card represents the least important comment for you. Do not allow team members to see your card ranking until signaled to reveal one card at a time, starting with your most important comment.

Striving for quality map wording, format, and intra-alignment is important because we will be reading maps *without map writers present.* 	**Collaboration and curricular dialogue add depth to *needed communication* regarding our students' learning continuum.** 
I am not the only one struggling with *doing this right.* Having an opportunity to assist one another in writing quality maps is helpful. 	**Having to first individually read and review map data *before attending a meeting* adds a dynamic reflective dimension to the collaborative process.** 

6

What Should We Know Before Creating Consensus Maps and Essential Maps?

A verbal agreement isn't worth the paper it's written on.

—Samuel Goldwyn

Consensus Maps and Essential Maps provide written agreement of the collaborative, agreed-on planned learning. These maps are intended to inform all stakeholders, including teachers, administrators, students, parents, board members, and the community, regarding students' mandatory or compulsory learning expectations. Many learning organizations have replaced traditional course description handbooks with the ability to view these types of maps within the selected online mapping system. Most mapping systems allow stakeholders outside the schools to use a guest entry code to access the system and stay informed regarding the planned student learning expectations.

MAP TYPE DIFFERENTIATION

A Consensus Map represents school-site learning expectations. An Essential Map represents districtwide expectations. Each map type portrays a level of consistency while allowing for autonomy and flexibility.

Consensus Maps

A Consensus Map is designed by two or more teachers. The design may involve the collaborative efforts of teachers in the same grade level or department, a series of grade levels, or a cross- or interdisciplinary team. A collaborative team configuration is not meant to convey exclusivity. For example, a team designing a Grade 4 mathematics Consensus Map may not consist of only the fourth-grade teachers. A special education teacher or a math resource teacher may also be part of the team designing the planned learning. Likewise, while a Consensus Map represents a particular grade level or discipline course, it is not intended to be an isolated map. Inter-alignment articulation across grade levels or across a series of courses is an important step in consensus mapping. In other words, a Grade 7 science Consensus Map needs to be aligned with the planned learning included in science Consensus Maps for the seven years prior to Grade 7 and the five years after. Likewise, an Algebra II Consensus Map needs to be aligned with the courses prior to taking Algebra II and the courses following it. Therefore, conducting alignment reviews is a critical component when designing Consensus Maps and is explained later in this chapter.

Elements Included

A Consensus Map is not as detailed as a Projected Map or a Diary Map so as to allow for individual teacher autonomy. The elements included in a Consensus Map are considered compulsory and are designed according to national, state, district, or self-created standards' proficiency targets. As previously mentioned, textbooks and materials are resources and are included as such when appropriate in a collaborative map.

When first drafted, a Consensus Map typically includes the following intra-aligned elements for each month and unit based on the breaking apart the standards process (see Chapter 9) and engaging in collegial dialogue and collaborative decision making:

- unit name
- content
- skills
- standards

When these elements have been aligned across grade levels or courses, the following elements may be added initially or over the course of a few years depending on the resources available to all teachers teaching the course and the level of collegial assessment practice among the teachers:

- resources
- common or same assessments

All wording, format, and intra-alignment norms for these elements, which were explained in Chapter 4, apply to Consensus Maps, with one caveat: Intra-alignment *number* coding is only included in the skills field for content-skill statements that are being measured using a common or same assessment. If a skill is not being included in the collaborative measurement(s), it will not have a number coding until a teacher personally adds a number to each skill within his or her Projected/Diary Map to intra-align the skill(s) to the appropriate assessments and evaluations using the appropriate letter-number coding. If teachers agree that a Consensus Map will not include collaborative assessments, there will be no numbers included in the skills' intra-alignment coding (see Figure 6.1).

As each year progresses, if the teachers come to agreement on common or same assessments for one or more content skills, the Consensus Map will reflect this agreement using intra-alignment letter and number coding for the appropriate content-skill listing(s) (see Figure 6.2). To do so may mean that the manner in which the skill statements were originally ordered will need to be revised to accommodate the inclusion of common or same assessments. Such revisions are natural and a part of the ongoing nature of mapping. Remember that a map represents the big picture of the learning. The data within a map's month or unit may not necessarily be in an exact sequential order of instruction. Notice in Figure 6.2 that one A skill statement and two B skill statements have been moved down to the bottom of the appropriate letter listing since these skills are not included in the letter-number sequence that represents the content-skills being measured using the two same assessments.

The more collegial a team is regarding its collective planned learning, the more likely that a Consensus Map will include additional data regarding content, skills, assessments, evaluations, resources, and other included elements. If the opposite is true, and teachers are not collegial, a Consensus Map will initially contain only that which can be agreed on. At a minimum that must include intra-aligned unit name, content, skills, and standards.

Conducting a Collaborative Map Initial Read-Through

At the onset of a curriculum-mapping initiative, if teachers are learning to write map elements via consensus mapping rather than diary mapping or projected mapping, conducting an initial read-through to check for writing quality map elements is still important and necessary. The directions for conducting an initial read-through in Chapter 5 can still be used, with one exception: Each teacher will not have an individual map; instead each team will have one collaborative map. Small-group team meetings will need to reflect this configuration. Each collaborative team should have its members on different initial read-through review teams, with each member using a copy of a drafted Consensus Map month. Doing so enhances the opportunity for multiple-perspective feedback for each design team and allows for individual personal growth.

What If Other Types of Maps Exist?

If Diary Maps exist prior to designing a Consensus Map, they will provide evidence of what each teacher currently values and can aid in the teachers' collaborative conversations regarding a Consensus Map's design. Diary Maps can be formally or informally reviewed as teachers evaluate connections between what is currently valued, what breaking apart the standard statements reveals regarding explicit and implicit learning expectations (see Chapter 9), and the above and below grade-level or course learning requirements as evidenced in other grade levels' or courses' Diary Maps and drafted Consensus Maps.

If an Essential Map exists, it means that some of the design process has already been completed since this map contains mandatory learning and is oftentimes designed based on learning organizationwide selection of power

Figure 6.1   High School Communication Arts Consensus Map Month—Year One

Month	Content	Skills	Assessment	Standards
February	**PUBLIC PRESENTATIONS II**			
	A. Informal Speech: Eulogy	A. Summarize orally and in writing 7 presentation phrases:		A.
		--attention getter (posing a question)		LA 2.3 (D)
		--credibility of speaker (why I know this)		LA 2.5 (D)
		--establishing purpose of speech (death of person)		LA 2.6 (D)
		--previewing points of the speech (attributes of person)		HS 5.1 (R)
		--using details (e.g., facts, anecdotes)		HS 8.4 (R)
		--summarizing (main points to know)		
		--clincher (something memorable)		
		A. Identify aurally at least 5 presentation-phrase concepts in given speech using orated examples to support identification		
		A. Justify in writing planned speech outline based on presentation terms		
		A. Orate while focusing on 3 vocal aspects: volume, pacing, inflection		
		A. Orate while focusing on 3 mannerisms: eye contact, hand motions, posture		
	B. Formal Speech: PowerPoint Enhancement	B. Identify aurally and in writing 4 organizational speech structures: introduction, body, conclusion, transitions		B.
				LA 2.3 (D)
		B. Research electronically self-selected topic based on personally created survey of current-event issue		LA 2.5 (D)
				LA 2.7 (D)
		B. Outline in writing planned speech and visual connections using storyboards/note cards		T 2.3.1 (R)
				T 2.3.3 (R)
		B. Construct technologically presentation slides including introduction, body, conclusion, bibliography, proper citing (Note: Slides are guides—not copy of speech)		
		B. Pace orally speech using balance of slide incorporation and oration		

148

Figure 6.2   High School Communication Arts Consensus Map Month—Year Two

Month	Content	Skills	Assessment	Standards
February	**PUBLIC PRESENTATIONS II** A. Informal Speech: Eulogy Resources --Local Toastmasters Guest Speakers	A1. Summarize orally and in writing 7 presentation phrases: --attention getter (posing a question) --credibility of speaker (why I know this) --establishing purpose of speech (death of person) --previewing points of the speech (attributes of person) --using details (e.g, facts, anecdotes) --summarizing (main points to know) --clincher (something memorable) A2. Identify aurally at least 5 presentation-phrase concepts in given speech using orated examples to support identification A3. Orate while focusing on 3 vocal aspects: volume, pacing, inflection A4. Orate while focusing on 3 mannerisms: eye contact, hand motions, posture A. Justify in writing planned speech outline based on presentation terms	A1-A4. SAME Famous Historical Person Eulogy (Evaluation: Peer Review/Rubric)	A. LA 2.3 (D) LA 2.5 (D) LA 2.6 (D) HS 5.1 (R) HS 8.4 (R)
	B. Formal Speech: PowerPoint Enhancement Resources --Computer Lab	B1. Identify aurally and in writing 4 organizational speech structures: introduction, body, conclusion, transitions B2. Construct technologically presentation slides including introduction, body, conclusion, bibliography, proper citing (Note: *Slides are guides—not copy of speech*) B3. Pace orally speech using balance of slide incorporation and oration B. Research electronically self-selected topic based on personally created survey of current-event issue B. Outline in writing planned speech and visual connections using storyboards/note cards	B1-B3. SAME 8-12 Slide Show/ 4 Minute Oral Presentation (Evaluation: Peer Review/Rubric including A3-A4)	B. LA 2.3 (D) LA 2.5 (D) LA 2.7 (D) T 2.3.1 (R) T 2.3.3 (R)

standards (see Chapter 9). Within the mapping system, a school-site team replicates the Essential Map into a Consensus Map account and studies it in terms of the required learning expectations and adds planned learning (e.g., content-skill sets based on breaking apart non-power standards), common or same assessments and evaluations, and resources for existing planned learning or entirely new units of study. Since an Essential Map has even less data than a Consensus Map, it encourages each school site's autonomy without jeopardizing the integrity and consistency of the required districtwide curriculum.

Some learning organizations choose to have teachers design a course-specific Consensus Map before having them individually create a Projected Map or a Diary Map for that course. Others prefer a reverse process and have teachers first create Diary Maps and then create a Consensus Map. While both directions have pluses and minuses regarding process and necessary map revision concerning the map elements, regardless of which direction a learning organization takes, eventually there will be an ongoing relationship between a course's Consensus Map and each teacher's Diary Map (see Figure 6.3).

Figure 6.3   Relationship of Operational and Planned Learning Evidence

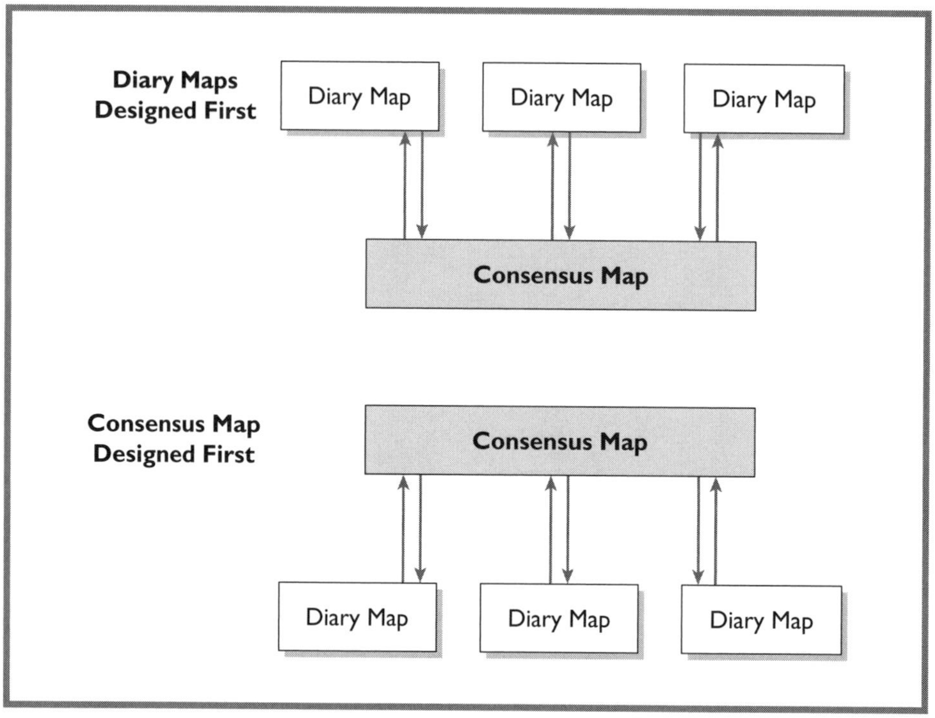

The ongoing documented relationship between the current and archived years of both the planned and operational learning plays an active role in conducting curriculum reviews and collegial decision making regarding student learning expectations.

An Isolated Teacher

When a school is learning the processes of designing Consensus Maps, I am often asked, "What if I am the only one teaching a course?" Here are some actual statements I have heard from teachers:

- I am the only band teacher in the middle school. What I decide happens, happens.
- I am the only one teaching third grade. We are a small elementary school and only have one teacher per grade level.
- I am the only one who teaches the Current Events AP course. What do I do when the course learning is my own decision?
- I am the only art teacher in the elementary school. Honestly, I do not get along with the middle school or high school art teachers. We think very differently about what students need to learn.

Please remember that a Consensus Map is not meant to represent the operational curriculum. It is the planned-learning curriculum representation void of the present calendar year and the present instructor(s). Projected Maps and Diary Maps provide evidence of each present teacher's current student needs in the current school year.

I am the only band teacher in the middle school. What I decide happens, happens. When this teacher shared this with me, I responded that the Grade 7 Band Consensus Map's planned learning expectations must be applicable regardless of who the current band teacher may be. If the students' planned-learning knowing and doing is to be measured and evaluated by participation in a spring recital as a course requirement, then the appropriate unit name, content, skills, assessment, evaluation, standards, and resources would be included in the Consensus Map. If, however, the spring recital is an event that the present school year's band teacher chooses to present because it enhances the current school culture or climate, the unit-based event would not be included in the Consensus Map and would instead be documented in this teacher's personal Projected/Diary Map.

I also told this teacher that even though he may be the only band teacher in the middle school, he is not the only music teacher in the district. I suggested that he and the two other music teachers (i.e., the district's entire music department—one teacher per school [one from elementary school, one from middle school, one from high school]) give final approval not only to the designed Grade 6, Grade 7, and Grade 8 Band Consensus Maps but also to the Grade 9 through Grade 12 Band Consensus Maps since they truly represent the two schools' planned learning, vertically articulated Band courses, not an individual teacher's courses.

I am the only one teaching third grade. We are a small elementary school and only have one teacher per grade level. I shared with this teacher that she should not be working on the grade-level planned learning in isolation. The school's K–5 Consensus Maps can be designed by a teacher team that consists of all six teachers. The Consensus Maps will then automatically be vertically inter-aligned and articulated by the very nature of the design team's membership.

I am the only one who teaches the Current Events AP course. What do I do when the course learning is my own decision? When talking to this advanced placement (AP) teacher, I recommended that he invite the entire social studies department to be involved in the decision-making process about this course's base learning since there is a non-AP version of this course, two courses must be taken as a prerequisite to taking the AP course, and there needs to be a foundation to this course's learning regardless of who the current instructor is.

I knew my suggestion was a difficult one for him to hear because his department engages in parallel-play relationships (Barth 2006). Since consensus mapping requires teachers to engage in collegial relationships, suggesting that the department work as a collaborative team to approve all of its offered courses was at least a first step toward working as true colleagues.

I am the only art teacher in the elementary school. Honestly, I do not get along with the middle school or high school art teachers. We think very differently about what students need to learn. I actually felt sad when I heard this. I instantly thought of Jacobs's (2004b) empty chair analogy. Is it in the students' best interests to not have an explicit learning connection between 13 years of art learning? When these three teachers were finally brought together, the tension proved to be not so much about students' expected knowing and doing (i.e., content and skills), but about wanting autonomy when choosing desired projects and performances (i.e., assessments) as well as pedagogy. Slowly but surely these teachers began to work collegially and eventually designed K–12 Consensus Maps for their three-school district.

To summarize, any time an isolated teacher needs to design a technically collaborative Consensus Map, make certain that the following things happen:

- The teacher must mentally remove personal intimacy regarding the course's planned learning and focus on each unit of study's content and skills that must be learned regardless of who is instructing the course.
- The teacher should invite other teachers in the department, related learning departments, grade levels, or throughout the learning organization to participate in designing or reviewing the drafted Consensus Map and to offer advice or final approval for the designed course.

Fresh Insights and Perspectives

At some point in the collaborative design process, dialogue across grade levels and disciplines is necessary. Conducting a review that includes teachers outside a course's discipline is important to this process. As Jacobs (2004b) explains,

> One of the most revealing and engaging steps in the mapping process is the mixed-group review, in which members of the faculty who do not regularly work together have the opportunity to do so. This interfacing creates a series of "jigsaw" review groups comprising of faculty members who rarely get a chance to step out of the box and view the experience of students from new perspectives. (p. 27)

The inclusion of those who do not teach the course allows the course designers to gain fresh insights and perspectives from others. For example, if a junior high school science department is designing Consensus Maps, it may invite the mathematics teachers to join in the approval process. Conversations during the review may lead to not only revision of the Consensus Maps but also in-depth, cross-disciplinary discussions and instructional planning. While mixed-group review members may not be official members of the Consensus Map's design team, their suggestions often prove invaluable.

Consensus Maps are critical for providing evidence of the collaboratively planned learning within a particular school site. When and how these curriculum maps are implemented and incorporated into the ongoing mapping process and connected to other types of maps (i.e., Projected/Diary Maps and Essential

Maps) need to be explored and discussed by the Curriculum Mapping Cabinet members, and potentially the Curriculum Mapping Council members, during the preplanning and prologue.

Essential Maps

Essential Maps are not necessarily needed in all learning organizations. The key purpose of Essential Maps is to provide districtwide curriculum consistency by (a) ensuring equity for all students irrespective of campus; (b) combating student intra-attrition rates throughout the learning organization; (c) providing newly hired teachers with districtwide learning expectations; and (d) informing students, parents, and community members about learning expectations regardless of neighborhood.

This collaborative map is only necessary when there are two or more like schools (e.g., Pinnacle Peak School District; see Figure 6.4) or two or more like courses available on two or more campuses (e.g., Solarium School District).

Figure 6.4   Pinnacle Peak School District and Solarium School District Configurations

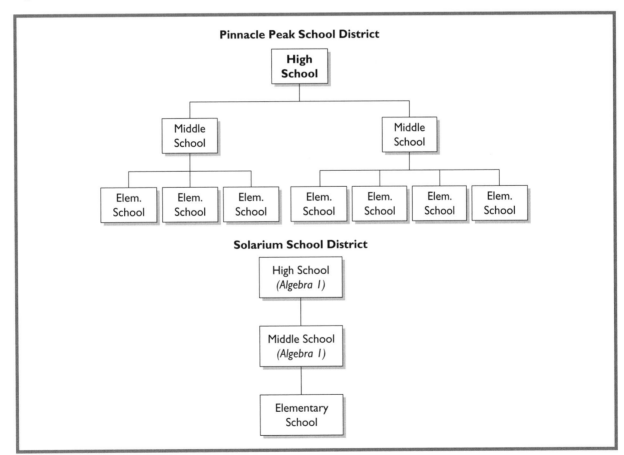

While Pinnacle Peak School District is just starting its curriculum-mapping initiative, at some point in the mapping process, it will need to design Essential Maps since there are seven elementary schools feeding into two middle schools that feed into one high school. One reason the district decided to implement curriculum mapping is that its schools have a history of site-based management to the point that learning expectations per site now have large inequities. The district administration and the Curriculum Mapping Cabinet agreed that there needs to be a vertically articulated essential curriculum for all three learning tiers (i.e., elementary, middle, high). To begin their mapping initiative, the Curriculum Mapping Cabinet determined that the right choice for this district is to first have all its schools provide evidence of what they individually value via school-site, course-specific Consensus Maps, which will then play an active role during the Essential Maps design process.

Solarium School District does not need like-school Essential Maps since there is only one school per learning tier. Vertically articulated Consensus Maps are sufficient. However, Essential Maps will be necessary for any like courses offered in two tiers. For example, Algebra I is an identical course taught on two campuses. Therefore, an Algebra I Essential Map needs to be designed by teachers from both schools' mathematics departments regarding the course's essential learning.

Elements Included

Essential Maps have the least amount of data in comparison to the other types of curriculum maps. However, this does not mean that the least is not the greatest. The learning included in this type of map represents the essential or indispensable expectations. As mentioned previously, many learning organizations base Essential Map learning on what has been determined to ensure student success, often referred to as *power standards* (Ainsworth 2003). A procedure for determining power standards is addressed in Chapter 9.

While Essential Maps can be designed based solely on teacher-selected power standards and breaking apart the standard statements, it is wise to also incorporate the review of existing curriculum documents, and, if available, Consensus Map or Diary Map entries. Imagine that only Diary Maps exist when a task force begins to design K–12 mathematics Essential Maps. The district has 132 mathematics teachers, which translates into potentially reviewing 132 Diary Maps. Having them available in the mapping system for the task force members to review when necessary is the key. If Consensus Maps exist, the same is true, except now a task force has evidence of collaborative planned learning expectations rather than individual evidence.

Once an Essential Map is published in a mapping system, each school site's Consensus Map design begins by first replicating the Essential Map. As mentioned previously, grade-level or department teams then collaborate and agree on additions that may include the following:

- content, skills, and related standards
- common or same assessments
- resources available to all teachers teaching the course
- potential reorganization of when learning will take place if flexibility within a grading period is permitted
- entirely new units of study

Each individual teacher teaching the course then replicates the agreed-upon Consensus Map planned learning data in his or her map account and adds learning or details based on personal student expectations and pedagogical practice.

DEVELOPMENTAL CONSIDERATIONS

Timelines for designing, revising, and refining Consensus Maps and Essential Maps can fluctuate due to a number of variables:

- existence or nonexistence of various types of curriculum maps
- preexisting curriculum data and documents used as resources to aid in the design of the collaborative maps
- length of time taken to break apart standards or determine power standards (see Chapter 9)
- collegial teaming experiences, both positive and negative, prior to designing collaborative maps
- emotional and intellectual composition of current team members
- familiarity and comfort with writing map elements and the procedures for recording maps within a mapping system
- amount of uninterrupted time dedicated to working through the developmental stages of designing a collaborative map

The most significant variable is often time. Collaborative mapping is formal work and takes concentration and adequate blocks of time to delve deep into exploring one another's perception of student learning expectations. I rarely find teachers who do not want to do such in-depth work; in fact, they revel in such opportunities. Rather, their frustrations lie in the inadequate time allotted to this critical work. Results are most productive when teachers are provided uninterrupted blocks of time, preferably without having to write substitute lesson plans, such as three to five full days consecutively in the summer or three to five full days before the school year begins.

Designing Consensus Maps

When designing Consensus Maps, establishing school board–approved late-start or preferably early-release days, or even better, a full day built into each school month affords teachers the respect and time needed to conduct this worthwhile and necessary curriculum design. It must also be pointed out that designing Consensus Maps is not the end; rather it is just the beginning. Ongoing reviews and dialogue about curriculum and related issues will naturally fill the time originally dedicated to developing Consensus Maps. Meeting times will then be utilized to discuss established and innovative pedagogical practices based on new or revised student learning expectations, evaluate student work using common formative and summative assessments, determine immediate learning interventions and extensions, discuss the impact of breakthroughs in education and societies (and how to apply them appropriately), and consider potential refinement of the established planned learning based on Diary Map–Consensus Map comparisons.

Designing Essential Maps

When the time allotted for designing Essential Maps includes full days, a task force can often draft K–12 specific-discipline maps and have them ready for review and approval in four to five days per discipline. But please be aware that this design process requires that preliminary collaborative work has already been completed regarding standards clarifications (e.g., determining power standards, breaking apart standards, reviewing existing Consensus Maps) and that the task force size is large enough to equally distribute the workload. Therefore, the Essential Map design process takes preplanning. A timeline, step-by-step procedures, and formulation of grade-level teams and, if appropriate, cross- or interdisciplinary review teams are components of the preplanning action plan. The Curriculum Mapping Coordinator, Cadre, Cabinet, and Council members, as well as school-site administrators, usually share in the preplanning and serve as facilitators. Many learning organizations conduct the preliminary work during the school year and design and record the Essential Maps in the mapping system during the summer.

After the implementation of Essential Maps, the task force's work is still not quite complete. During the first year or two, the task force periodically conducts implementation reviews, which include (a) using comparison reports included in the selected mapping system to view Essential Map implementation in relation to learning expectations included in Consensus Maps and Diary Maps, (b) obtaining feedback from teachers based on comments made in implementation surveys, and (c) studying local or state assessment results in comparison to the Essential Maps' learning expectations to monitor and possibly adjust the newly implemented districtwide learning expectations. While modifications to the Essential Maps will most likely not be drastic, when changes are made they must be immediately announced to the affected school-site grade-level or course teachers since Essential Map revisions may affect Consensus Map learning expectations. When the Essential Maps have reached an acceptable stability, the task force is officially disbanded.

If Essential Maps are designed later in a mapping initiative, each school site may need to modify a specific course's Consensus Map to reflect the newly established essential learning now evident in the Essential Maps. Likewise, each teacher's Projected Map and Diary Map may also need adjusting.

Articulation Reviews

As mentioned previously, collaborative maps are not meant to be designed in isolation, void of considering other grade levels' or courses' learning expectations. To ensure school-site or districtwide articulation, adequate time must be set aside for conducting articulation reviews. Some disciplines and courses will need vertical inter-alignment articulation, some horizontal inter-alignment articulation, and still others relational articulation (see Figure 6.5). Therefore, thoughtful preplanning regarding review team configurations is paramount.

Figure 6.5   Articulation Review Sample Focuses

Vertical Inter-Alignment Articulation	Horizontal Inter-Alignment Articulation	Relational Articulation
K–12 mathematics	All Grade 3 courses	Math and science courses
High school technology strand	All college freshman academy courses	Writing across the curriculum
K–12 art	All Grade 11 required courses	Project-based assessments

Do not allow representation gaps to happen when creating grade-level review teams. For example, there are three representation gaps in the following review configuration: K–2/3–5/6–8/9–12. The first is between Grades 2 and 3, the second between Grades 5 and 6, and the third between Grades 8 and 9. Therefore, it is recommended to have vertical review teams based on overlapping grade-level teams to ensure a continuous flow of represented learning (see Figure 6.6).

Figure 6.6   Overlapping Vertical Team Configurations

PK	K	1	2	3	4	5	6	7	8	9	10	11	12	13+
▓	▓	▓	▓											
			▓	▓	▓									
					▓	▓	▓							
							▓	▓	▓					
									▓	▓	▓			
											▓	▓	▓	▓

Whenever possible, include local preschool centers and the most frequently attended two- and four-year colleges and universities in vertical curriculum articulation review teams' conversations and collaborations.

When conducting articulation reviews, the number of members per team varies depending on the number of courses being reviewed, the number of staff members involved, and the degree of like or mixed grouping. While in-person interaction during the review meetings allows for nonverbal communication such as body language and facial reactions, review teams pressed for in-person meeting time can use the mapping system as a hub for preliminary review tasks and incorporate e-mail correspondence, videoconferencing, or online meetings into the process before in-person meetings are conducted.

CONCLUSION

In a world where time and pressures are not an issue, some might say that the following is how the curriculum map design process should unfold:

- Each teacher individually designs a course's Projected/Diary Map to provide documented evidence of what is personally valued.
- Collaborative teams review Diary Maps and analyze state standard statements to reach collective agreement and design a course's Consensus Map, which documents articulated school-site values.
- A task force with single- or multiple-discipline expertise reviews the collective school sites' Consensus Maps, revisits broken-apart state standard statements and established power standards, and studies any other pertinent data that may affect decisions regarding Essential Map design.

While this linear process may work for some, it may not work for all. Also, do not be surprised if what is originally planned regarding the process for developing the various map types changes once implementation begins—not only for the learning organization as a whole but also for specific disciplines within the organization.

Jacobs (1997) explains that "curriculum mapping amplifies the possibilities for long-range planning, short-term preparation, and clear communication" (p. 5). The beauty of both collaborative map design and instant access to all of the planned and operational learning recorded in a mapping system is that they positively impact the ongoing growth and education of both students and teachers.

SAMPLE CONSENSUS MAPS AND ESSENTIAL MAPS

Figures 6.7–6.8 and 6.9–6.10 are sets of relational Essential Map and Consensus Map months. As a reminder, notice that the Essential Maps have less data than the Consensus Maps do.

REVIEW QUESTIONS

Collaborative planned-learning maps provide documentation of a learning organization's teacher-designed curriculum. Discuss your responses to the questions below with a partner or in a small group.

1. Having now read about teacher-designed Consensus Maps and Essential Maps, as well as personally designed Projected Maps and Diary Maps, considering your learning organization's past and present professional climate, culture, and student needs, what do you currently think is the best developmental progression* for designing the various types of maps? (Support your reasoning.)

   Note: May be a different progression for different disciplines.

2. When designing Consensus Maps, teachers need to work collegially, not only in one grade level or for one course but also for articulation across grade levels or series of courses. Will this be a problem for all teachers, some teachers, or just a few teachers in your school? What about throughout your entire district? What do you believe needs to strategically happen to support design teams that may not be collegial at this point in time? What about the necessity for adequate amounts of time for teachers to collaboratively design the curriculum? How do you think this will be possible? (Support your reasoning.)

3. Your learning organization (select one) does/does not need Essential Maps. If it does, will the need be based on two or more like schools, like courses offered on two or more campuses, or both? Given your response to Question 1, what variables or factors do you perceive will affect the Essential Map design process? (Support your reasoning.)

Figure 6.7 Environmental Science Essential Map Month

Month	Content	Skills	Assessments	Standards
October	(First Quarter) **ECOSYSTEMS** A. Biomes: Land/Aquatic	A. Locate hemispheric, continental, regional examples of each biome: land (Taiga or Coniferous Forest, Temperate Deciduous Forest, Temperate Rain Forest), aquatic (Euphotic Zone, Littoral or Intertidal Zones, Coral Reef) A. Summarize relationships between latitude, altitude, soil, temperature, precipitation ranges, inhabitants of land biomes A. Justify effects of 4 variables (salinity, light, penetration, nutrients) on aquatic biomes' inhabitants		A. S10.3.1 (D) S10.3.4 (D) S10.3.6 (I)
	B. Scientific Method: Graphic Representations	B. Translate textual data information into numeric representation		B. S10.6.8 (D) M10.2.2 (R)

Figure 6.8 Environmental Science Consensus Map Month

Month	Content	Skills	Assessments	Standards
October	*(Oct 1-Oct 15)* **ECOSYSTEMS** A. Biomes: Land/Aquatic Resources --Chapter 3 --Virtual Field Trip: *The Biosphere* --Computer Lab Internet Research	A1. Locate visually and in writing hemispheric, continental, regional examples of each biome: land (Taiga or Coniferous Forest, Temperate Deciduous Forest, Temperate Rain Forest), aquatic (Euphotic Zone, Littoral or Intertidal Zones, Coral Reef) A2. Summarize in writing relationships between latitude, altitude, soil, temperature, precipitation ranges, inhabitants of land biomes A. Justify visually and in writing effects of 4 variables (salinity, light, penetration, nutrients) on aquatic biomes' inhabitants A. Analyze visually and in writing biomes' present and future evolution based on topographic features, population data, plant diversity and distribution using primary/secondary sources	A1-A2. COMMON 30 Question Quiz	A. S10.3.1 (D) S10.3.4 (D) S10.3.6 (I) S10.3.8 (I) T 10.2.1 (R)
	B. Scientific Method: Graphic Representations Resources --Student Biomes Internet Research Data	B1. Translate in writing textual data information into numeric representation B2. Determine in writing highest/lowest values based on graphed data	B1-B2. SAME 10 Problem Test	B. S10.6.8 (D) M10.2.2 (R) T10.2.1 (R)

Figure 6.9   Grade 6 Library Science Essential Map Month

Month	Content	Skills	Assessment	Standards
September	**ORIENTATION**			
	A. Library Facilities: Personal Use	A. Check out, renew book/materials		A.
		A. Access card/electronic catalog		I-2a
				I-2b
				I-2c
				I-3a
	RESEARCH			
	B. Library Layout: Materials Accessibility	B. Locate materials in nonfiction, references, periodicals (current/archived), video sections		B.
		B. Search for materials using circulation program and Dewey Decimal call numbers		III-1b
	C. Citations: Hard Copy, Internet	C. Identify copyright laws to recognize instances of plagiarism versus fair-use guidelines		C.
		C. Locate necessary information on verso page: copyright date, publisher, city of publication, edition		II-1b
		C. Cite hard-copy/Web-based information sources using proper MLA format/conventions for endnotes/parenthetical citations		III-1a
				III-1c
				III-d

Figure 6.10 Grade 6 Library Science Consensus Map Month

Month	Content	Skills	Assessment	Standards
September	**ORIENTATION** A. Library Facilities: Personal Use	A1. Check out, renew electronically book/materials with minimal or no help from library staff A2. Access manually or electronically card/electronic catalog to locate desired book or materials	A1-B2. SAME Selection/Check-Out Procedures (Evaluation: Library Staff Ob/Checklist)	A. I-2a (R) I-2b (R) I-2c (R) I-3a (R)
	RESEARCH B. Library Layout: Materials Accessibility	B1. Locate kinesthetically materials in nonfiction, references, periodicals (current/archived), video sections using electronic catalog B2. Open, scan, search manually for materials using circulation program and Dewey Decimal call numbers		B. III-1b (D)
	C. Citations: Hard Copy, Internet	C1. Identify visually and in writing copyright laws to recognize instances of plagiarism versus fair-use guidelines C2. Locate visually and in writing necessary information on verso page: copyright date, publisher, city of publication, edition C3. Cite in writing hard-copy/Web-based information sources using proper MLA format/conventions for endnotes/parenthetical citations C. Self-check visually recorded citations for accuracy by looking up in appropriate materials	C1-C3. SAME* Citation Project (Evaluation: Rubric) *Grade 6	C. II-1b (R) III-1a (D) III-1c (I) III-d (I) LA6.5.4 (R)

7

How Should We Be Using Our Created Curriculum Maps?

The practice of "reviewing" . . . has nothing in common with criticism.

—Henry James

Curriculum maps are meant to be used to aid ongoing curriculum conversations and decision making. Jacobs (1997) states that "a curriculum map is like a school's manuscript. . . . With a map in hand, staff members can play the role of manuscript editor, examining the curriculum for needed revision and validation" (p. 17). Examining the curriculum means *reviewing* the curriculum. This chapter addresses Jacobs's Seven-Step Review Model and the potential focuses for conducting reviews.

CONDUCTING DATA-DRIVEN REVIEWS

Curriculum-mapping reviews are based on five meeting principles that may affect how teachers currently attend to students' curriculum needs and concerns (see Figure 7.1).

Figure 7.1   Five Review Meeting Principles

1. Based on a predetermined review focus (i.e., problem, issue, concern), a large group is formed with small groups predefined within the large group.

2. Appropriate curriculum maps and/or other forms of data are first studied individually by each review team member. Personal notes are taken and brought to a small-group meeting.

3. Individual findings are collaboratively shared and discussed during the small-group meeting. Key discussion points, comments, and suggestions are recorded. Each small group's meeting summary is given or made available to each large-group member. Each member individually reads the collective commentaries before the large-group meeting commences.

4. The large group collaboratively discusses the data, findings, and commentaries. Decisions made are either immediately implemented or designated as needing further exploration. If exploration is necessary, the focus is revisited until decisions can be effectively made.

5. Once decisions have been made and actions taken, the large group is disbanded. The review team may someday meet again if a new or previous focus warrants participation from the same large-group members.

Two Review Scenarios

The beauty of these principles is that they can be applied to any formal or informal review process, even when curriculum maps are not involved. Here are two examples.

New Science Kits

Park Central Elementary School utilized grant monies to purchase a series of Grade K–5 science kits. The entire faculty attended a one-hour orientation presented by the publishing company. A company representative explained the kit components and supplementary materials.

After the meeting Mrs. O'Donnell, Mrs. Isaac, Ms. Friedman, and Mr. Peroni walked back to their classrooms with kits and materials in hand. Mrs. Isaac inquired, "When can we meet?" They talked over schedules and decided to meet after school on the following Thursday.

Mrs. Issac asked, "What should we focus on in the new kits?"

Mr. Peroni commented, "The company rep said the supplementary readers are divided by readability levels. I think we should read them and focus on how they can fit into our student-led reading meetings."

Ms. Friedman added, "I think we need to look at how the lessons are set up and sequenced. The man talked about the lessons, but just briefly."

After a few more ideas were exchanged, Mrs. Isaac recapped, "So, do we agree that we will focus on two issues? One, analyzing the student readers; and two, looking at how the lesson structure fits, or doesn't fit, how we currently teach our units."

Everyone responded, "Yes." They ended their conversation deciding who would meet in small groups and what time to start.

On Thursday afternoon Ms. Friedman and Mr. Peroni met in Mr. Peroni's room, and Mrs. O'Donnell and Mrs. Issac met in Mrs. Issac's room. After sharing personal reflections, they discussed their thoughts and wrote collaborative summary notes. A timer buzzed after 20 minutes.

Soon Mr. Peroni and Ms. Friedman joined Mrs. Issac and Mrs. O'Donnell. They took a few moments to read each small group's summary notes and then began their large-group meeting.

They decided to address the student readers first. After a few rounds of comments, conflicts, and compromises, they came to agreement on how the readers could best be used during the reading meetings. Mrs. Issac said that she would generate a master list of the readers, code them by reading level and meeting use, and e-mail a copy to everyone.

Next they discussed the kit's lesson-plan structure. They decided the best way to truly know if the lessons needed adaptation was to individually try out a lesson or two. They agreed to do so in the next two weeks.

When it was time to meet again, they followed the same review principles, including writing personal notes, sharing in teams of two, and then meeting as a large group. During the large-group comparison time, they decided to divide up the lessons and make notations about how each lesson needed to be adapted to fit their preferred instructional style.

Orchestra Tryouts

It was time once again for senior orchestra tryouts at Hoce High School. In the past each student trying out played one time in front of the music department during two days of afterschool auditions. The teachers discussed each applicant's performance and tried to reach an agreement on which students to select. The decision-making process never seemed to run smoothly. It often took a full week of deliberations before the selection process came to a close.

This year the department decided to conduct tryouts in a slightly different manner. Mr. Tuna, the department chair, set up a mutually agreed-upon meeting sequence and e-mailed it to each department member:

Student/Last Name A–O Tryouts*

- May 2—Mrs. Evans, Mrs. May, Ms. Searle (Music Room)
- May 3—Mr. Tuna, Mrs. Joanele (Music Room)

Student/Last Name P–Z Tryouts*

- May 4—Mrs. Evans, Mrs. May, Ms. Searle (Music Room)
- May 5—Mr. Tuna, Mrs. Joanele (Music Room)

Miniteam Meeting

- May 6—Mrs. Evans, Mrs. May, Ms. Searle (Music Room)
- May 6—Mr. Tuna, Mrs. Joanele (Room M104)

Department Meeting

- May 9—Mrs. Evans, Mrs. May, Ms. Searle, Mr. Tuna, Mrs. Joanele (Music Room)

Note: Each student will try out twice; each day with a different teacher team.

(Continued)

(Continued)

> The department met just prior to May 2 to focus on the use of a new scoring sheet and scoring criteria designed by the department. The newest teachers, Ms. Searle and Mrs. Joanele, appreciated spending time hearing about the past experiences and discussing the new selection process.
>
> From May 2 to May 5, the teachers listened to students play. By late afternoon on May 5, each teacher had input personal scores and criteria commentaries in a networked computer file. Mr. Tuna compiled the data and e-mailed the results to each teacher to preview before the May 6 miniteam meetings.
>
> Each miniteam conferred based on the collective scores and commentaries. Each team's designated recorder e-mailed everyone in the department a prospective student-selection list to preview prior to the May 9 meeting.
>
> The final meeting went smoothly and quickly. The list of selected students was finalized and posted on May 10. During a debriefing discussion the teachers said that they felt this year's process had been more objective than in the past, and no one experienced frustrations or hurt feelings during the process.

The five meeting principles are infused into Jacobs's (1997) review model. As mentioned previously, they can be incorporated into current meeting structures prior to maps being created. Doing so affords teachers time to become familiar with the meeting protocols and routines. When maps are eventually created, it will be a natural progression to begin to include them when conducting reviews.

The Seven-Step Review Process

Jacobs's review model consists of seven phases, or steps (see Figure 7.2).

Figure 7.2 Seven-Step Review Process

1. Collecting the data

2. First read-through

3. Small-group review

4. Large-group comparison

5. Immediate revision

6. Research and development

7. New review considerations

Reviews are not conducted simply for the sake of conducting reviews. There must be a problem, issue, or concern in need of investigation and resolution. A review may take a few hours, a few days, or a few weeks. It may even take several months if the focus is complex and involves large-scale decision making and potential alteration to the current curriculum design or environment (e.g., moving from traditional to block scheduling, incorporating a freshman academy model).

There are four components involved in the preplanning stage of a review:

1. Determine what the review's focus will be, based on a specific problem, issue, or concern.

2. Decide who needs to be included in the review's large group and determine the most effective large-group configuration:

   - Horizontal = One grade level
   - Vertical = Across a series of two or more grade levels
   - Like = One discipline
   - Mixed = Cross-disciplinary or interdisciplinary

   These four configurations are often combined to best meet the needs of the review focus:

   - Horizontal—Like (e.g., Grade 3 mathematics)
   - Horizontal—Mixed (e.g., Grade 3 mathematics, science)
   - Vertical—Like (e.g., Grades 3–6 mathematics)
   - Vertical—Mixed (e.g., Grades 3–6 mathematics, science)

   A large group can be any size, as it will depend on the focus and who should be part of the review. In the two non-map-use scenarios shared previously, the large groups did not exceed five people. If a schoolwide review focus is planned, and there are 50 faculty members, the large group will consist of 50 people. If a focus is specific to a high school social studies department that has seven teachers, the large group would include seven teachers unless other discipline-specific teachers are invited to join in the review process.

3. Determine how the large group will be subdivided into small-group review teams. While the subdivision may appear obvious given the large-group configuration, it is important to think outside the box. For example, if a K–8 school consists of one teacher per grade level and the review focus pertains to the most frequently and infrequently used assessment types evident in Diary Maps, the small-group teams could be vertical with a twist—K, 3, 6; 1, 4, 7; 2, 5, 8—to allow those who do not normally get to meet and discuss student learning and assessment practice to do so.

4. Develop specific focus questions to direct inquiry and guide collaborative dialogue. Oftentimes the large-group team members are provided an informational or procedural packet prior to the start of the review and may include the following:

   - the problem, issue, or concern on which the review will focus
   - pregenerated focus questions
   - space for personal note taking
   - each small-group review team's member names
   - the name of the large group's comparison facilitator(s)
   - meeting dates, times, and locations
   - specific data to be reviewed and the necessary retrieval process (e.g., specific curriculum maps, search and report features, assessment results, student work samples)

Step 1: Collecting the Data

The review focus will determine the necessary data. The data may include one type of map or multiple types as well as other data sources. At times, collecting data may be figurative rather than literal when using various search and report features in a mapping system. Unless hard copies are personally desired or requested for the small- or large-group meetings, the data may not need to be printed out from the mapping system.

When curriculum maps are involved in the review, the mapping system's search and report features often play a role during Step 2's first read-through. Therefore, each team member must independently become familiar and comfortable with using the system's features. If there are additional sources involved in the review process, each member needs to be provided hard-copy documents or given information regarding how to personally retrieve the data prior to Step 2.

Step 2: First Read-Through

Each review team member privately reads through the designated maps and, if appropriate, other data sources. Members may choose to print out specific search and report results from the mapping system and bring them to the small-group meeting. This can be done at the discretion of the reviewer, or it can be a part of the review process. If the latter, indication of the type of report(s) needed is included in the informational or procedural packet. During this personal reflective inquiry time, each member responds in writing to the predetermined focus questions.

Step 3: Small-Group Review

A small group usually consists of two to eight members. Exceeding eight members is not recommended because it can lead to a decrease in total-group participation and interaction. A small-group leader may be preselected or designated at the onset of the meeting.

A recorder takes notes based on individual findings and collaborative comments. These notations may be recorded longhand or in an electronic format such as Microsoft Word.

If a network server is accessible to all large-group members, each small-group team's electronic document may be saved to a predesignated networked file. All members can then access the file to read each small-group review team's notes. If each team's notes are recorded longhand, a hard copy needs to be distributed to each member of the large group.

The length of time for this meeting is dependent on variables such as the focus, the amount of data to be discussed, the number of and collegial abilities of team members, and the drafted timeline for the entire seven steps. Whatever time limit is established for conducting the small-group review, selecting a timekeeper is advised.

Step 4: Large-Group Comparison

All small-group review teams' notes are personally read and compared by each team member before the large-group meeting begins. If a facilitator has not already been determined, when the large group commences its meeting, a facilitator should be selected to keep the review focus in the forefront of the group conversation. A designated large-group recorder takes notes to document the conversations and decisions made or planned.

Depending on the total number of review members, everyone may be able to work together as an entire group throughout the meeting. However, if the group is quite large, when discussing specific points it may be best to subdivide into smaller groups using the same or different configurations from those used in Step 3.

Given the focus, this step is intended for the review team to determine the best solution(s) by comparing and discussing the small-group findings. If the solution(s) can be integrated straight away regarding curriculum design, instructional practice, or environmental changes, the review begins to incorporate Step 5 into the large-group meeting. If the large group determines that the focus needs further or expanded exploration before solutions can be reached, the review team first follows the procedures involved in Step 6.

Step 5: Immediate Revision

Now that the large group has collaboratively come to agreement on a solution or solutions, actions can be taken. Once everyone is clear on what those actions are, the recorder documents the decisions made. If necessary, a timeline for the actions and faculty members who will be the accountability leaders are determined.

Once Step 5's discussions have been completed and actions have been documented, which may take more than one meeting, the review process moves to Step 7.

Step 6: Research and Development

As mentioned in Step 4, if the large group cannot yet come to agreement on an immediate solution or solutions, it must identify the area or areas of concern that need research and development. The large group forms a temporary task force to investigate. It may not be possible to officially determine the task force members during the large-group meeting since people who are not members of the review team may need to be invited to participate in the task force. During the large-group meeting, what can be determined are the task force's expectations, timelines, and management for disseminating new information.

The initial large-group meeting concludes by announcing the next planned large-group meeting date. All members should receive periodic research and development information from the task force via e-mail or hard copy that is individually read before attending any new meetings.

Step 6 may take a few meetings or longer, depending on the depth of the task force's assignment, before the large group is able to reach a final solution or solutions. When finally accomplished, procedures in Step 5 are carried out and the review proceeds to Step 7.

Step 7: New Review Considerations

There are no long-term committees in curriculum mapping. The right people meet for the right reason at the right time (Jacobs 1997, 2004b). Therefore, once the problem, issue, or concern has been resolved and appropriate actions have been carried out, the large-group review team is disbanded. The same is true for a task force that may have been formed during Step 6. This is not to say that a large group or a task force will never meet again. A future problem, issue, or concern may warrant the same people being involved in another review. Likewise, the same large group may need to reconvene to revisit an earlier review focus.

Multiple Reviews

There may be times when teachers and administrators are involved simultaneously in more than one review. For example, a teacher may be a member of a horizontal, grade-level team focusing on science; a school-site, vertical-mixed team focusing on mathematics; and a districtwide task force focusing on K–12 vocabulary development. While participation in multiple formal reviews is an exception rather than a rule, never assume that only one review can happen at one time.

INVESTIGATING THE CURRICULUM

Examining the curriculum is an ongoing endeavor. Any aspect of student learning can be investigated to verify that current learning, methods, and practices are going well or are in need of minor or major improvement.

Review Focuses

There are many problems, issues, or concerns that can be investigated using created curriculum maps. Jacobs (1997) mentions having teachers "identify curricular gaps, find repetitions, target potential areas for integration, match assessment with standards, and review for timeliness" (p. 17). Learning organizations often choose identifying gaps and finding repetitions as the focus of a desired review to aid in the design of a rigorous, vertically aligned curriculum.

Identifying Gaps and Finding Repetitions

A *gap* is an interruption of continuity. When reviewing a series of curriculum maps, a gap is recognized as a longer-than-expected time break for specific learning. If curriculum maps are recorded by year, identifying the actual length of a gap is nearly impossible. While maps recorded by grading periods provide a better chance of finding gaps than do maps recorded by year, accuracy in identifying a gap is most precise when evaluated by month.

> Based on state standards, two-dimensional geometric shapes are learned in Grades 2 and 3 in a private primary school. The teachers wanted to investigate *when* the learning specifically takes place in their school site since this information will aid in determining whether a true gap in the curriculum is in need of revision.
>
> The teachers conducted a curriculum review using a keyword search report in the mapping system. The results revealed that, based on the Grade 2

mathematics Consensus Map, four two-dimensional shapes (rhombus, parallelogram, trapezoid, and kite) are learned in September and other two-dimensional shapes (polygons) are learned in December. The search results also revealed that, based on the Grade 3 mathematics Consensus Map, three two- and three-dimensional shape relationships (square/cube, circle/sphere, and triangle/prism) are learned in April.

For these teachers, the data raised two concerns:

- Is a total of 16 months (i.e., from December of Grade 2 to April of Grade 3) too long of a gap?
- Since the Grade 3 state testing is considered a benchmark year and is given in March, should learning wait until April in this grade?

The teachers collegially discussed these questions and researched the latest testing blueprints as well as the previous year's testing results. They collaboratively agreed that minor adjustments needed to take place regarding when geometric shapes need to be learned in Grade 3. Grade 2 teachers also agreed to make a slight revision and include triangles since Grade 3 learns about a variety of prism types.

A *repetition* is a superfluous, nonspiraling redundancy. When reviewing a series of curriculum maps, a repetition is recognized as unplanned identical learning beyond one academic year or course. A repetition can often be misidentified if curriculum maps are not written with quality, especially regarding the content and skill descriptors. If teachers do not provide detailed descriptors, a learning expectation may appear as if a redundancy is occurring when actually it is not (see Figure 7.3).

Figure 7.3   Content Listings: Repetitions or Meaningful Spiral

Grade Level	Content Listings Appear Repetitive	Content Listings Appear to Spiral
Grade 1	Parts of Earth	Earth: Soil, Water, Air
Grade 3	Earth: 3 Parts	Earth: Crust, Mantle, Core
Grade 5	Earth: 3 Parts	Earth's Compositions/Properties: Soil, Atmosphere

I find that teachers who have not been trained well regarding how to write quality maps early on in the mapping process often get frustrated when trying to conduct a repetition review focus because the learning often appears repetitive when, as stated previously, it actually is not. For this type of review focus to be successful, it is recommended that teachers use the writing norms explained in Chapter 4.

Adequate Data. Identifying gaps and finding repetitions districtwide cannot take place if there is not a full school year of map data for all grade levels and courses relating to the selected discipline focus. Likewise, the initially selected map type and discipline may affect the amount of time it takes to collect the necessary data for a districtwide review. For example, if a K–12 mathematics vertical review focus is desired and teachers first designed mathematics Consensus Maps, assuming that the maps are written with quality, a review could potentially take place in the latter half of the first year of designing the Consensus Maps. If instead teachers were asked to diary map language arts (which would include all elementary teachers in the district), K–12 vertical review regarding mathematics could not happen for at least two years. While the middle schools and high schools' Mathematics Departments can be working on alignment in and between their schools, an entire K–12 articulation cannot happen without the elementary schools' teachers providing evidence via either Consensus Maps or Diary Maps.

From experience I have found that most teachers are not usually comfortable with or confident in their knowledge of writing quality maps, the mapping concepts and processes, and the mapping system until well into the second year of mapping. Because of this, finding large-scale gaps and repetitions is usually more meaningful and productive when teachers are given a second year to improve the quality of the maps and time to focus on clearly articulating student learning expectations.

Consideration must also be given to the teachers mapping other disciplines than what may have been selected as the initial districtwide focus. Vertical articulation for specialists such as those who teach art, music, physical education, or library science may also need more time before they can conduct these review focuses since these disciplines often have only a few teachers districtwide. Yet if all K–12 teachers in a given discipline, such as art, work as one team to create K–12 Essential Maps or Consensus Maps, an ongoing feature of their map design will be to constantly check for potential gaps and repetitions.

Finding Absences Regarding Standards Integration

An *absence* is unintentional missing content and skills based on state or local standards requisites. When reviewing curriculum maps regarding this focus, an absence can easily be revealed using a "What Standards Are Missing?" report included in most mapping systems. This report compares selected standard statements to selected courses and displays the standard statements that have not been addressed in the course. If the report is run midyear and teachers are in the first year of recording Diary Maps month by month, there is no doubt that standards will be absent given that all the months have not yet been recorded.

Typically, if standards are absent in a Projected Map or a Consensus Map, there are two common reasons why:

- A teacher or team of teachers has literally forgotten to follow the mapping system's procedure for aligning standards to the appropriate content, skills, and assessments.
- A teacher or team of teachers made a conscious decision not to include a missing standard statement and its related content–skill learning within the curriculum map.

If the first item is the reason for a missing standard statement, the teacher or teachers simply revise the standards' documentation with the curriculum map. If the second item is the reason, and the teacher or teachers stand by their reasoning for not including the standard statement and relational content–skill learning, the in-question standard statement will remain unaligned. However, during a standards absence review, if other grade-level or course teachers question any absences, collegial dialogue and decision making must ensue.

Assessments, Integration, and Timeliness

A mapping system's search and report features can also be used to analyze curriculum maps regarding assessments, integration, and timeliness. While each can be a separate review focus, there are times when two or all three may overlap, depending on the purpose of the review. The following is an example of combining timeliness with assessment practice.

> Technology is timely given the fact that 21st-century children are growing up in a techno-savvy world. Jacobs (2006b) tells of a school where the teachers realized they needed to embrace this fact and include more technology-based assessments. They felt their students' acquisition-of-learning performances and products needed to demand that students use electronic graphic organizers, slide-show presentations, podcasts, videos, and other media presentation formats.
>
> To begin the review process, the teachers studied their Projected Maps' assessment fields and discovered that the current use of technology-driven assessments was negligible. During a large-group comparison meeting, each teacher committed to dedicating at least one major summative assessment per grading period to the new requirement of timely assessments. They planned a checkpoint meeting for just after the first grading period to study student samples of the newly integrated technology-based products and performances.

Assessments. A specific assessment focus review may be conducted to analyze the coherency of an assessment or assessments in relation to the aligned content-skills learning. For example, if student learning involves orally critiquing and taking stances, a mock court trial assessment is a coherent measurement, while a written-response essay is not.

Another assessment focus may be to study the most often-used assessment formats or types in a school or throughout a learning organization. For example, a horizontal-mixed task force was involved in a high school ACT prep review focus since many students were electing to take this college entrance exam. A search of Grades 10–12 English, mathematics, and reading assessments included in Diary Maps revealed that students were asked to respond to, on average per assessment, 25 selected-response items. The task force asked the teachers for samples of the tests as well as time limits for taking the tests to conduct a comparative study with the ACT requirements. Based on the compared data, the task force generated a report of its findings and recommendations to revise the current assessment structure. They e-mailed the document to each high school teacher in preparation for participation in upcoming small-group review meetings.

Integration. An integration review focus is an excellent way to explore an academic environment wherein students shift from teacher to teacher throughout the day. By running comparison reports using a mapping system's appropriate features, teachers from various course disciplines are able to visually review maps to find ways they can support and reinforce what students must know and be able to do based on the learning expectations in each other's courses. This review often results in teachers agreeing that there needs to be a shift in *when* learning takes place to best enhance opportunities for primary learning and reinforcement opportunities.

If teachers at a particular grade level are collegial and willing to do so, modifying current practice by designing cross- or interdisciplinary units of study is a wonderful way to embrace integrated learning. Often, teachers who do so design a final product or performance assessment that causes students to combine the learning expectations from all the disciplines involved. Each student receives a grade in each discipline based on the one collective assessment.

Timeliness. Timeliness does not pertain only to student and teacher use of technology; it also encompasses connecting student learning to local, national, and global current events and breakthroughs (Jacobs 1997). When using maps for this review focus, the included resources play a critical role in addressing such questions as the following:

- What Web sites, webcasts, software programs, videos, DVDs, magazine articles, books, and other text formats are students reading, viewing, or interacting with?
- How do our units of study involve current events as well as historical-perspective primary and secondary resources?
- Is the large-scale and smaller equipment in lab rooms and workshops antiquated or state of the art?

When timeliness review focuses reveal a need for items such as adequate laptops for each student and teacher, new science lab equipment, subscriptions to various magazines and periodicals, or subscriptions to webcasts, acquisition of these resources may not happen instantaneously. Awareness is the first step. Having evidence that there is a need may cause a learning organization to consider appropriating funds directly to school sites so that teachers and administrators can resolve the timeliness concerns by purchasing what is needed the most for students to be successful learners.

Bilevel Item Analysis

Bilevel item analysis is an investigative term. The word *bilevel* refers to specific data in two learning tiers. The first tier is the specific subject matter that the test item is measuring, and the second tier is the linguistics involved in comprehending the item's task. *Analysis* refers to comparing and contrasting the information gathered pertaining to the two tiers in relation to the student learning evidence in curriculum maps (Jacobs 2004b, 2006a).

Figure 7.4 is a test item that was frequently missed by Grade 6 students in a district-designed, mid-year benchmark assessment.

Figure 7.4   Grade 6 Mathematics Test Item

Just as the men entered the woods, a sow walked toward her cub. What was the approximate angle of the bear's back as she protected her cub?

(A) 30°
(B) 90°
(C) 150°
(D) 155°

The sixth-grade teachers deconstructed the test item based on the two tiers of mathematics and linguistics. Regarding the concept of *angles,* students had to know (a) acute angle, (b) unmarked angle degrees, (c) approximate distance, and (d) degree symbol. Students also had to be able to determine an angle regardless of directionality and ignore secondary visual data (i.e., bear and cub). The team felt that their students learned the content and skills the item required mathematically and was validated when they reviewed their Consensus Map and personal Diary Maps.

The teachers then began to discuss the language involved in the item's text. They felt that problem points may have included (a) having to begin reading with a subordinating conjunction, (b) continuing to read an irrelevant-to-the-task sentence, (c) the term *sow,* and (d) the term *approximate*. The teachers discussed each point and decided that even though the term *sow* may have been problematic for some, the most problematic item may have

(Continued)

(Continued)

> been the subordinating conjunction. They conducted a keyword search for this term in the mapping system using Grades 3–6 language arts Consensus Maps and Diary Maps. The results revealed that two Grade 5 teachers had this term in their Diary Maps. The teachers decided that this language concept needed further investigation and approached the other grade levels' teachers to participate in a vertical-mixed group review.

Here is another example of bilevel item analysis in which both tiers involve language arts.

> Four teachers selected the three most frequently missed test items in the reading portion of the state test (first tier). The three items were associated with two different nonfiction reading passages (second tier). The teachers read the passages and began to deconstruct the test items regarding what students must know and be able to do. They determined that the students had to infer based on the ability to connect three or four details within the selection in order to draw a conclusion.
>
> The teachers ran a keyword search report for their Diary Maps using the terms *infer, inference, draw, conclusions* (first tier), and *nonfiction* (second tier). They found that one teacher's Diary Map explicitly addressed these learning expectations three times throughout the school year and another teacher addressed the expectations one time. They also noted that few resources in anyone's Diary Map revealed a strong use of nonfiction text; the majority of listings were fiction selections.
>
> The teachers were conducting the bilevel item analysis as part of the process for collaboratively designing a language arts Consensus Map. From this and other bilevel item analysis results, breaking apart the comprehension-related state standard statements, and speaking to grade-level teachers above and below them, they designed the desired specific student learning expectations, which they documented in their Consensus Map's appropriate months and units of study. They also committed to demanding that students' anchor their reasoning more often in nonfiction text passages by incorporating the Consensus Map learning expectations into their classroom lessons for the coming school year.
>
> During the first grading period of the following school year, the teachers began to investigate the protocols and procedures for designing common assessments. They agreed that this was the best next step for them as a team to aid in their ongoing collective evaluation of their students' learning progress based on the Consensus Map's learning expectations and the reality that students learn at different rates.

Focusing on explicit and implicit expectations of both discipline-specific learning (e.g., mathematics, science, social studies) and critical language and literacy demands involved in test items *plus* making connections between what is discovered by studying assessment items and curriculum map evidence makes bilevel analysis a valuable review focus. As Jacobs (2004b) recommends, teachers must "analyze both tiers if we are to determine a sustained prescriptive approach that will enable learning to achieve success" (p. 117).

Universal Commitment

Curriculum maps can also be used to focus on comparative reviews regarding a universal commitment. *Universal* refers to a strategy or instructional practice that every teacher commits to implementing throughout the school year in one school or throughout a learning organization. The following is an example of a universal commitment made by a middle school regarding vocabulary terms.

Based on the past three years of state testing results and one year of district benchmark testing results, the Grades 6–8 faculty at a middle school decided they needed universal agreement on processing vocabulary. They believed that if all teachers in all grade levels, regardless of content area, began to incorporate agreed-upon selected terms into students' operational learning, the students would have a better chance at success when taking the required state tests.

A vertical-mixed task force was formed, consisting of three teachers per grade level, four specialists, and one administrator. The 14-member team worked collaboratively to narrow down potential grade-level-specific and cross-grade-level terms using the state standards' discipline-specific process vocabulary as well as the past three years of released state test items. The task force's final criteria for generating a prospective vocabulary for Grades 6–8 was based on a vocabulary term's predominance in state test items and the ease of incorporation across the curriculum.

After e-mail correspondence and one faculty meeting, the task force generated a drafted list for all teachers to review. During a full faculty meeting the task force facilitated the final decision-making process. The Grades 6–8 Process Vocabulary Terms list was approved, and the faculty agreed that they would conduct a formal review at the end of the first semester to see whether, based on Diary Map evidence, inclusion of the terms was taking place.

To make the agreed-upon terms easy for all to access, the task force added a Grades 6–8 Process Vocabulary Terms document as a link within the mapping system. Figure 7.5 lists the Grade 7 terms. Boldface words signify vertically aligned vocabulary that appears in all three grade levels' lists of terms.

Figure 7.5   Grade 7 Process Vocabulary Terms

Analyze	Express
Apply	**Formulate**
Check	Indicate
Determine	**Justify**
Develop	Summarize
Estimate	**Support**
Evaluate	Test
Explain	**Verify**

(Continued)

(Continued)

> At the end of the first semester, the entire staff conducted a vertical-mixed, large-group review. Using the mapping system's keyword search-and-compare feature to locate incorporation of grade-level and across-grade-level terms, each teacher focused on when and how the terms had been incorporated in the maps and in student learning to prepare for conversation in the small-group review meetings.
>
> Figure 7.6 represents one teacher's November Diary Map. This particular teacher chose to include the vocabulary terms as a resource listing.
>
> The small-group review teams' discussions revealed usage trends regardless of how each teacher chose to document term usage within a Diary Map. During the large-group comparison meeting, it was noted that some terms were being focused on heavily, others slightly, and some not at all. The faculty collaboratively discussed potential ways to incorporate the least-focused-on terms and broaden use and application of the other terms.
>
> No revisions were made to the Grades 6–8 Process Vocabulary Terms list at this time. The teachers agreed that they wanted to wait until they had a full school year's worth of data, as well as the current school year's state test results, before making decisions regarding modifications to the list.
>
> The remainder of the large-group meeting, as well as additional conversations that took place within departments, focused on strategies and activities that were proving most successful in encouraging students' use of the terms in reading, writing, listening, and speaking situations.

Informing New Teachers

It must not be overlooked that curriculum maps can be used to inform newly hired teachers of districtwide curriculum (Essential Maps), school-site curriculum (Consensus Maps), and the operational learning curriculum (Diary Maps). Jacobs (2004b) points out that "the K–12 curriculum path provides the big picture. . . . As experienced teachers retire, they can pass on a legacy of their maps and their plans. Indeed, mapping is a way of electronically passing the torch" (p. 8).

Hussar (1999), a statistician for the National Center of Education Statistics, predicts that "projections for the number of newly hired public school teachers needed by 2008–09 ranges from 1.7 million to 2.7 million. Some of these newly hired teachers will be needed to replace those leaving the profession, and others will be needed as enrollments continue to increase" (p. iii). Based on Hussar's formula, these numbers are only expected to increase in subsequent years. Knowing this, it is wise to create a living legacy for the next generation of teachers by designing curriculum maps that represent both the planned and operational student learning evidence.

In addition, teachers switching from one grade level to another, or starting to teach a course they have never personally taught before, appreciate having instant access to both the archived history and current student learning expectations.

Figure 7.6   Grade 7 Language Arts Diary Map Month

Month	Content	Skills	Assessment	Standards
November	**READING COMPREHENSION** A. Short Story/Fables Elements: Characterization, Morals Resources --Aesop's Fables --Modern Fables --Vocabulary Terms in Oral Discussions/Test Taking: *express, indicate, determine, analyze, formulate* B. Nonfiction Text: Summarization, Outline Resources --*Time* --*Teen People* --Vocabulary Terms in Oral Discussions/Test Taking: *check, develop, explain*	A1. Compare and contrast in writing positive/negative attributes of main characters using supporting explicit and implicit details A2. Summarize and infer in writing similarities and differences in traditional versus modern morals A3. Justify in writing impact traditional morals may have had on original-era readers compared to present-day readers A4. Compose in writing a life-lesson fable using animals as main characters with anthropomorphic characteristics B1. Summarize in writing central idea of current event articles using at least 5 supporting details B2. Outline in writing current event articles using Roman numeral and decimal structures to sequence order of information or events	A1. FOR 3 Paragraph Essay (Evaluation: Peer Review/ Checklist) A2. 5 Open-Ended Questions Quiz A3. Morals Venn Diagram (Evaluation: Checklist) A4. Original Fable (Evaluation: Peer Review/Rubric) B1. Summary Paragraphs (Evaluation: Peer Review/Student-Created Rubric) B2. FOR *Do Teens Need Sleep?* Outline (Evaluation: Self-Critique/Feedback)	A. ELA7.2.1 (D) ELA7.2.3 (D) B. ELA7.3.1 (D) ELA7.3.3 (D)

CONCLUSION

Curriculum reviews are based on inquiry and are driven by two fundamental questions:

- What learning expectations and instructional practices are in place that consistently prove to be in students' best interests?
- What learning expectations and instructional practices need to be started, stopped, or modified to enable or enhance students' success?

While a learning organization is first introduced to the mapping process by learning how to write quality maps and using a mapping system, it is important to be proactive and start exposing teachers to the various ways that maps can and will be used to conduct collaborative reviews that enable and empower teachers to study and resolve school-site-specific or districtwide curriculum and related problems, issues, and concerns.

REVIEW QUESTIONS

The more opportunities teachers have to use curriculum maps to conduct reviews, the more likely it is that they will begin to see the intended systemic nature of curriculum mapping. Independently, answer the first question and complete the two tasks. Share your responses with a partner or in a small group.

1. What problems, issues, or concerns do you know of that currently exist in your school or throughout your learning organization that conducting a specific mapping review may help resolve? (Support your reasoning for selecting a specific review focus. *Note*: You may have more than one review focus to share.)

2. Think of one specific problem, issue, or concern that currently needs to be addressed at your school site or throughout your learning organization. Outline in writing a seven-step review process that includes (a) the reasoning for your selected review focus, predetermined guiding questions, and the necessary map or map types and/or other resources necessary for conducting the review; (b) designating participants to be involved in the large-group comparison and how the large group will be subdivided into preplanned, small-group review teams (include your reasoning for the small-group team member configurations); and (c) outlining the anticipated timeline for each step.

3. Since the five meeting principles in Figure 7.1 can be applied to any meeting's focus, as demonstrated by the two scenarios following the figure, plan an upcoming meeting that you will actually be participating in where you can use the meeting process based on the five principles. When you write your step-by-step plan, include your reasoning for how conducting the meeting using the five principles' protocols can foreseeably enhance decision making and outcomes based on the manner in which such a meeting has been conducted in the past.

What Data Is Often Incorporated When Refining Curriculum Maps?

Desire of knowledge, like the thirst of riches,
increases ever with the acquisition of it.

—Laurence Stern

Curriculum maps that include the five common initial elements emphasized in Chapter 4 provide a learning organization with a firm foundation for curriculum design, documentation of learning expectations, and data-driven decision making. Once teachers are comfortable and confident in writing quality maps based on these elements, incorporating additional data can expand curriculum design and instructional awareness. The supplementary data chosen to be incorporated may differ from one learning organization to another. This chapter emphasizes the most common additional elements.

ADDITIONAL MAP DATA

Most mapping systems allow a learning organization to name additional element fields included in a map template. When adding a new element, be cautious in naming the element field. Since mapping is an ongoing process, as years progress the supplemental data collection focuses may vary. Therefore, using a broad element name allows for data-collection flexibility. For example, if an element is titled *Strategies*, as opposed to a specific topic such as *Big 10 Reading Strategies*, data included in this field can include a wide variety of strategies.

Regardless of what an additional element is titled, an element is never added just to be added. There must be a problem, issue, concern, or collegial desire that warrants its addition. Before an element is officially added, a school-site Curriculum Mapping Council or districtwide Curriculum Mapping Cabinet, with teacher input via in-person meetings or surveys, determines its inclusion. Once an element is added, it is meant to remain. In other words, an additional element does not appear for one year and then go away the next. There may be some years during which the added element's data collection is emphasized more than in other years, but the element field is always available for use.

Strategies

Strategies included in a map may vary from school to school. For example, one school may focus on mapping when specific strategies included in *Classroom Instruction That Works: Research-Based Strategies for Increasing Student Achievement* (Marzano, Pickering, and Pollock 2001) are being incorporated in the learning, while another school may have just completed a book study on *Active Literacy Across the Curriculum: Strategies for Reading, Writing, Speaking, and Listening* (Jacobs 2006a) and plans to begin mapping note-taking strategies. Another school may want to include *I can* statements that are aligned to assessments and standards (Chappuis et al. 2004), while another school chooses to include problem-solving and cooperative learning strategies.

There is no limit strategy-wise regarding what a teacher, team of teachers, school site, or district may choose to include in this element field. The point is that whatever is collected in this element field is meant to enhance collegial discussions and decision making regarding student learning expectations and instructional practices that ensure student success.

Modifications/Accommodations

Since a Diary Map represents students' operational learning, there may be times when teachers want to make note of students who are learning at different rates than the majority of the learners. A teacher or team of teachers may choose to document this information in a Modifications/Accommodations element field regarding general education, special education, or gifted students. Recorded modifications or accommodations may be related to content, skill, or assessments. Figure 8.1 represents a Kindergarten mathematics Diary Map that informs readers of content differentiation for five students. Each student's initials directly follow the modification data. If one or more skill statements were modified, the teacher would indicate this by using the appropriate letter-number coding(s).

In Consensus Maps this element field is often used to include possible student adaptations to support remedial or extension learning. While a Consensus Map's content and skills are considered compulsory, the data in the

Figure 8.1 Kindergarten Mathematics Diary Map Month

Month	Content	Skills	Assessments	Modifications/ Accommodations	Standards
October	**NUMBER SENSE** A. Patterns: 3 Attributes Resources --Chapter 2, pp. 31–35 --Attribute Bears --Vocabulary: core = identifiable "beginning" of a pattern's chain B. Number Sets: 0-10 Resources --Chapter 1, pp. 10–20 --Math Mats --Generic and Seasonal Manipulatives --Teacher-Created Worksheets	A1. Identify orally and create manipulatively 3-attribute core pattern A2. Extend manipulatively core pattern 2 times to repeat core pattern A3. Verify orally identifiable core pattern within a self-created extended pattern B1. Identify visually and orally individual/collective members of given set B2. Write numeral to match corresponding set B3. Justify orally reasoning for created set based on simple recited numeric "story" (e.g., 3 fish swam into a pond; 2 more swam in. . . . How many fish are in the pond now?)	A1.-A3. Pattern Train Performance Task (Evaluation: Teacher Ob/Rubric) B1.-B2. 10 Set Identification Performance Task (Evaluation: Teacher Ob/Checklist) B3. FOR Small-Group Storytelling Problems (Evaluation: Teacher Ob/Checklist)	A. 2 Attributes (JT, LL) B. 0-5 Sets (JT, LL, WS, FR, SS)	A. K1.3 (D) K1.4 (I) B. K2.1 (D) K3.3 (I)

Modifications/Accommodations field are considered recommendations. After a teacher duplicates the Consensus Map into a personal map and begins diary mapping the current school year, the teacher removes any adaptations that weren't used and may need to add adaptations that were not originally included in the Consensus Map.

Essential Maps do not usually include data in this additional field. If a learning organization chooses to do so, the included modifications or accommodations are meant to be incorporated districtwide.

Activities

Activities highlight teachers' instructive practices. If teachers choose to include an activities element, they should include only those activities that truly enhance the learning. An activity's description in a map is meant to summarize the activity's key point(s). For intra-alignment coding purposes, activities are aligned to the appropriate skill(s). Figure 8.2 is a Prekindergarten Diary Map that informs readers of key activities that students participated in during the unit of study.

Most mapping systems have the ability to attach full explanations and related handouts regarding an included activity summary. If teachers choose to include entire lesson plans, it is recommended that they come to collective agreement regarding placement of the plans so that there is consistency regarding input and data retrieval. One mapping system has a predesignated field for lesson plans. For the remaining systems, inclusion of a full lesson plan may be accomplished by attaching the document to the appropriate activity description, skill(s), or resource listing.

Adding Data to Established Elements

The term *refining* refers to using precise distinctions. There may be times when teachers choose to refine maps by incorporating more precise data within an existing map element field rather than adding new elements. For example, when teachers initially learn to map the five elements, evaluation notification is included in parentheses after an appropriate assessment:

- A1-A3. Plant Genetics Lab (Evaluation: Teacher Ob/Checklist/Student Journal Entry)

To refine map data, teachers may choose to focus on removing the written parenthetical data and replace it with an attachment of the actual evaluation documentation and assessment process. The document-attachment procedure varies depending on the mapping system used.

Another choice may be to focus on refining current resource listings by including or updating previously recorded uniform resource locators (URLs), attaching teacher-created learning packets or worksheets, or adding key vocabulary terms pertinent to the unit of study.

Teachers will naturally begin to generate their own desired refinement focuses for existing and, if incorporated, additional elements. When curriculum maps are used to provide evidence of established or new school-site or districtwide initiatives, teachers can record the pertinent data needed for collaborative reviews and ongoing decision making.

Figure 8.2 Prekindergarten Thematic Unit Diary Map Month

Month	Content	Skills	Assessments	Activities	Standards
October	**PUMPKIN HARVEST TIME** A. Fine Motor Skills: Hand-Eye Coordination Resources --Child-Safe Scissors	A1. Cut straight trace line holding paper with opposite hand A2. Cut curved trace line holding paper with opposite hand A3. Trace straight and/or curved line A4. Place small objects on glue line or in glue area	A1-A2. 7-Inch Lines Performance Task (Evaluation: Teacher Ob/Checklist) A3-A4. Jack-o'-Lantern Shape Tracing/Seed Pasting Project (Evaluation: Teacher Ob/Checklist)	A1-A2, C1, D1. --Cut out pumpkin shape, triangle eyes, crescent mouth; paste on paper and color A3. --Trace capital/small "p" "j" --Pumpkin-seed letters "Pp" "Jj" gluing project	A. PKFM1.1 (D) PKFM1.2 (D)
	B. Informational Text: Photographs Resources --*It's Pumpkin Picking Time* --*Jack-o'-Lanterns*	B1. Identify visually and orally photographic main idea per page/in series of pages B2. Identify aurally key words in text that match main idea of photograph or photographs per page/in series of pages	B1-B2. FOR One-on-One Performance Task (Evaluation: Teacher Ob/Checklist)	B1. --Guess covered photograph after teacher or aide reads matching text/reveal photograph	B. PKR1.5 (D) PKR1.6 (D) PKR1.7 (D) PKL1.2 (D)

(Continued)

Figure 8.2 (Continued)

Month	Content	Skills	Assessments	Activities	Standards
	C. Shapes: Circle, Triangle, Crescent Resources --Jumbo Pencils/Crayons	C1. Identify visually and orally shape by its characteristics C2. Draw named shape using pencil or crayon	C1. Shape Identification (Evaluation: Teacher Ob/Checklist) C2. FOR Flower Drawing (Evaluation: Teacher Ob/Checklist)	C1. --Determine shapes included in a collection of pumpkins and jack-o'-lantern faces	C. PKM2.1 (D)
	D. Color Recognition: Orange, Green, Black Resources --*What Color Is It?* Jumbo Color Cards	D1. Identify visually and orally specific color when presented in a series/set of colors D2. Color general and seasonal shapes using 1 to 3 named colors	D1-D2. Recognition/Color Performance Task (Evaluation: Teacher Ob/Checklist)	D2. --Draw a jack-o'-lantern using shapes and colors	D. PKR4.1 (D) PKFM 1.4 (D)
	E. Number Recognition: 0-5 Resources --Pumpkin Candies	E1. Identify visually and orally numerals in environmental/textual print E2. Count orally a set of objects in numeric sequence E3. Write number for given object set	E1-E3. One-on-One Performance Task (Evaluation: Teacher Ob/Checklist)	E2. --Play pumpkin patch game by counting, adding, and removing pumpkins using cupcake holders	E. PKM1.1 (D) PKM1.2 (D)

186

Month	Content	Skills	Assessment	Activities	Standards
	F. 5 Senses: See, Smell, Hear, Taste, Touch Resources --*Farm Life* DVD --Fresh/Canned Pumpkin	F1. Identify visually and orally body part or parts used for each sense action F2. Identify visually and orally items close versus far away F3. Identify olfactorily and orally pungent versus sweet smells F4. Identify aurally and orally sounds from 4 environments: transportation, home, work, zoo F5. Identify sweet/sour/salty tastes using a variety of edible food items F6. Identify tactually and orally objects felt with/without eye contact	F1-F6. FOR Senses Stations Rotations (Evaluation: Teacher-Aide Ob/Anecdotal Records)	F3. --Smell different scents from jars/match to pictures F4. --Listen to farm animal sounds/discuss different sounds (low, high, long, short) F3, F6. --Carve pumpkin to examine it with senses --Compare pumpkin pulp with canned pumpkin --Bake/eat pumpkin seeds	F. PKS3.1 (D)
	G. Plant Growth: Life Cycle Resources --*Pumpkins Grow* Video --*Pumpkin, Pumpkin* Song --1/2 Day Field Trip: Henderson's Pumpkin Patch	G1. Identify visually and orally 4 plant parts: seed, plant, flower, fruit G2. Sequence 6 cycle steps: seed in ground, seed sprouts, plant grows, flower blooms, fruit grows, seeds go back in ground	G1. Plant Parts Recognition (Evaluation: Teacher Ob/Checklist) G2. Pumpkin Cut-and-Paste Sequence Sheet (Evaluation: Teacher Ob/ Checklist)	G2. --Sequence steps in growth of a pumpkin using cut/paste worksheet ***Culminating Unit Activity*** --Visit local farm to integrate real-world shapes, colors, numbers, senses, and plant growth in small-group/one-on-one conversations and observations; pick pumpkins for class and personal family	G. PKS2.1 (D)

Dual Roles

Sometimes faculty members may have the dual role of teacher and administrator. I have seen some choose to add more information to help map readers differentiate the dual roles. Figure 8.3 is a high school counselor's map wherein he devised a personal small-letter symbol and key (i.e., *c = counselor expectation versus student expectation*) to aid readers' understanding of student expectations versus his administrative duties.

As long as teachers adhere to the established wording, format, and intra-alignment norms, any supplementary data included in any type of map, via an additional element or refinement to existing elements' data, continually expands and enhances a learning organization's curriculum and instruction knowledge as a part of the ongoing curriculum-mapping process.

ESSENTIAL AND SUPPORTING QUESTIONS

There are a variety of models that advise the use of essential questions to drive learning and instruction (Erickson 2001, 2007; Jacobs 1997; Schmied 2004; Wiggins and McTighe 1998). While there may be diversity regarding the definition and construction of the questions, there is agreement that essential questions should cause lingering learning—learning that stays with students for a lifetime.

Essential questions are not meant to be made up on a whim. They are intended to (a) be stimulating and thought-provoking, (b) drive content and skills learning, and (c) influence assessment products and performances. As Jacobs (1997) notes, "the essential question is conceptual commitment . . . it is a declaration of intent. In a sense you are saying, 'This is our focus for learning. I will put my teaching skills into helping my students examine the key concept implicit in the essential question'" (p. 27).

Teachers should not include essential questions in curriculum maps simply because a mapping system includes this element field. It is recommended that teachers first receive in-depth professional development based on a preferred model. The following information is intended to present an overview of what needs to be considered when using conceptual questions to drive learning within units of study.

Conceptual Questions

Instructional models' names for conceptual questions vary. For this overview, the two types of questions addressed are *essential questions* and *supporting questions.* Conceptual questions are based on big ideas (Wiggins and McTighe 1998) or conceptual understanding (Erickson 2001). Erickson (2007) states that conceptual understanding causes "integrated thinking. . . . [S]tudents see patterns and connections between the facts and related ideas that transfer through time, across cultures, and/or across situations" (p. 129).

Figure 8.3 High School Counselor Diary Map Month

Month	Content	Skills	Assessment	Strategies
April	**COLLEGE AND CAREERS**	c = counselor expectation versus student expectation		
	A. National College Fair: Self-Exploration Resources --Field Trip to Fair in Downtown Chicago	A1. Determine in writing self-selected critical information shared by representatives from colleges, universities, trade/technical schools, military academies A2c. Assist students in making transition decisions toward "life after high school"	A1. FOR Personal Notations A1. College Application Submission Drafts A1. ASVAB Preparation A2. Counselor-Student Dialogue	*Literacy* A1. Write admission essays/personal statements based on personal notes and personal interpretations
	B. PSAE/ACT: Retest	B1. Interpret, analyze, apply in writing personal knowledge acquired during school tenure to test-taking environment B2c. Conduct retesting	B1. Prairie State Examination/ACT Exam B2. Retest Examination	*Literacy* B1. Read informational text/write sample answers for weakest exam subsections; group-discuss answers
	C. College Tours: In State Resources --Various Campus Field Trips	C1. Compare in writing institution and program best suited for individual needs based on visit to college campuses (talk to faculty/meet with college students) C2. Assess in writing pros and cons for self-selected prospective colleges, universities, military programs, or special academic opportunities	C1–C2. College Placement Acceptance Notification	*Literacy* C2. Write narrative summary based on gathered information
	D. Career Path: Exploration Resources --Student Portfolios --Local-Sponsored Youth Motivation Programs Guest Speakers --Media Center Computer Lab	D1. Hypothesize in writing personal career opportunities based on variables including past/present grades, scholarship opportunities, work experiences, mentorship, college opportunities	D1. Career Portfolios (Evaluation: Peer Review/Rubric)	*Literacy/Technology* D1. Conduct Internet searches, make phone calls, write e-mail exchanges, and take notes about educational requirements and potential personal concerns for career choices

Direct-answer questions are not conceptual questions because they require straightforward, recall answers. They do not require students to link or transfer understanding. Here are four examples of direct-answer questions:

- What is an adjective?
- What are the five parts of a friendly letter?
- Who was the first president of the United States?
- How do you know the outdoor temperature has reached 100 degrees Fahrenheit?

Each answer is very specific. No introspection is necessary to justify or support the responses.

Essential questions are divergent questions that can be generalized and applied to multiple disciplines. They are universal and timeless:

- How do patterns affect changes?

Patterns and *changes* are concepts involved in mathematics, social science, science, art, and other disciplines. Regardless of grade level or discipline, teachers can use this essential question to frame content-and-skill learning.

Similar to an essential question is a supporting question, which incorporates terminology that is specific to a discipline's unit of study topic or theme. This type of question is not as generalized as an essential question. The terms used in a supporting question affect the appropriate content-and-skill learning. As you read each of the following questions, notice that specific discipline learning for each question becomes more identifiable:

- Why do economic patterns affect changes in lifestyles?
- Why do energy consumption patterns affect changes in global warming trends?
- How do harmonic frequency patterns affect changes in metal structural fatigue?
- How do mathematical patterns affect changes in outcomes?

Depending on grade-level-appropriate learning, the last supporting question's content-skills focus may be skip counting, the counting principle, input-output function tables, or slope comparisons.

Therefore, when designing essential or supporting questions, teachers must determine (a) the big idea or concepts involved in the learning, (b) what students must specifically know and be able to do, (c) the reasoning and processing abilities involved in the learning, and, most important, (d) the formative and summative assessments that demand students independently respond to the conceptual essential or supporting questions.

Essential and supporting questions must always be age-appropriate. While conceptual questions make sense for all grade levels, they may be too abstract for younger learners. Early learners may have difficulty connecting various facts and information to formulate reasoning and justify answers independently. I mention this simply to ensure that the questions created and used are cognitively appropriate for the literal and maturational age and abilities of the students involved in a unit of study.

When creating conceptual questions some teachers find the following structural formula helpful (Schmied 2004):

- How *or* Why phrase + conceptual noun + relational action verb + conceptual noun?

To begin the question-creation process using this formula, some teachers prefer to first brainstorm conceptual nouns related to the unit of study's predetermined learning expectations, and then brainstorm a potential list of relational action verbs.

When developing essential questions, conceptual nouns are not proper or personal nouns, and the relational action verbs are not past, past perfect, or present perfect verbs (Erickson 2002, 2007). Supporting questions, which usually include specific topic terms, may include proper nouns, but relational action verbs stay the same as in essential questions.

The following generalized essential question and supporting topic-based questions were created using Schmied's (2004) structural formula and noun-verb-noun guidelines:

- EQ How can interdependence affect systems?
- SQ How can allowances affect family chores? (Grade 2)
- SQ How can micro-organisms affect human beings' systems? (Grade 4)
- SQ Why can economic costs affect delivery systems? (Grade 8)
- SQ Why can time sensitivity affect organ transplant operations? (Grade 10)

Using Schmied's formula is not a requirement; it is a recommendation. What is required is that essential questions be conceptual, universal, and timeless, whereas supporting questions are meant to be conceptual and topical, but not direct-answer questions. Remember that conceptual questions help students (a) discover patterns and build personal meaning, (b) discover deeper meaning rather than relying mainly on deductive lecture methods, and (c) involve thinking and reasoning on more complex levels (Erickson 2007). Here are supporting questions that meet Erickson's threefold criteria but are not written using the formula:

- What do colors tell us about people, places, and things?
- Considering past election patterns, what is on the horizon politically for our township?
- How are scientists applying the Fibonacci Sequence to natural and man-made patterns?

Planning a Unit of Study

A conceptually based unit of study's content-and-skills learning is generally driven by one essential question and one to three supporting questions. The number of supporting questions is dependent on the length of time devoted to the learning and the students' eventual ability to independently and adequately respond to the questions through product or performance assessments.

Some teachers find it helpful to visualize an essential question as a frame for the supporting question(s). An essential question frame may be the same in multiple units within one school year or over a period of years, while the supporting questions within the frame are different (see Figure 8.4).

Figure 8.4   Essential Question and Spiraled Science Supporting Questions

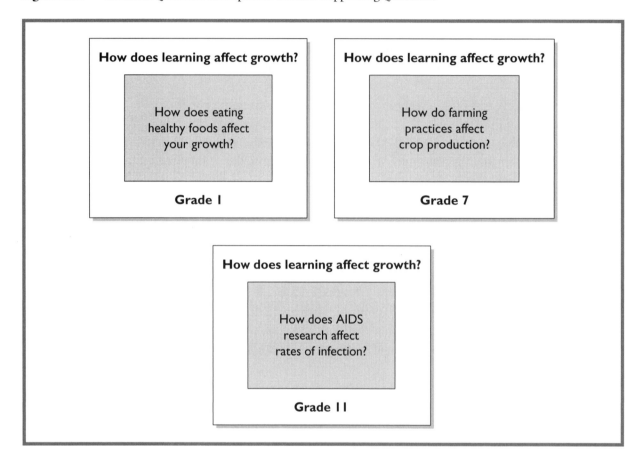

Backwards Design

When student learning is going to be based on conceptual questions that are added to a preexisting unit's content and skills, teachers must think differently about the unit's new assessment needs and the levels of cognition regarding action or abilities (i.e., measurable verbs). Are the current assessments consistent with the divergent-thinking expectations the conceptual questions demand? Are the current content-skills and reasoning expectations adequate for involvement in new or adapted products or performances? In other words, does the current unit of study need to be reworked with the conceptual learning outcomes in mind? Wiggins and McTighe (1998) refer to planning the outcome assessments first as "application of backwards design" (p. 13). Assessment and evaluation processes are equally important while rethinking or initially designing a conceptually based unit of study. As Erickson (2007) comments, "the scoring guide addresses criteria describing 'quality performance' for conceptual understanding as well as for content knowledge and skills. Too often the conceptual expectations for performance are missing from the scoring guide" (p. 72).

Keeping the Students in Mind

Jacobs (1997) outlines eight criteria for generating student-friendly essential questions:

1. Each child should be able to understand the question.
2. The language of the questions should be written in broad, organizational terms.
3. The question should reflect your conceptual priorities.
4. Each question should be distinct and substantial.
5. Questions should not be repetitious.
6. The questions should be realistic given the amount of time allocated for the unit or course.
7. There should be a logical sequence to a set of essential questions.
8. The questions should be posted in the classroom. (pp. 30–32)

Although number five states that an essential question should not be repetitious, an essential question may be repetitive if it frames different supporting questions in a given school year or over a series of years.

Number eight is critical. When a teacher begins a unit of study framed by essential and supporting questions, each question needs to be posted at the onset of the learning and referred to often throughout the unit study.

Mapping the Questions

Some mapping systems include a preset Essential Questions field. Others allow this field to be added when teachers are ready to begin using conceptually based units of study. If the mapping system allows, teachers often prefer to use italic type for the essential questions and include the letters SQ before each supporting question:

THE EARTH MOVES UNDER OUR FEET
How do disturbances affect environments?
SQ How do rock cycles affect land formations?
SQ How do plate shifts affect land formations?

Figures 8.5 and 8.6 are sample map months that include essential and supporting questions.

Designing learning based on conceptual, question-driven units of study takes thoughtful preplanning to ensure a knowing-and-doing focus that guarantees that students reach the necessary depth and insight to independently address the essential and supporting questions. Jacobs (1997) notes that "given the limited time you have with your students, curriculum design has become more and more an issue of deciding what you won't teach as well as what you will teach. . . . [A]s a designer, you must choose the essential" (p. 27).

While designing conceptual, question-based units of study is not meant to be difficult, it may be for some teachers. It is recommended that teachers be provided adequate opportunities to study various unit-design models and

Figure 8.5   Life Science Unit Diary Map Month

Essential Questions	Content	Skills	Assessment	Standards
How do environmental conditions impact life? SQ How do abiotic factors impact plant growth? SQ How do plants adapt to survive in different environments? SQ How do plants depend on animals to survive?	**PLANT INQUIRY** A. Scientific Inquiry: Abiotic Conditions Resources --Grow Light --Variety of Soils --Bean Seeds --Potting Materials --Variety of Watering Solutions	A1. Formulate in writing hypothesis describing impact of abiotic variables on plant growth A2. Identify in writing dependent and independent abiotic variables A3. Design in writing and conduct abiotic experiment following 7-step scientific method A4. Formulate and support in writing conclusion based on analysis of collected data A5. Create and present orally and in writing technological report of scientific investigation results	A1-C2. How Do Environmental Conditions Impact Life? Position Notes/Oration (Evaluation:Teacher Ob/Peer Review/Six Facets of Understanding Rubric/Life Science Checklist) A1-A5. FOR Tri-Team PowerPoint Abiotic Report (Evaluation:Teacher Ob/Rubric/ Feedback) A1-A4, B1-C2. EQ Persuasive Essay (Evaluation: Persuasive Rubric/SQs Concept Integration Rubric) A1-A2. 10 MC Test	A. 9.A.3a (D) 9.A.3g (R) 9.7.10 (D) T9.1.3 (R)
	B. Reproduction: Sexual/Asexual Resources --Petunias --Magnifying Lens --Pins --Paper Towels --Videotaped Assessment: Tech Lab	B1. Differentiate in writing sexual and asexual reproduction of plants by providing at least 3 examples for each category B2. Illustrate and label in writing reproductive organs of sexual reproduction and explain in writing pollination process B3. Analyze orally and in writing variables in life cycle of flowering plants based on interdependency between plants and animals	B1. Comparative Essay (Evaluation: Science Checklist/Writing Rubric) B2. COMMON Petunia Lab (Evaluation: Lab Sheets/Checklist) B3. Life Web Poster Presentation (Evaluation:Video Self-Critique/Rubric)	B. 9.7.19 (I) 9.7.20 (D) 9.7.21 (D) 9.7.29 (D)
	C. Plant Processes: Photosynthesis Resources --New Directions Online Teaching Unit: Lives of Plants --Green Power Video --BioCoach: 9 Interactive Animations --BioCoach: Photosynthesis	C1. Distinguish in writing 5 plant structures involved in photosynthesis: chloroplast, chlorophyll, stomata, leaves, vein C2. Compare and contrast orally and in writing environmental survival adaptation of plants from 3 different habitats (e.g., cacti have spines instead of leaves, tropical rainforest plants on forest floor require less light, temperate forest broadleaf trees lose leaves in fall)	C1. 25 MC Online Quiz C2. FOR Science Display Board Presentation (Evaluation: Peer Review/ Rubric/Feedback)	C. 9.7.15 (D) 9.12.7.16 (I) 9.12.7.17 (D)

Figure 8.6 U.S. History Unit Diary Map Month (Five-Week Unit)

Essential Questions	Content	Skills	Assessment	Standards
How do choices influence actions? *SQ Why can multiple perspectives lead to common compromises?* *SQ How may have past governments influenced the Constitution's context and wording?* Vocabulary Terms: - compromise - legislative, executive, judiciary - separation of powers	**CONSTITUTIONAL CONVENTION 1787: DEBATES AND COMPROMISES** A. Annapolis Conference 1786: Rethinking Articles of Confederation Resources --http://bensguide.gpo.gov/6–8/documents/constitution/background.html (*Constitution* Web Site) --*America Rock* Schoolhouse Rock Video B. Multiple Perspectives: Virginia Plan, Connecticut Great Compromise, New Jersey Plan, Pinckney Plan, British Plan, Pinckney Plan Resources --Student Internet Research Teams --*The Constitution* Decisions, Decisions Tom Snyder Interactive DVD	A1. Analyze in writing 3 critical Confederation document weaknesses: commerce facilitation, establishment of standard rights/rules/regulations, authority of Congress A2. Hypothesize in writing weak representation of states B1. Analyze orally and in writing 5 plans focusing on similarities/differences: legislative, executive, judiciary B2. Justify orally and in writing key compromises per plan based on primary/secondary sources and personal stance B3. Analyze orally and in writing personal and political strengths/weaknesses of Madison, Sherman, Paterson, Hamilton, Pinckney B4. Justify in writing 2 secret agreement behaviors: taxation conflicts, small versus large states	A1-E4. FOR EQ/SQs Inner-Outer Circle Debate (Evaluation: Dual-Teacher Ob/Peer Review/SS Rubric/Listening-Speaking Rubric) A1-A2. Persuasive Essay (Evaluation: SS Checklist/LA Rubric) B1-D2. Plans/Compromises 4-Team Debate (Evaluation: Peer Review/Presentation and Stance Rubric) B1-C3. FOR *The Constitution* DVD Simulation (Evaluation: Program Teacher's Guide)	A. SS8.1.A.2 (D) SS8.1.A.5 (M) SS8.1.A.6 (D) LA8.4.1.4 (R) B. SS8.1.A.2 (D) SS8.1.A.3 (D) SS8.1.A.5 (M) SS8.1.A.7 (D) SS8.1.A.8 (M) LA8.4.1.5 (R)

(Continued)

Figure 8.6 (Continued)

Essential Questions	Content	Skills	Assessment	Standards
- checks and balances - House - Senate - Supreme Court - Electoral College - veto - Federalists	C. Questions of Power: Branches/Presidency Resources --*Electoral College: From Birth to Present Video*	C1. Analyze in writing 2 schools of thought: grant federal government general powers with interpretation left up to congress/grant specific powers to the federal government C2. Define in writing purpose for forming Committee of Detail and influence on decision making C3. Analyze in writing influences of royal governors and king of England in Framers' decision making; single individual or committee?/appointed or elected?/people or legislature? C4. Explain in writing purpose and process of Electoral College	C1–C4. 20 MC/10 Short-Answer Test C1, C3. FOR Personal Note-Taking Cards Discussion (Evaluation: Teacher Ob/ Teacher-Peer Feedback)	C. SS8.I.A.2 (D) SS8.I.A.3 (D) SS8.I.A.5 (M) SS8.I.A.7 (D) SS8.I.A.8 (M)
- Antifederalists - article - amendment - Constitution - Preamble - Bill of Rights	D. Slavery: Full or Three-Fifths Count Resources --http://www.crf-usa.org/lessons/slavery_const_guide.htm (*Slavery Debate Lesson*)	D1. Analyze in writing 3 slave trade factors on Framers' decision making: capitation, taxation, representation D2. Evaluate in writing reasoning for 2 details of South compromise: slave trade continue for 20 years, taxation	D1–D2. FOR Small-Group Note Cards Debates (Evaluation: Teacher Ob/Student Self-Critique/Feedback)	D. SS8.I.A.2 (D) SS8.I.A.3 (D) LA8.4.1.5 (R)
	E. Democracy: Constitution/Bill of Rights Resources --Constitution/Bill of Rights Reproductions --*Inspiration Software* (Timelines)	E1. Sequence in writing final action and timeline steps of ratification for both documents, including relevance of Bill of Rights E2. Translate in writing Preamble into personal words to convey intended message E3. Explain in writing context for Constitution's 7 Articles E4. Explain in writing purpose of Letter of Transmittal and Continental Congress, 2 major acts: establishment of first federal elections, new government operations in New York City	E1. Ratification Timeline (Evaluation: Checklist) E2. Preamble Translation Paragraph (Evaluation: Rubric) E3–E4.12 Item (7 Matching/ 5 Short-Answer) Test	E. SS8.I.A.8 (M) SS8.I.A.9 (M) LA8.4.1.5 (R) M8.2.1.3 (R) T8.2.A.5 (R)

196

examine personal pedagogical practices in relation to the various models' demands on both teachers and students. Since all models require that students be engaged in higher-level thinking and reasoning, it is critical to give teachers enough time to also explore their current instructional practice in comparison to the requirements involved in refining student learning expectations through incorporating essential and supporting question–based units of study.

Some learning organizations find it advantageous to form action-research teacher teams at various school sites to serve as the trailblazers by designing and incorporating conceptual question–based units of study. From collegial dialogue, surveys, feedback, and open forums, the involved teachers provide insight and recommendations that the Curriculum Mapping Cabinet and Council members can use to collectively determine implementation throughout the learning organization.

CONCLUSION

Refining curriculum maps most often affects Consensus Map and Projected/Diary Map entries. While curriculum mapping may begin as a districtwide initiative, it is important to remember that curriculum mapping is equally meant to be a school-site initiative (Jacobs 2006b). In other words, school-site autonomy should be allowed regarding refinement of map data in relation to when and how additional elements or details are added to existing maps. Some systems do not allow each school site to determine additional element field titles. If the map template must remain the same throughout the learning organization, be certain that any additional element fields are titled only after Curriculum Mapping Cabinet members determine, based on school-site input, the best titles for newly added elements.

For refinement regarding the already-recorded five common initial elements, each school site should be given the right to focus on what to refine as a school, by grade level, or by department. What is specifically worked on should be noted annually in school-site curriculum-mapping action plans.

REVIEW QUESTIONS

Answer the following questions to spark conversation related to refining curriculum maps. Discuss your responses with a partner or in a small group.

1. Why is it important for teachers to feel confident in their ability to write quality maps based on the initial five common elements before adding supplementary data? (Support your reasoning.)

2. If the teachers in a school or district felt confident in writing the initial map elements and you were asked to advise the Curriculum Mapping Cabinet or Council members regarding what supplementary data should be in focus, what would you suggest and why? (Support your reasoning.)

3. Cover the answers near the bottom of the page before continuing. After answering the three bulleted questions, uncover the answers. First, study the questions in the following figure:

Figure 8.7 What Type of Question?

1. Why do businesses think critically about customer service?

2. What do you think will happen if I put this seed in a pot with soil and water?

3. Why do choices alter results?

4. How do rains affect ecosystem interactions?

5. Why did Elisha Gray and Alexandar Graham Bell clash over the invention of the telephone?

6. How does algebra prove that number tricks work?

7. How do revolutions repeat in structures?

- Which ones are essential questions (i.e., can be generalized to any discipline)?
- Which ones are supporting questions (i.e., still general, but contain topic- or theme-specific discipline terms)?
- Which ones are direct-answer questions (i.e., demand basic knowledge or recall responses)?

Answers

Questions three and seven are essential questions.

Questions one, four, and six are supporting questions.

Questions two and five are direct-answer questions.

Share Your Thoughts

Do you see conceptual essential and supporting question–based units of study as part of the short- or long-term goals for your learning organization's curriculum-mapping initiative? (Support your reasoning.) If yes, when do you think that professional development should begin based on a desire to have teachers design conceptual-based units of study? What instructional-design models are you considering for teachers to study and potentially use in the design process (e.g., *Understanding by Design* [Wiggins and McTighe 1998]; *Concept-Based Curriculum and Instruction for the Thinking Classroom,* [Erickson 2007])?

How May Interpreting Standards Influence Our Curriculum Design?

With reference to the narrative of events,
far from permitting myself to derive it from the first source that came to hand,
I did not even trust my own impressions,
but it rests partly on what I saw myself, partly on what others saw for me.

—Thucydides

There are many professional books dedicated to the study of standards and their impact on learning and curriculum design. This chapter focuses on two standards-interpretation procedures that teachers may choose to use when collaboratively designing or refining Essential Maps or Consensus Maps. The first is *breaking apart standards.* This procedure asks teachers to collegially discuss and determine standard statements' explicit and implicit concepts, content, and skills, and to develop formative and summative assessments that accurately measure the designed planned learning. The second is *determining power standards.* Ainsworth's (2003) criteria for determining power standards aids teachers in selecting the standard statements that can have the greatest impact on improving student learning. This process can be carried out using Jacobs's (1997) seven-step review process, which is demonstrated later in this chapter.

Regardless of whether national, state, local, or self-generated standards are used when designing or refining planned-learning curriculum maps, it is recommended that textbooks not initially be included in either procedure. Once a collaborative curriculum map is designed, discussing and recording available resources is appropriate. It is never in students' best interests to modify standards-based curriculum expectations to meet available resources. If new or refined curriculum does not currently have adequate resources to support the planned learning, procurement is the logical next step.

I am often asked which of these two procedures should be conducted first. Just as there is no single sequential order for creating the various map types, the right time and purpose for using either procedure is dependent on what is best for helping teachers improve their abilities to collaboratively design curriculum maps.

Breaking apart the standards is a critical cognitive process used when designing collaborative maps. For example, if teachers have collegially developed power standards that will serve as the base for designing discipline-specific Essential Maps, the next logical step is for the task force to break apart the power standard statements. When a grade-level or course-specific Essential Map is copied to a school site's Consensus Map, the appropriate teachers work as a team to break apart the non-power standards and make critical decisions about how to best include the explicit and implicit learning required by the remaining standards. The teachers add these expectations to new or already existing units based on the Essential Map's mandatory learning.

STANDARDS AND CURRICULUM

You have previously read that textbooks are not the curriculum. Standards also are not the curriculum. They are proficiency targets. As Erickson (2007) clarifies,

> Academic standards are not a curriculum: they are a framework for designing curriculum. A curriculum is a coherent, teacher-friendly document that reflects the intent of the academic standards. When teachers mistakenly think that the state academic standards are the curriculum, they may start checking off benchmarks one by one, which can lead to pellet-gun teaching. (p. 48)

How teachers interpret standards is critical to improving student learning. O'Shea (2005) observes that

> there is a distinct difference between alignment with the topics of the standards and achievement of the expectations included in the standards. Standards are written to raise expectations of students' intellectual engagement with the subject matter. . . . Mere topic coverage, or the alignment of topics . . . does not ensure achievement of the higher expectations described in state standards. (p. 16)

When designing collaborative curriculum, dialogue must be focused on the *collective interpretation* of standard statements' explicit and implicit expectations to ensure that students experience a well-planned, rigorous curriculum.

Throughout this chapter the term *standard statement* is used in reference to an individual proficiency target. For example, in Figure 9.1 what is in italics is one standard statement in a set of relational standard statements.

Figure 9.1   Standard Statement

Understand and apply the basic concepts of probability
• Name the possible outcomes for a probability experiment.
• *Predict the most likely or least likely outcome in probability experiments (e.g., Predict the chance of spinning one of the 2 colors on a 2-colored spinner).*
• Predict the outcome of a grade-level-appropriate probability experiment.
• Record the data from performing a grade-level-appropriate probability experiment.
• Compare the outcome of an experiment to predictions made prior to performing the experiment.
• Compare the results of two repetitions of the same grade-level-appropriate probability experiment.

From the onset of a mapping initiative, it is imperative that teachers are never told or encouraged to simply copy a standard statement in its entirety and paste it in either the content or skills field of the map. Doing so indicates a misunderstanding of both the purpose of the standard statements and how to interpret the statements as student learning expectations.

BREAKING APART STANDARDS

In the field of education, there are a variety of *–ing* expressions used when considering student learning, such as unwrapping, unpacking, and breaking apart. All of these terms have a specific purpose and meaning to those involved in any one of the *–ing* processes. For the purpose of this book's emphasis on designing collaborative curriculum maps, the term *breaking apart* refers to isolating one or more standard statements' specific terms—nouns, verbs, and adjectives—and disaggregating and analyzing them to collegially formulate concepts, content, skills, and assessments that represent horizontal and vertical student learning expectations in the form of a curriculum map.

Disaggregating Standards

Disaggregating refers to teachers agreeing on the explicit and implicit content-and-skills learning included in a standard statement or series of statements. If choosing to incorporate essential and supporting questions into the learning and instructional design, teachers may also determine conceptually based questions that link a series or set of statements together. Success in using the breaking-apart procedure depends on variables, including the following:

- general versus in-depth understanding of and familiarity with the standard statements
- professional development and support for the mapping process and designing collaborative maps
- teachers' capability to work collegially
- adequate time to work (e.g., full or half days versus trying to find a half-hour here and there)

The standard statements selected to be broken apart also play a significant role. For example, design outcome will vary if teachers focus on one standard statement within one discipline, a series of relational standard statements within one discipline, or multiple standard statements across and within disciplines.

Another variable to consider is the fact that each member of a collaborative team will have a personal history regarding the selected standard statements. Teachers may have varying degrees of personal understanding regarding content, skills, topics, and themes associated with the standard statements. The similarities and differences may affect the interpretation process as well as map-design outcomes.

Interpretation Outcomes

Based on the fact that the aforementioned variables may affect interpretation, consider an example of two teacher teams within the same learning organization, but in different schools, who broke apart the following standard statement: *Identify how scarcity requires people to make choices due to their unlimited wants and needs.* The first team focused on one standard statement in one discipline. Their interpretation resulted in the following:

- *Content:* Basic Economics: Wants and Needs
- *Skill:* Identify in writing how scarcity affects people's goods and services choice making

The second team focused on a series of standard statements in one discipline that included the standard statement. Their interpretation resulted in the following:

- *Essential Question:* How does supply affect demand?
- *Supporting Question:* Given the United States' economic rise and fall pattern in the latter half of the 20th century, what is your prediction for the first half of the 21st century?
- *Content:* Basic Economics: Wants and Needs
- *Skill:* Justify orally and in writing how scarcity affects people's goods and services choice making

While both sets of content–skill elements may appear similar, they are in actuality quite different regarding students' cognition level expectations. The formative and summative assessments to measure the learning requisites will be higher-level at one school than the other. The point is not to say that one interpretation is appropriate and the other is not but rather to illustrate the reality that the potential variables may affect the breaking-apart procedure and curriculum-design outcomes.

Explicit Versus Implicit

Critical to the breaking-apart procedure is focusing on the implicit standard statements' expectations. Teachers must come to agreement on what the unspoken learning expectations are and contemplate how these unspoken expectations will be incorporated in a curriculum map.

> **Standard Statement:** Use geography concepts and skills to find solutions for local, state, or national problems.

A teacher team breaking apart this standard statement, given their students' maturational and grade-level expectations, may interpret and conclude that this proficiency target implies that students must have the following:

- a conceptual understanding of affecting variables (e.g., migration, man versus nature, shortage of natural resources)
- content knowledge of geographical attributes (e.g., rivers, mountains, deserts, forests, climate)
- content knowledge of human activity (e.g., transportation routes, settlement patterns, mining or other types of production using natural resources)
- process performance: make connections
- skill abilities:

  o compare and contrast
  o evaluate
  o critique
  o hypothesize
  o justify

Once a team agrees on the implicit concepts, content, process, and skills along with the explicit learning expectations, the next step focuses on when or if the implied or explicit learning expectations take place in any previous academic years, future years, or the current year based on relational standard statements.

If curriculum maps exist in a mapping system, teachers may choose to review appropriate maps using keyword searches based on the implicit and explicit learning expectations. If maps do not exist, teachers will have to communicate with previous grade levels or related courses in person or by using electronic or written correspondence.

Once the team members have determined what the planned learning map elements will be, they need to decide whether the learning expectations need to be included in a stand-alone, in-depth unit of study or a spiraled series of shorter units that build upon previous learning throughout the school year or a portion of the year.

To summarize the procedure, the process of breaking apart standards includes (a) predetermining the standard statement or statements involved in the design process, (b) breaking apart the standard statement(s) to determine explicit learning, (c) brainstorming and listing the standard statement or statements' implicit learning expectations, (d) investigating when and if the explicit and implicit learning occurs in previous or future academic years, (e) designing the curriculum using stand-alone or spiraling units of study, and (f) recording the units of study in a curriculum map within a mapping system. Built into this sixfold process are four recommended phases, which are presented in the next section, that aid teachers in this collaborative-agreement process.

The Breaking-Apart Procedure

The term *standards* is often used in reference to all proficiency targets from global to specific criteria. In the United States it is up to the discretion of each state's Department of Education to name each criteria tier. For example, Arizona state standards' global-to-specific terms, in a descending order of tiers, are *standards > strands > concepts > performance objectives*. Ohio's descending tier terms, on the other hand, are *standards > benchmarks > indicators*.

Therefore, to begin the procedure of breaking apart standards, teachers must agree on the standard statements at each tier that will be involved in designing one or more units of study. For example, if teachers are designing mathematics-specific units, they may select a probability strand of standard statements similar to those included in Figure 9.1. Another team may choose to include not only probability statements but also relational data analysis and statistics statements. Likewise, one teacher team may choose to focus on topic-related statements in a science strand, such as *the earth,* while another team chooses the theme of *interdependency* and combines various science-strand statements that relate well to the chosen concept.

Once a team has selected the standard statement(s) to break apart, it is ready to move on to Phase One.

Phase One

Two nonnegotiable elements in a curriculum map are content and skills. Content is what students must know and is most often noun based. Skills are what students must do in relation to the knowing and include three parts: measurable verb, target, and descriptor.

A team, therefore, first breaks apart each standard statement to reveal the explicit nouns, verbs, targets, and descriptors. To visually represent the explicit learning, each statement's text is highlighted. Some teachers prefer to do so using colored highlighters, while others prefer to use a pen or pencil (see Figure 9.2).

Some teachers prefer to conduct the highlighting process individually before meeting as a team, while others prefer to work on the breaking-apart process together. Regardless, commentaries and questions are recorded when the team discusses the highlighted text.

Here are a few discipline-specific examples that provide a visual breakdown of a standard statement, followed by teacher commentaries in italics.

Figure 9.2   Breaking Apart Standard Statement Coding

Skills	Content or Concept	Targets or Descriptors
Highlighter Color #1 *Use broad side of highlighter* or Draw a box around text	Highlighter Color #2 *Use broad side of highlighter* or Draw a circle around text	Highlighter Color #2 *Use tip point to underline text* or Draw a line under text
Verb relating to student action or ability	Key noun or noun phrase	*Text providing specific details

*Sometimes a standard statement includes text (oftentimes in parentheses) that has an abbreviation directly in front of the information:

- If the text is preceded by *e.g.*, which in Latin means "for example," it indicates that the learning term or terms are not considered compulsory unless otherwise indicated in the standards document. Teachers, therefore, may or may not choose to include the expectations as required learning.
- If the text is preceded by *i.e.*, which in Latin means "that is," it indicates that the learning term or terms are compulsory and must be included as a required learning expectation.
- If *e.g.* or *i.e.* is not written prior to a target or descriptor, the information is equivalent to *i.e.* and is considered required learning.

- Compare structures in plants (e.g., roots, stems, leaves, flowers) and animals (e.g., muscles, bones, nerves) that serve different functions in growth and survival.
  - *There is a lot of learning involved here. Given that this is a school-year's worth of learning, we need to decide on the month(s) during which we'll focus on plants versus animals, and eventually both. How should we plan to scaffold the implicit learning as content and skills? What are the "different" functions expected to be learned since not stated? "Serve" how? Since there are e.g.s, are we going to stay with just these, expand, or include different ones altogether?*

- Identify models or illustrations of prisms, pyramids, cones, cylinders, and spheres.
  - *Pretty clear cut as far as what students must know. The doing is not very high-level cognition (identify). We should consider comparisons of concept of planes (2-D versus 3-D) even though it is not in our academic year since it is heavy in the following year's standards. Will models and illustrations include studying real objects and drawn objects? Also, are we going to bring technology into the learning expectations? If yes, how? Assessments?*

- Recognize how art (e.g., porcelain, poetry), architecture (e.g., pagodas, temples), and inventions (e.g., paper, fireworks) in Asia contributed to the development of their own and later civilizations.
  - *Recognize means students are going to have to compare, contrast, and make connections because of the included details: their own and later. What "later" civilizations should we have students compare to and make connections with? (Note: Check social studies standards/maps.) Should we consider changing*

how we've been teaching this to a theme-based unit of study given that we can base the art, architecture, and inventions studied in time periods and connect with social studies and maybe even science? We could have students comparing contemporary Asian influential artisans and inventors to a specific era or eras.

- Construct a paragraph that groups sentences around a topic.
  - ○ *Only one paragraph? We really need to get students to three paragraphs given the next grade level's state testing requirements. Do we need to agree on how many sentences are considered adequate for a paragraph? Update our rubric? What is really meant by "groups sentences around"?*
- Use estimation to verify the reasonableness of a calculation (e.g., Is 4.1×2.7 about 12?).
  - ○ *This statement should actually be: Verify in writing reasonableness of a calculation using estimation. Will we want to assess using word problems, numeric problems, or both? What will our expectations be when they are asked to write a verification? Logic, process, support, or all three? Is there a specific concept, content, or skill that is implied and needs to be scaffolded in this learning that we need to consider when designing the learning expectations?*

While the teacher comment in the last example indicates that the target will be *in writing* when the skill expectation is included in the map, this step is not meant to formally focus on translating broken-apart standard statements into actual map element configurations. That is part of Phase Two. Phase One is meant to be a time of both personal and collaborative focus on the explicit learning expectations included in a standard statement or statements, as well as a time to begin considering the implicit expectations.

Phase Two

Based on the broken-apart standard statement(s) and commentaries, team discussions focus on four design points:

1. What are each statement's implicit learning expectations? In other words, what do they infer that students have to know and be able to do? What must be implicitly learned in order to master or move toward mastery of the statement's explicit expectations? The team determines all of the implicit content and skills that need to be included in the map along with the standard statement's explicit learning expectations.

2. What statement or statements do not include a measurable verb or verbs? The team determines appropriate measurable action or ability verbs to replace any nonmeasurable verbs. Likewise, if a standard statement's verb or verbs are measurable but the team believes the expectation is at a lower level of cognition than desired, the team determines an appropriate higher-level-thinking measurable verb or verbs that will be included in the map's learning expectations. When necessary, the team determines each measurable verb's target or targets (e.g., in writing, orally, aurally) in relation to the desired assessment mode(s).

3. A broken-apart statement may or may not include explicit descriptors. To design a rigorous, spiraled curriculum, both horizontally and vertically, curriculum maps must contain clear expectations regarding

content and skill descriptors. This is critical for learning expectations that appear in a series of units in one academic year and those that spiral over a series of years. If any standard statement does not contain specific descriptors, the team determines the implied descriptors that will become explicit in the curriculum map.

4. Content or concept learning in a standard statement may or may not be explicit. Therefore, there may need to be discussion regarding what students are truly expected to know (i.e., key noun: descriptor). If appropriate, discussions may focus on whether the content of a standard statement or statements is topic based or concept based (Erickson 2007). If teachers' desire is to design or refine units of study to reflect concept-based learning, team members may need to take time to study Erickson's (2001, 2002, 2007) model or other conceptual learning models such as *Understanding by Design* (Wiggins and McTighe 1998; see also McTighe and Wiggins 2004) to determine how to transform the topic-based learning to concept-based learning.

During the time taken to address the four focuses, there most likely will be a need to review relational standard statements both above and below the focused grade level or course to aid in the decision-making process. Likewise, in-person discussions or e-mail correspondence with teachers who instruct using relational standard statements may be necessary, especially when considering the implicit learning involved in the statements' learning expectations.

It is a common practice to have a team member designated as a recorder to take notes longhand, or preferably electronically, regarding discussions and decisions made. Be aware that Phase Two, and the upcoming Phase Three, will take time, especially if this procedure is a new concept for teachers. Just as with any new learning, it takes time and experience to get comfortable with the procedural phases.

Phase Three

The third phase involves translating the broken-apart explicit and implicit learning expectations into a curriculum map's scaffolded or spiraled elements within a mapping system. Some teachers prefer to generate a first draft in a Microsoft Word document and eventually copy the information to a curriculum map; others prefer to record the draft within the mapping system from the onset.

A Translation Example. An elementary team is in the process of designing a series of spiraling science units of study that will be taught every other month over the course of a school year. The teachers focus on a set of three relational standard statements and two process standard statements that include the broken-apart standard statement:

- Compare structures in plants (e.g., roots, stems, leaves, flowers) and animals (e.g., muscles, bones, nerves) that serve different functions in growth and survival.

Based on Phases One and Two, as well as collegial discussions and agreement, the teachers have decided to do the following:

- Create a series of five units; the first four units focus separately on plants and animals, and the last unit combines and extends previous learning:

  o GROWTH: PLANTS
  o SURVIVAL: PLANTS
  o GROWTH: ANIMALS
  o SURVIVAL: ANIMALS
  o GROWTH/SURVIVAL: PLANTS/ANIMAL/DISEASES

- Each unit's focus will include the concepts of *structures* and *functions*. While the essential question will relate to both concepts in all the units, specific structures will be included as content descriptors and functions as skills descriptors.

  o While the standard statement does not mandate that students learn roots, stems, leaves, and flowers in relation to plant structures, or muscles, bones, and nerves for animal structures, they will be included in the learning expectations along with others to be collegially determined.
  o The standard statement does not provide any suggestions or mandates regarding plant or animal functions. Functions relating to growth and survival will be determined based on above and below grade-level expectations.

- Before students can compare as indicated in the statement, they first must be able to identify and explain, which will be a skill focus in the first two units. The *compare* skill expectation will be incorporated for the first time in the third unit when students begin to compare and contrast plant and animal growth. A *making connections* processing ability will play a significant role in learning during the last unit, when diseases will be included in the unit of study.
- For the first year of implementation, formative and summative assessments will be left up to the discretion of each classroom teacher. Therefore, no assessments will initially be included in the Consensus Map. During the implementation year, the teachers will periodically meet to discuss the effectiveness of the map, student work, and assessments used. Revision to the Consensus Map for the second year may lead to determining common or same assessments.
- Standards intra-alignment will include collaborative agreement on the level of learning expectation for each statement within each unit of study.
- When appropriate, as each unit is recorded in the mapping system, current textbooks, materials, or kits available to all teachers will be included.

Figure 9.3 represents a very small portion of the first unit of study. Notice that the skill statement has additional expectations (i.e., implicit made explicit) beyond the standard statement's learning regarding each plant structure's function.

Figure 9.3 Growth: Plants Unit of Study

Content	Skills
GROWTH: PLANTS A. Plant Structures: Roots, Stems, Leaves, Flowers	A. Identify in writing individual function of each structure: roots--absorb nutrients, stems--provide support, leaves--synthesize food, flowers--attract pollinators and produce seeds for reproduction A. Explain visually and in writing relational functions of each structure

Phase Four

Once an academic year's Consensus Map or Essential Map units of study have been recorded in the mapping system, vertical review teams check for unintentional gaps, repetitions, or absences in the maps. As mentioned previously, during the first year of implementation a design team periodically evaluates the effectiveness of the learning expectations based on the planned learning.

Changes to any expectations in a planned-learning map can be made with one stipulation. If specific learning has already happened in real time, the data may not be adjusted within the current year's map. Adjustment notations can be recorded either in a separate document or by using a notes feature if one is included in the mapping system. After the map has been archived for the current school year and rolled over to the next school year, appropriate adjustments can be made. This process ensures documentation of accurate evidence of a course's planned-learning curriculum evolution from year to year.

If teachers want to make changes to any learning expectations in units of study before the actual month takes place in the current calendar year, doing so is acceptable and appropriate.

DETERMINING POWER STANDARDS

As mentioned previously, research has clearly pointed out that it is statistically impossible for a student to reach a point of independent mastery for national or state K–12 standards in every discipline within 13 years of schooling. It takes approximately 23 years to master multidisciplinary learning (Marzano 2003). Therefore, teachers must come to agreement on what standard statements are the most powerful and must be included in a collaboratively designed map.

Ainsworth (2003) refers to power standards as

a *subset* of the complete list of standards for each grade and for each subject. They represent the "safety net" of standards each teacher needs to make sure that every student learns prior to leaving the current grade. . . . Once the Power Standards are identified through school and/or district consensus, educators agree to teach these particular standards for depth of student understanding. . . . Meaningful classroom, school, and district assessment are aligned to the Power Standards. (p. 2)

The "complete list" that Ainsworth refers to includes every standard statement within a particular discipline. For example, the Grade 5 Arizona state standards' five mathematics strands include a total of 100 standard statements. Ainsworth suggests that power standards should narrow "the standards within one content area for a particular grade to *approximately one-third* of the total number" (p. 98; italics added). Therefore, a team of teachers would reduce the Grade 5 mathematics total number to approximately 33 standard statements. I find that most learning organizations see this reduction as appropriate for a districtwide Essential Map, but prefer that Consensus Maps be designed based on at least half, if not two thirds, of the total number of appropriate standard statements.

Power standard statements serve as the foundation for the requisite learning. The key is for teachers to come to the agreement that they will focus on the agreed-upon standard statements to a greater learning depth. Students are thereby guaranteed instruction and support to reach independent mastery of the selected power standards.

There are various ways to determine the safety net standards. Ainsworth (2003) gives direction and identification criteria for determining if a standard statement is worthy of power. The identification criteria include the following:

1. *Endurance:* A standard statement that provides knowledge, skills, and proficiency not only for the academic years but for a student's professional and personal life as well.

2. *Leverage:* A discipline-specific standard statement that enables a student to be proficient or excel in one or more other disciplines.

3. *Readiness:* A standard statement that provides a student with essential knowledge and skills needed for the next grade level or series of grade levels or courses.

Given assessment accountability, when appropriate, learning organizations may also include a fourth criterion: *mandatory testing.* Teachers are not allowed to immediately say, "Every statement!" Testing every standard statement given current testing methods is statistically improbable. Teachers must use state-provided data to support any selected standard statements based specifically on this criterion.

This decision-making procedure does not mean that the standard statements not included in an Essential Map or Consensus Map are free from being taught or learned. On the contrary, the inclusion of non–power standard statements is simply left up to the individual teacher's discretion regarding when they will be included in the learning within the school year. Evidence of inclusion appears in each teacher's Diary Map.

Seven-Step Review Focus: Determining Power Standards

The following example of a power standards selection review process was conducted by a middle school mathematics department in preparation for designing Consensus Maps for Grades 6–8. The department prepared for the review by doing the following:

- determining the large-group team members:

  o the entire mathematics department of five teachers
  o one special education teacher

- determining small-group configurations:

  o Team 1: two mathematics teachers *(Focus: Grade 6 Standards)*
  o Team 2: two mathematics teachers *(Focus: Grade 7 Standards)*
  o Team 3: one mathematics teacher and one special education teacher *(Focus: Grade 8 Standards)*

Step 1: Collecting the Data

The large-group team first met collectively to discuss the purpose and the goal of the review. They revisited Ainsworth's (2003) statement that power standards are *"prioritized* standards that are derived from a systematic and balanced approach to distinguishing which standards are absolutely essential for student success from those that are 'nice to know'" (p. 3). They agreed on a marking system for indicating a statement's worth based on four criteria: endurance, leverage, readiness, and testing:

√ Yes, statement should definitely be a power standard.

+ Maybe, but not certain if it should be a power standard.

− No, it should not be included as a power standard.

? Cannot decide.

The review team agreed that a potential power standard statement may meet one or more criteria. Also, if a portion of a detailed statement warranted inclusion, notations should be made regarding the acceptable specific portion of the statement.

Team members were reminded to read relational standard statements in the above and below grade levels to aid in the selection process. A large-group facilitator and a recorder were selected, and an agreed-upon timeline was generated with the understanding that it may need modification once the task got under way.

Step 2: First Read-Through

Each team member privately coded each statement in preparation for the small-group meeting. Here is a sample of one of Team 2 teacher's coding:

√ 7.4.1 Understand coordinate graphs and use them to plot simple shapes; find lengths and areas related to the shapes; and find images under translations (slides), rotations (turns), and reflections (flips).

+ 7.4.2 Understand that transformations such as slides, turns, and flips preserve the length of segments, and that figures resulting from slides, turns, and flips are congruent to the original figures.

Step 3: Small-Group Review

Each small group's designated recorder marked each member's individual coding on one standard-statement Microsoft Word document. Here are the coding results for two statements:

√ + 7.4.1 Understand coordinate graphs and use them to plot simple shapes; find lengths and areas related to the shapes; and find images under translations (slides), rotations (turns), and reflections (flips).

+ −7.4.2 Understand that transformations such as slides, turns, and flips preserve the length of segments, and that figures resulting from slides, turns, and flips are congruent to the original figures.

Each small-group member reviewed the collective coding for each statement and began the selection process based on the following criteria:

- all check marks: collaborative agreement that the statement should be a power standard (in draft form)
- all minus signs: collaborative agreement that the statement should not be a power standard (in draft form)
- all plus signs: further discussion needed
- mixed coding: further discussion needed
- all question marks: statement may need to wait to be addressed in the large-group meeting

After acknowledging unanimous yes's (all check marks) and no's (all minus signs), the floor was open to discussion about the remaining statements. These were the protocols:

1. Be respectful and courteous concerning one another's thoughts and opinions.

2. Set aside a statement if five minutes have been spent on its discussion. Readdress any set-aside statements after remaining statements have been discussed.

After all the statements were collegially discussed, and agreement or nonagreement was determined, each small-group recorder saved the document as an electronic file on the district network server in a folder titled "Grades 6–8 Mathematics Power Standards Review," which had been created by the large-group recorder.

Depending on variables including (a) number of statements, (b) number of initial unanimous agreements, (c) group dynamics and personality types, and (d) educational beliefs, the time needed to complete Step 3 varied slightly per small group.

Step 4: Large-Group Comparison

Prologue to Large-Group Meeting. The large-group recorder created a document that represented the compilation of all three small groups' coding of the Grades 6–8 mathematics standard statements. The recorder sent a copy via district e-mail to each member. Before meeting as a large group, each member read the compilation document and took notes concerning the collective coding, pertaining to not only horizontal learning but also vertical trends, patterns, and concerns about relational statements. Each member was asked to add a personal coding mark for each relational standard statement in the two grade levels not in focus during the small-group meeting.

Comparison Meeting. When the meeting began, the large-group facilitator asked members to share their personal coding for the three grade levels of statements. The recorder added all members' coding to each statement. Here are the comparison results for three Grade 7 statements:

√√ √ √ √ √ 7.4.1 Understand coordinate graphs and use them to plot simple shapes; find lengths and areas related to the shapes; and find images under translations (slides), rotations (turns), and reflections (flips).

√ + –√ √ + 7.4.2 Understand that transformations such as slides, turns, and flips preserve the length of segments, and that figures resulting from slides, turns, and flips are congruent to the original figures.

+ + + + + + 7.4.3 Know and understand the Pythagorean Theorem and use it to find the length of the missing side of a right triangle and the lengths of other line segments. Use direct measurement to test conjectures about triangles.

The large-group facilitator acknowledged the unanimous check-marked statements. The teachers worked through the remaining statements using the same open-floor small-group discussion protocols. It took two one-hour meetings to accomplish the task of determining the power standards for each grade level.

Step 5: Immediate Revision

To see whether there was a need for immediate revision to the drafted power standards, a vertical review of the potential Grade 6–8 mathematics power standards was conducted with teachers from Grades 5 and 10. Their input was provided via e-mail and a few phone calls. The drafted power standards were accessible to all on the district network server, and the large-group facilitator served as a liaison between the team members and the additional reviewers.

Based on the Grade 5 and 10 teachers' recommendations, a few slight modifications were made and the final draft of the middle school mathematics power standards was approved by the middle school mathematics selection review team and shared with the CM Council.

Step 6: Research and Development

Given that the immediate revisions made to the drafted middle school mathematics power standards were agreed on by all, there was no further need for dialogue, discussion, or research. Therefore, this review step was not applicable to the purpose and focus of this review.

Step 7: New Review Considerations

The middle school power standards selection review team was officially disbanded, but the teachers did discuss the possibility of incorporating an official review process when they begin the process of designing Consensus Maps' common assessments, which is part of the next school year's departmental curriculum-mapping action plans.

The preceding example demonstrates that Jacobs's (1997) Seven-Step Review Model is applicable to a variety of curriculum review focuses. Determining power standards can be accomplished using this model or any collaborative model that aids teachers in reaching collective agreement.

CONCLUSION

Both procedures discussed in this chapter are examples of how a learning organization may choose to work toward collaboratively designing planned-learning Consensus Maps and/or Essential Maps. While an emphasis on aligning student expectations to standard statements plays a role in all types of curriculum maps, it is important to remember that standard statements are not *the* learning; they are proficiency targets. By intimately studying and analyzing these targets, teachers can choose to aim for or extend beyond the explicit and implicit student learning expectations. Collaboratively, teachers must work together to design a horizontally and vertically aligned rigorous curriculum whose learning expectations are clear and concise—for teachers, students, parents, and the community.

REVIEW QUESTIONS

Based on your learning organization's long- and short-term mapping goals, answer the following questions. Share your responses with a partner or in a small group.

1. How do you perceive the process of breaking apart standards benefiting teachers in your learning organization when they are ready to collaboratively design curriculum and create Consensus Maps or Essential Maps? (Support your reasoning.)

2. Do you perceive that the breaking apart standards procedure can be used by individual teachers when designing Projected Maps? (Support your reasoning.)

3. At what stage in the mapping process do you think determining power standards may be the most advantageous to designing collaborative curriculum?

4. Given that the goal of collaborative map design means creating an agreed-upon, rigorous horizontally and vertically aligned curriculum, what other educational models or procedures can you think of that would also support the processes and procedures necessary for teachers to come to collective agreement on planned learning expectations beyond the two included in this chapter? (Support your reasoning.)

10

What Should We Consider Regarding Technology?

*Our Age of Anxiety is, in great part, the result of
trying to do today's job with yesterday's tools.*

—Marshall McLuhan

Maps were, for a time, recorded using the tools of paper, pencil, and butcher paper. Gradually recording maps moved to software programs such as Microsoft Word and Excel. Technology capabilities have advanced exponentially in the last 10 years and will only continue to do so (Friedman 2006). Regarding curriculum mapping, Jacobs (2006a) states "the power of the model is its employment of *technology as a key communication device*" (p. 118). The communication device—a 21st-century tool—is a specific-to-mapping system, an interactive, integrated database of maps.

While I have mentioned using a mapping system frequently in the previous chapters, this chapter focuses on selecting a mapping system and includes a comprehensive list of questions to aid in the selection process.

COMMERCIAL ONLINE MAPPING SYSTEMS

All 21st-century mapping systems are Web based. A user enters a specific uniform resource locator (URL) and, when prompted, enters a personalized name and password or guest pass. Most learning organizations choose to purchase a subscription to a commercial online mapping system.

Featured Commercial Systems

The three subscription-based mapping systems featured in Figure 10.1 are not the only commercial systems available. New companies start up annually, and some private and not-for-profit groups choose to develop their own customized systems. The rationale for featuring these three companies is that they were the pioneers in mapping technology and continue to be trailblazers in advancing mapping system capabilities. Likewise, they are leaders in developing and providing multiple-tool options, including assessment management systems and grade book systems.

Ongoing feedback, focus groups, and suggestions from users influence and direct these systems' semiannual updates. Company representatives are knowledgeable in the field of curriculum mapping and passionate about both the mapping process and helping learning organizations improve student learning.

To locate or contact additional mapping system companies, enter *curriculum-mapping system* or *curriculum-mapping software* in an Internet search engine. I must offer a word of caution regarding any additional mapping system companies you find via a keyword search. Be thorough in your questioning, listen closely to company representatives' responses, and be acute when observing the visual aspects of a prospective company's mapping system configuration and search and report features during a demonstration. Make certain the system accurately portrays Jacobs's (1997, 2004b) curriculum-mapping model and the information detailed in the previous chapters.

Figure 10.1 Commercial Mapping System Contacts

Curriculum Mapper	**Rubicon Atlas**	**TechPaths**
Collaborative Learning, Inc.	Rubicon International	Performance Pathways, Inc.
825 N. Cass Avenue, Suite 101	One World Trade Center, Suite 1200	5010 Ritter Road, Suite 119
Westmont, IL 60559	121 SW Salmon Street	Mechanicsburg, PA 17055
Phone: (630) 455-4141, (800) 318-4555	Portland, OR 97204	Phone: (717) 790-0170, (866) 457-1990
Fax: (630) 455-4144	Phone: (503) 223-7600	Fax: (203) 452-8095
info@clihome.com	Fax: (503) 224-7474	info@perfpathways.com
www.clihome.com	www.rubiconatlas.com	www.techpaths.com

Selecting a Mapping System

Selecting a mapping system is part of the prologue. If a large learning organization is engaging in a curriculum-mapping initiative, the mapping system selection process usually involves the Curriculum Mapping Coordinator, Cadre, and Cabinet members. If a mapping initiative is for one school or a small learning organization, a Curriculum Mapping Council or Councils may serve as the selection team. Regardless of size, it is recommended to also have appropriate representation from technology staff (e.g., district level and school site levels) on the selection team.

Since a mapping system is an integral part of the mapping process, selection should not be made quickly or haphazardly. Thoughtful consideration and contemplation should include the following:

- phone or Web conferencing with prospective mapping companies, including asking questions and observing demonstrations of each system's capabilities
- conversing with teachers and administrators in districts already using the potential mapping systems to gain firsthand insights regarding pros and cons of the systems once implemented
- conducting a trial-use period during which each system-selection team member or designated members record, edit, and view a Projected Map month or Diary Map month to grasp each system's ease-of-recording process (e.g., How long did it take to enter the same map data in each system? Was it easy or difficult to enter the elements based on the wording, format, and intra-alignment norms? Was the overall procedure simple or complex? Was it easy or difficult to find and view one's own map and each other's map?)

While all three featured systems are based on Jacobs's (1997, 2004b) Curriculum Mapping Model, each one has distinctive structural interpretations. All three systems offer most of the capabilities displayed in Figure 10.2.

MAPPING SYSTEM CONSIDERATIONS

Effectively selecting a system can be a bit overwhelming if you're still trying to fully grasp curriculum-mapping terminology and concepts. Before contacting any mapping companies, those involved in the selection process need to have a comfortable understanding of the curriculum-mapping basics, including (a) the purpose for each type of curriculum map, (b) how to write the initial common map elements, (c) implementation and sustainability plans regarding the first type of map to be recorded in the system, and (d) the initial problems, issues, or concerns that will be addressed using a mapping system's search and report features.

Questions, Questions, and More Questions

In the fable "Seven Blind Mice," each mouse individually travels to investigate a mysterious *something*. Upon returning, each mouse expounds on the unique features of what it felt, yet each describes a different small creature or item.

Figure 10.2 Mapping System Capabilities

Record and Edit (Modify)	Projected Maps, Diary Maps, Consensus Maps, Essential Maps • Common and additional elements • Discipline-specific, cross-curricular, or interdisciplinary standards • Document attachments • Hyperlinks
Replicate (Copy)	Essential Maps to Consensus Maps Consensus Maps to Projected Maps
Roll Over (Year to Year)	Diary Maps, Consensus Maps, Essential Maps
View	All current and archived curriculum maps
Search	Curriculum maps by keyword, phrase, course title, subject area, teacher, or demographics
Compare	Two or more courses to generate horizontal and vertical reports focusing on one or more elements, disciplines, or teachers Intra- and inter-alignment of content, skills, assessments, evaluations, resources, and additional elements or data
Conduct	Reports for when, where, and by whom standards are or are not addressed; frequency of standard statements, including a breakdown of level of expectations Various reports that focus on specific grading periods, courses, months, units, or elements
Graph	Results of various search and report features using bar, pie, and table configurations

Not until the seventh mouse touches the something, while combining all the individual features, do they correctly conclude that they were actually touching a large elephant. The fable ends with this moral: "knowing in part may make a fine tale, but wisdom comes from seeing the whole."

This moral is applicable to selecting a mapping system. Each set of focus questions in Figures 10.3 and 10.4 represents an individual part of the whole. Final selection should be based on considering the whole mapping system's capabilities. Some of the questions may, at this time, not appear to make sense based on your current knowledge and understanding. Once you begin to observe and study the potential systems, as well as speak to company representatives, the questions and their responses will become clearer and aid in your decision-making process. Figure 10.3 includes questions pertaining to a potential mapping system's specific capabilities. Figure 10.4 includes questions that, when answered, may affect a learning organization's financial and technology structure for supporting the ongoing use of a particular mapping system.

(Text continues on page 228)

Figure 10.3 Mapping System Questions

System Entry and Security	<ul><li>Does the system have a generic URL, or does the company create a specific address for our learning organization?</li><li>What if a user forgets a portion of the entry code such as user name or password?</li><li>Do all learning organization users have access to viewing all types of curriculum maps?</li><li>Do all learning organization users have equal access and ability to record all types of curriculum maps within the system?</li><li>How does the system ensure that only an authorized map writer or writers can record maps or modify existing maps?</li><li>What about students, parents, and the community? How do they gain entry into the system to access and view planned learning maps (e.g., Consensus Maps, Essential Maps)?</li></ul>
User Accounts	<ul><li>How are new user accounts added or created for those joining the learning organization after the initial system setup?</li><li>What about user accounts for commuter teachers or administrators who travel between two or more schools and need the ability to record maps at each school site?</li><li>What happens when a user leaves one school permanently and moves to another school in the district? Does this user need a new account at the new school, or can the existing account be transferred to the new school within the system?</li><li>What about a user who retires or leaves the district entirely? Is this user's account given to the replacement user, or is the account terminated and an entirely new account created for the new user?</li><li>How does a user who is moving to another school between school years, or who is permanently leaving and getting a replacement, affect the annual per-user subscription fee?</li></ul>
Map Type Distinctions	<ul><li>Are Projected/Diary Maps, Consensus Maps, or Essential Maps referred to by a different name within the system or by the company?</li><li>How are the various types of maps distinguished within the system?</li><li>Are users' entry codes identical or different when entering the system to record and edit the various types of maps?</li></ul>
Course Titles	<ul><li>How are course titles initially entered in the system?</li><li>What is the procedure if new course titles need to be added or deleted after the initial entry process?</li><li>Can any school-site user automatically create a new course title? If not, what is the procedure to allow key school-site teachers or administrators to create or modify a course title? If this is not an option, who is allowed to add/edit course titles in the system—a designated person at the district level or someone in the company office?</li><li>Is there a different procedure for entering course titles for a school site versus the entire district, or for each type of map?</li><li>What if a course no longer exists and is terminated in the system, but archived years have maps using the course title? Can the archived maps still be accessed and viewed?</li><li>Does a course title have a procedure for including a course description? If not, where is this information housed within the system?</li></ul>

(Continued)

Figure 10.3 (Continued)

Map Viewing	• How do users access and view their personal Projected/Diary Maps? • How do users access and view one another's Projected/Diary Maps or Consensus Maps at a school site? How do users access and view districtwide Essential Maps? • How do users contact one another regarding viewed map data? By standard e-mail or an intra-system communication procedure? If by an intra-system procedure, how does a user know there is a message to be retrieved? • Can a viewed map's data be reconfigured to fit the monitor screen to maximize the ability to see all included elements simultaneously? • If all viewed element fields are not yet in use, can each element be individually minimized when viewing a map? • Can a map be viewed by a specific month or unit, or must a user view an entire year at one time? Does the ability to view by month or unit change depending on whether the user is viewing his or her own map or viewing another person's map? • Can a viewed map be exported to another format (e.g., Microsoft Word, PDF) and saved to a hard drive or an external source?
Map Replicating and Rolling Over	• How are entire maps or specific months or units replicated (copied) within a current school year? Is there a different procedure depending on what type of map is being replicated (e.g., Essential Map to Consensus Map versus Consensus Map to Projected Map)? • Are there limitations for replicating someone else's Projected/Diary Maps? • How are the various types of maps rolled over from the current school year to the next school year? Is this procedure date sensitive (i.e., must it take place during a specific window of time during the school year)? • Does the system automatically roll over the current year's maps into the next school year's database on a given date, or do users manually roll over the desired maps from year to year? Are there options for how a school or district wants this feature set up or maintained?
Archived Maps	• Where are previous years' (archived) maps stored within the system? • How many previous years of maps can be retrieved and copied into the current school year's map database? • How are archived maps accessed to be viewed? • Can archived maps be accessed and incorporated into the current year's search and report features, or are archived maps only viewable as standalone documents?
Creating a Month or Unit	• Can maps be recorded only by individual months, or does the system have optional settings to record units of study by weeks or grading periods? • Is a unit name optional, or does the system require entering a unit name before any elements can be recorded? • What is the procedure for a user to create a specific month or unit when recording a Projected Map or a Diary Map? • How does a user return to and modify (i.e., edit) data within a previously created Projected Map or Diary Map month or unit? • What is the procedure for a collaborative team to record a specific month or unit for a school-site Consensus Map or a districtwide Essential Map?

	• Can a collaborative team add/edit data in a collaborative map simultaneously, or can only one person be working within a collaborative map at a time? • How do users return to and modify (edit) data within a previously created Consensus Map or Essential Map month or unit?
Map Elements	• Does the system come with predesignated element fields? • Is there flexibility in naming the element fields initially as well as in the future? • Is there flexibility in arranging the order of the element fields? • Is there a limit to the number of element fields the system allows? • Will modifications to a current year's element field's name affect the name of the same field in archived maps? • If we started our mapping process by having teachers first create Microsoft Word or Excel map documents, what is the procedure for copying an existing map month's or unit of study's elements into the system's map element fields?
Text Enhancements	• Are font enhancements such as bold, italic, underline, or color included? • Are scientific or mathematical symbols included? • Are foreign language marks or characters included? • Is there a spell-check feature?
Standards	• How do users access standards to be embedded in (added to) a map? • What is the procedure for embedding standard statements in a map? Is it the same procedure regardless of map type? • Is there flexibility regarding where standard statements can be embedded in a map? • How are standard statements denoted in a map (e.g., symbol, number, full text)? • How are standard statements visually intra-aligned to a map's content, skills, and assessment data? • Can users toggle between and access all grade levels' and disciplines' standard statements to embed in a map regardless of a designated course's primary discipline? • Are all disciplines' standard statements automatically included and accessible within the embedding-standards feature regardless of course, or must the learning organization inform the company of standard statements to be included for a course that are outside of the course's primary learning focus? • Are level-of-learning expectations (e.g., introduce, develop, mastery, reinforce) available for each standard statement? Can multiple levels be selected simultaneously for a standard statement? How do the selected level-of-learning expectations appear visually in a viewed map? • What types of standards (e.g., state, national, specialty, self-created) are initially included in the system's embedding-standards feature? • What if, initially or over time, we want to add standard types that are not originally input by the company? Can someone in the learning organization enter the desired standard statements manually? If yes, what is the procedure? • What happens if state or other types of standard statements change? Does the system automatically update the affected standard statements? If yes, when does the update occur in relation to the release date? Will changes to the standard statements affect the accuracy of embedded standards data made in past years' archived maps? • Does the system have specific search and report features regarding embedded standard statements? If yes, what is the intent of each included report?

(Continued)

Figure 10.3 (Continued)

Attachments	• Can an attachment be added to data included in any element field? • What is the step-by-step procedure for attaching a document within a map? • What type of attachments can be uploaded? • How do users access an attached document when viewing a map? • Where and how are attached documents stored within the system? • Do users have access to manage (e.g., categorize, remove, modify) an attached document collection? • If a user removes an attachment from a current year map that was rolled over or copied, does this action also get rid of the attachment in the archived or copied map? • How much storage space is initially designated per user? Can the initial storage space per user be expanded? If yes, is there an additional fee per user? • Are the actual attached documents read by the system during a search or report request, such as a keyword search?
Hyperlinks	• Can a hyperlink be added in any element field? • What is the procedure for embedding a URL within a map? • How does a URL need to be recorded within a map to activate the hyperlink? • Is an entire hyperlink's visual text seen when viewing a map?
Reference Links	• Are reference links (e.g., Bloom's verbs, differentiated instructional strategies) automatically included in the system? If yes, where are they located? If not, can Web-based reference links be added by an individual user, a school site, or the district? • How are reference links accessed by users when recording maps?
Search Features	• What is the procedure for conducting a systemwide search using keyword or Boolean search strategies? • What is the procedure for conducting a systemwide search using filters to narrow or isolate a search (e.g., one school site, a series of grade levels, one or more disciplines, one or more courses, a small set of teachers)? • How are search results configured? Do result formats vary depending on the type of search conducted? • Do any search features' results have graphic display options that translate textual results into chart or graph views? • Do search results allow users to drill deeper by linking result data to a specific teacher, course, unit, or month?
Report Features	• How many report features are included in the system? What is the intent of each type of report? • Can report results be memorized and reaccessed within the system in the current or future school years? If yes, how is this accomplished? • Are report results displayed textually, graphically, or both? • Can viewed report results be exported to another format (e.g., Microsoft Word, PDF) and saved to a hard drive or an external source? • Do teachers and administrators have access to run the same report features? • Are there additional report features only for administrators? If yes, what is the intent of each administrative report? How are these reports accessed?

Printing	<ul><li>What is the procedure for printing a viewed map?</li><li>Can a viewed map be printed by individual month or unit, or must an entire school year be printed out?</li><li>How do users print archived maps? Can users print one month or unit, or must an entire archived year of months or units be printed?</li><li>If a map is reconfigured to a see-all-the-fields screen view, will elements be cut off when printed?</li><li>Are landscape and portrait options included in the system, or must an option be manually selected within a printer's properties prior to printing a map?</li><li>What if one or more element fields are not currently part of the focus during a mapping review? Can an element be excluded for printing purposes?</li></ul>
Backing Up Map Data	<ul><li>When users are recording a map's element data, does the system automatically back up the inputted information periodically (e.g., instantaneously, every 10 minutes, every half hour), or do users have to do so manually? Are users reminded to back up data periodically if this needs to be done manually?</li><li>How does the company ensure or guarantee that the system's data will not permanently be lost due to power outages or other unforeseen minor or major electronic or technology crises?</li><li>Has the company ever had the system hacked into and lost data because of such an infraction?</li></ul>
User Support References and Services	<ul><li>Are procedural manuals included in the system? If so, are they Web-based and downloadable to hard drive or flash drive? Printable?</li><li>Are there different procedural manuals for teachers versus administrators?</li><li>Are audio/video tutorials included in the system? If so, where are they located? Are there specific technology requirements to run the tutorials?</li><li>Can users make a phone call to reach a live technical support employee? If so, what are the hours for this service, and in what time zone are the support employees?</li><li>Can users submit a question via e-mail? If so, how long before a reply can be expected?</li><li>How often does the company update the system's capabilities? How does the company inform systemwide users that an update is occurring soon? Does the system need to be dormant (e.g., not in use) when an update occurs?</li><li>How are users informed of any new or revised features, reports, or system configurations affected by an update?</li></ul>
Administrative Abilities	<ul><li>Are district-level administrators' features and capabilities different from site-level administrators' features and capabilities? If so, how and to what extent?</li><li>Do school-site administrators, designated lead teachers, or department chairs have the ability to create or modify course titles or map element field names? Can these people manage user accounts and access capabilities for users or guests? If not, who has the ability to do so?</li><li>What percentage of the system's ongoing modifications can be accomplished by the learning organization, school-site or districtwide, versus the company (e.g., 90% learning organization, 10% company)?</li></ul>

Figure 10.4   Learning Organization Support Questions

Italicized questions are those that need to be answered within the learning organization, although the mapping system company may have worthwhile advice.

System Cost	• Given our learning organization's configuration needs, what are the projected initial costs? Are costs calculated per user? Does it matter if a user is a teacher or an administrator? • What if a user works in two or more schools? Is that user's fee still based on a one-user account? • Are there initial or ongoing implementation or maintenance costs outside initial development costs? • Is there an annual subscription fee? • Do subscription fees increase, decrease, or stay the same annually once we have committed to purchasing? • Are there additional costs for the system's new features, reports, or system configuration updates?
Company System-Specific Support	• How many company employees are designated and available for system-specific troubleshooting and maintenance needs when they occur? • Will we be working with a specific person or persons regarding system-specific technology issues or concerns? Is there an additional fee for this service or time spent for assistance? • Is system-specific technical support offered during school hours only or during evening hours as well? What time zone are these technical support employees in? • Can the system-specific technical support employees be reached by phone, e-mail, or both? Is there a company preference regarding how these employees are contacted? • What system-specific training materials are provided in print or online for our technology staff? Are there additional fees for any support materials provided by the company? • Is there a cost for our technology staff's professional development needs regarding system requirements and procedures, both initially and ongoing?
Bandwidth and Speed	• What do you suggest, or mandate, regarding requirements to best utilize the system given our current hardware and network capabilities? • *Is there enough bandwidth for the system to function at its maximum capability during the height of the school day when students, teachers, administrators, and clerical services are simultaneously accessing the Internet? If the speed of access will be lessened with the addition of the mapping system, to what degree?* • *If more bandwidth is deemed necessary, where will the funding come from for the expansion?* • *How long before the expansion can take place?*
System Interface	• Is this a dual-platform system (e.g., Windows and Macintosh)? Are there any issues if users have one platform at school and another at home? • Are there limitations in maximizing the ability to run the system due to certain types of computers, programs, or Internet portals? • Is the system intuitive for nontechnical users? If so, how?
Servers	• What type of system traffic is anticipated? Can the server handle it? • Where and how often will the data from the server be backed up? • Are the backups made over the previous version, or are multiple versions maintained? • Is the underlying database an Object Database Management System (ODMS; e.g., SQL, Oracle)?

Security	• Are both the server and the firewall set up to handle denial-of-service attacks? • Is the firewall on the provider's end monitored by software only or by both software and a human? • Will the system work with our existing firewall and proxy server structure? • Do pop-up blockers cause user issues? If so, how is this addressed by the company and the system?
District System-Use Technical Support	• *Will we need a specific technical system-support person at each school site or a few designated persons for the entire learning organization?* • *Will a specific company person(s) be assigned to our specific person or persons?* • *How will system issues be handled effectively and efficiently throughout the learning organization and at each school site?* • *Will a new paid position or an established person(s) be designated as full-time or part-time for implementing, maintaining, troubleshooting, and fielding technical, system-related questions?* • *Who can contact the inside technical support person(s) (e.g., all users, lead teachers at school sites, administrators)?* • *Will the technology support person(s) be expected to learn about the curriculum-mapping concepts and processes besides the functions of the mapping system?* • *Is the planned technical support person(s) patient and understanding when potentially being confronted by frustrated users?* • *Will this person or persons be able to communicate in nontechnical terms?* • *How will inside technical support be offered to our users (e.g., e-mail, phone, combination)?* • *Will inside technical support be offered during school hours only or during evening hours as well?* • *What will the expected response time be when assistance is requested?*
Optional Integrated Systems	• Can the mapping system be integrated with our existing assessment system or grading system? • If not, does the company offer subscription-based assessment, grading, or other curriculum-based management systems? If yes, what is the additional fee per system? Is this fee based on users, schools, or district? Is there an initial setup/implementation fee or fees? • After mapping is established and functioning well, if we want to explore adding one or more of the company's supplementary systems, is price bundling an option? • How often does the company update its optional integrated systems' capabilities? How does the company inform systemwide users that an update is occurring soon? Does the optional system need to be dormant (e.g., not in use) when an update occurs? • How are users informed of any new or revised features, reports, or system configurations affected by an update?

Developing a Web-Based Mapping System

While most choose to subscribe to a commercial mapping system, some learning organizations prefer to enlist the aid of in-house software developers to design a personalized Web-based mapping system. If there is still a desire to develop a personalized system after reading the questions outlined above and exploring the potential for purchasing a commercial system, it is recommended that a System Design Task Force be formed to accomplish this endeavor. The Curriculum Mapping Coordinator, Cadre, and some Cabinet members should be part of the task force, as should in-house technology experts who are educated in database construction, maintenance, and network security; firewall protection; and hardware systems.

Before beginning the process of developing an in-house mapping system, the task force members must be in mutual agreement regarding, at a minimum, (a) the use, purpose, and integration of each type of curriculum map; (b) initial and potential map element fields; and (c) which of the following system aspects are desired:

- user access to the system, including security features
- visual configuration for each type of map and element field
- course titles and information entry and access per school site as well as districtwide
- procedures for creating personal maps versus collaborative maps
- procedures for adding new maps or editing existing maps and inputting data within maps
- add/edit data features when recording map element text, such as font capabilities (e.g., bold, italics, underline, symbols) and spell check
- attachment capabilities and procedures, including storage space allotment per user
- initial entry of national, state, local, or self-generated standard statements into the system, as well as access in add/edit window, including embedding statements within map fields and a level-of-expectation feature for each standard statement
- configuration and accessibility for viewing personal maps and collaborative maps as well as one another's personal or collaborative maps
- configuration for accessing and viewing maps in a particular school versus throughout the learning organization
- capabilities and procedures for conducting keyword searches, including global-to-specific filters
- types of included report features, both individual and comparison, including how report results will be configured (e.g., textual and/or graphic display; drill-down to or within maps)
- retrieval and viewing of archived maps, as well as the ability to include archived maps in a current school year's search and report features
- method for contacting other system users (i.e., e-mail or in-system messaging)

These items do not represent all that needs to be agreed upon when developing a mapping system. They are intended to provide a beginning point for conversation with the task force's system developers.

The task force development process will also need to include the following steps:

- creating a step-by-step development plan and timelines
- designating the responsible people for each step or portions within a step
- designing a framework and a system-functions prototype to be field-tested online by task force members in order to provide input for necessary modification recommendations (Note: Field testing may need to take place several times before the prototype has reached a level of official use.)
- determining the technology support person(s) for ongoing system maintenance, troubleshooting, and innovations at both district and school-site levels

Developing a self-generated mapping system is not a simple task. If you are interested in this process, try to locate learning organizations that have developed their own system so you can discuss with them the pros and cons of such an enterprise. Regional educational service centers, state educational departments, or curriculum-mapping specialists may be able to assist in providing potential contacts.

CONCLUSION

A mapping system is central to the ongoing mapping process. A system selection team or task force needs to ask prospective companies a lot of questions, test the potential systems by entering maps and using some of the search and report features, and talk to learning organizations that are using the various systems.

While a mapping system is one of the most critical components for ensuring a curriculum-mapping initiative's success and sustainability, be aware that an effective system is not enough. There is synergy between *system* and *understanding.* If teachers are not well trained regarding the purposes and process of curriculum mapping, how to write quality maps, how to design curriculum, and how to use created maps and the mapping system to drive ongoing curriculum reviews and collaborative decision making, the system itself will not matter.

Be proactive. Conduct a thorough mapping prologue and thoughtful mapping system selection process. Likewise, when teachers are asked to map, make certain that they are thoroughly trained in both mapping processes and procedures and how to effectively use the selected mapping system.

REVIEW QUESTIONS

Discuss the necessity for ensuring that your learning organization is involved in 21st-century mapping. With a partner or in a small group, share your responses to the following statements and questions.

1. Since a mapping system is not commonly changed once a learning organization selects a specific company's tool, I am most concerned about the following points regarding the selection of a mapping system. (Support your reasoning.)

2. Although all the questions you ask prospective mapping system companies are important, of the questions listed in Figures 10.3 and 10.4, which ones seem most important to you? (Support your reasoning.)

3. Some learning organizations prefer to create a mapping system selection task force to review the different companies' systems and present their findings to the members of the established curriculum-mapping intra-organizations. Given the total number of members involved in your learning organization's prologue, do you believe you need to form a task force, or can you all play an active role in the system-selection process? (Support your reasoning.)

11

What Should We Focus on When Planning Our Implementation?

One must learn by doing the thing; though you think you know it,
you can't be certain until you try it.

—Sophocles

There is much to be aware of when considering how to best implement a systemic-change model within a learning organization. This chapter culminates the information shared in the past 10 chapters by spotlighting factors that may affect not only a successful implementation but also longevity and sustainability. As Sophocles's quote suggests, it is one thing to talk about getting mapping started; it is another to make it happen. By focusing on five critical components—vision, skills, incentives, resources, and action plans (based on Lippitt, as adapted in Villa and Thousand 2000)—an implementation team can discuss, deliberate on, and design a thoughtful plan and a step-by-step process.

Much of what is shared in this chapter has been mentioned or alluded to in previous chapters. Any mental or written notes you may have taken while reading those chapters may now rise to the surface and play an active role in collegial dialogue pertaining to the five components. Chapter 12 provides practitioners' insights into roadblocks and brick walls that may be encountered even with diligent planning. Some prefer to read Chapter 12 before reading this chapter, while others prefer to read Chapter 12 afterward.

SYSTEMIC CHANGE AND CURRICULUM MAPPING

In the process of examining the individual and collective settings, it is necessary to contend with both the "what" of change and the "how" of change. Meaning must be accomplished in relation to both of these aspects. It is possible to be crystal clear about what one wants and be totally inept at achieving it. . . . We are not only dealing with a moving and changing target; we are also playing this out in a social setting. Solutions must come through the development of *shared meaning.* (Fullan 2001b, pp. 8–9)

A learning organization is a social setting. Fullan's comment regarding explicitly developing shared meaning is critical to developing and executing a curriculum-mapping implementation plan since it involves systemic second-order change.

Shared meaning must be explored and established regarding the aforementioned five components—vision, skills, incentive, resources, and action plans. If any one of these critical components is absent or out of sync, implementation can waiver and ultimately, if not corrected, fail. While each component has its own attributes, they work together to form a synergistic environment.

VISION

If *vision* is a missing critical component, there will be *confusion*.

Shared vision is necessary because it sets the stage for the *what* and *how* Fullan (2001b) refers to regarding change. When members of a learning organization are asked why curriculum mapping was initially pursued, they often provide an answer based on one of the following reasons (Strangeway 2006):

1. **Issue-Motivated Initiative**—A learning organization turns to mapping to address specific problems, issues, or concerns, such as low test scores in a particular discipline or disciplines (e.g., reading, writing, mathematics) or group or subgroups (e.g., special education, free and reduced lunch). Certain members within the learning organization are looking for a quick fix and quick results in relation to the problematic area(s) of concern.

2. **Grassroots Initiative**—A learning organization turns to mapping after a small number of administrators, teachers, and/or parents learn about curriculum mapping at a conference or from other types of informational resources and believe mapping the curriculum will help students improve academically. The stakeholders realize or feel that the present curriculum has gaps, redundancies, and absences and want to

create stronger horizontal and vertical articulation and communication between teachers.

3. **Good to Great**—A learning organization is considered successful by its own criteria or current personal, local, state, or national criteria; however, it wants to stay competitive and continue to improve learning expectations for both students and teachers. Stakeholders look to mapping as an active tool and catalyst that will enable teachers and administrators to exceed current learning requisites and establish a deeper sense of rigor regarding the curriculum and learning environments.

When a learning organization is planning to implement curriculum mapping based on the first reason, trouble lies ahead. Curriculum mapping is not meant to be a quick fix. It is never intended to be implemented and then dropped after a few years. It is meant to be a forever model that requires a learning organization to conduct its curriculum business continuously in a new manner. It is a replacement model (Jacobs 2004b).

When a learning organization gets involved in mapping for the second reason, there is often not enough critical mass to gain momentum, which can make expanding a shared vision difficult. It is therefore important to expand capacity as soon as possible by inviting a consortium of teachers and administrators to gain or expand personal and collective curriculum-mapping knowledge and understanding through involvement in one or more of the mapping intra-organizations.

The third reason works well if everyone in a learning organization already has a shared vision and desires to move from good to great. Problems arise when this is not actually the case. There may be some or many who are happy and content resting on their laurels and do not want to expand their personal or collective horizons, which may cause them to make slight or significant changes. Therefore, thoughtful preplanning and prologue are still critical in a good-to-great learning organization.

Setting the Stage

Why Are We Mapping?

Given Strangeway's (2006) three reasons for building upon your learning organization's history of curriculum design, student learning success, and collegial decision making, a shared vision must be explicitly explored, formulated, and made clear to all stakeholders (e.g., administrators, teachers, students, board members, community) regarding why curriculum mapping is a worthwhile model and a long-term endeavor. Plan to revisit the shared vision often, especially in the first few years of your initiative's implementation.

Some people, even those involved from the onset, may lose sight of the *why* while attempting to gain deep understanding of the complexities of mapping and making sense of what the mapping processes and procedures ask of teachers throughout the learning organization. To help keep the shared vision in focus, many learning organizations create a link on their school or district Web site's home page that directs users and visitors to the selected curriculum-mapping system, various curriculum-mapping documents, and helpful resources such as a *reasons for curriculum-mapping* document.

What Are the Curriculum and Learning Concerns We Want to Focus on Immediately, as Well as Those We Anticipate Focusing on in the Future?

The problems, issues, or concerns related to why curriculum mapping is chosen for implementation can vary greatly. Specific reasons may become evident through the study of current testing results, previous and current curriculum review results, and/or existing but hushed problems. Current problems, issues, and concerns need to be explicitly discussed and ranked in order from the most to least concerning. The ranked order will influence your initial shared vision and focuses for both the short- and long-term implementation plans.

If possible, collegial conversations during this time should not be limited to preplanning members. Teacher surveys provide critical insight and input from those who work most closely with the students. Likewise, asking students for their thoughts and perspectives is at times quite revealing. They often express observations or opinions quite different from what teachers and administrators have perceived or presumed.

Who Will Be Responsible for Establishing Our Shared Vision and Our Mapping Initiative's Implementation, Monitoring, and Revision Needs?

This is a critical question. If the answer is not explicitly known, the uncertainty causes confusion and will affect the other four components. Jacobs (2004b) says that the best way to set the stage and create a clear and concise vision is to conduct a prologue:

> "Prologue" in Greek means "before the action of a play." Setting the stage, literally and figuratively, elevates the attention of all participants— the actors, the director, and the audience. As I have observed schools and districts develop their mapping projects, ample preparation time has characterized the most effective attempts. Clearly, the most successful education settings have crafted a prologue to their actions. They used advanced scouting reports, research, and discussion groups before they applied substantial effort and energy. Then they identified key people and charged those people with advanced planning for the new and dynamic shift in curriculum decision making. Those effective districts and schools gave themselves permission to find out what they needed to know in order to create the condition for success. (p. 1)

It is recommended that a prologue last approximately two-thirds of a school year, if not one full school year, before a learning organization begins an all-teacher implementation.

During the prologue responsible parties and their responsibilities are established through the incorporation of various curriculum-mapping intra-organizations. Members learn about the complexities of mapping, including the purposes for each type of curriculum map as well as how to write quality maps, use the selected mapping system, and conduct reviews involving the seven-step review process. They also serve as liaisons to share and establish the vision with the remaining teachers throughout the implementation process.

The teachers and administrators who are directly involved in the intra-organizations and prologue meetings need to become savvy in all aspects of curriculum mapping and the selected mapping system. It is recommended that they take advantage of multiple curriculum-mapping learning opportunities such as attending the national curriculum-mapping institute held each summer (www.curriculumdesigners.com), regional curriculum-mapping conferences and workshops, local educational service center workshops and trainings, and in-house trainings conducted by a curriculum-mapping consultant or trainer. Taking online courses; visiting, communicating, or networking with learning organizations that have already implemented a curriculum-mapping initiative; and leading book or video studies throughout the learning organization are beneficial ways to immerse preplanning members in expanding their personal and collective understanding of curriculum mapping.

The following information provides insight into each intra-organization's role and job description.

Curriculum Mapping Intra-Organizations

All four intra-organizations are necessary for a large multiple-schools learning organization. If a lone school is planning to begin a mapping initiative, forming a Curriculum Mapping Council and possibly a modified Curriculum Mapping Cadre is sufficient.

Curriculum Mapping Coordinator

The Curriculum Mapping (CM) Coordinator organizes and attends the CM Cadre, the CM Cabinet, CM Councils, and district-level curriculum task force meetings. The CM Coordinator serves as the liaison and key communicator between the collective CM intra-organizations, all levels of administration, board members, and the community. This person plays a significant role in strategic planning and development alongside the CM Cadre and CM Cabinet. The coordinator also assists in ensuring that necessary initial and ongoing professional curriculum-mapping training sessions are in place and attended. Along with the CM Cadre, this person takes on responsibility for becoming one of the learning organization's resident experts in both curriculum mapping and the selected mapping system.

The CM Coordinator may or may not be a district-level employee. If the person is an employee at the district level, he or she may already be in charge of controlling the monetary allowances designated for the prologue, the initial implementation, and ongoing curriculum-mapping needs, such as (a) the annual subscription cost for a selected commercial mapping system; (b) professional development costs and/or stipends for attendees and trainers; (c) substitute pay for release time so teachers can learn to map, map, or use created maps to drive curriculum discussions if board-approved early-release, late-start, or full mapping days have not yet been built into the official school calendar; and (d) intra-organization members' fees to attend various national, state, or local curriculum-mapping conferences or workshops.

If instead the CM Coordinator is a teacher who has been charged with an implementation administrative role, he or she will need to work closely with the administrator(s) in charge of budgetary and policy allowances.

Curriculum Mapping Cadre

The CM Cadre is a team of approximately five to seven people who meet certain criteria, including a high interest in curriculum and curriculum design and an understanding of administrative insights into the learning organization's past and present culture, climate, and curriculum issues and needs. The CM Cadre may not be made up solely of district or school site administrators. There is often a mix of administrators and key teacher leaders. CM Cadre members do the following:

- become resident experts in all aspects of curriculum mapping in order to help determine the learning organization's shared vision and the initial implementation processes and procedures as well as plan the ongoing next-steps progression
- become resident experts in the chosen mapping system once it has been selected by the CM Cabinet (or if only one school is implementing mapping, the CM Council) and help connect the use of the system's search and report features to the collection of map data and other data
- help train teachers and administrators in the complexities of mapping, including understanding the map types, writing quality maps, how to conduct seven-step reviews using curriculum maps, the mapping system, and, when appropriate, other data sources by utilizing a curriculum-mapping consultant or trainer's services, or determining appropriate in-house people (including CM Cadre members themselves) who will fill this role or roles
- meet to inform and establish curriculum-mapping relationships with key stakeholders such as curriculum and related superintendents, assistant superintendents, program directors, board of education, union representation, and the community
- attend all CM Cabinet meetings and, when appropriate, CM Council meetings; when necessary, cadre members also attend curriculum-related functions such as board meetings or community forums whose agenda items pertain to various aspects of the curriculum-mapping initiative

Curriculum Mapping Cabinet

The CM Cabinet is a districtwide team consisting of teachers from all school sites, each school-site administrator, the CM Cadre, the CM Coordinator, and the technology support person, all of whom represent a diversity of all grades and all curricular areas. Total membership will vary depending on each school site's faculty population. On average, there is a 1:15 representation ratio; 1 school-site teacher representative for every 15 teachers at the school site. For example, if a school has 60 teachers, three to four representatives will serve on the CM Cabinet. Please take note that this ratio is an estimate. If a district's average number of teachers per school site is 10, there should be 2 teachers per school serving on the CM Cabinet to allow for a better balance of personal perspectives, disciplines, and grade level representation.

CM Cabinet members become mentally and emotionally prepared and confident in all curriculum-mapping processes and procedures since they serve as liaisons between the collective school sites and their own school site. The CM Cabinet members are key players and decision makers regarding the initial and next steps concerning the learning organization's districtwide prologue and implementation plans, including, but not limited to, selecting the mapping system; determining the first in-focus districtwide discipline given current problems, issues, or concerns that need to be resolved; generating an anticipated timeline for when teachers will begin to map and begin to conduct reviews using created maps and the mapping system's search and report features; and determining the teachers' step-by-step training needs regarding the various aspects of mapping and the selected mapping system.

For the prologue, and at least through the first half-year of full-scale implementation, the CM Cabinet usually meets in person on a monthly basis. Into the second full-scale implementation year and beyond, the CM Cabinet usually meets in person bimonthly or once a grading period depending on districtwide implementation needs and concerns. CM Cabinet members do the following:

- agree to serve on the CM Cabinet for a two- to three-year commitment; after the initial construction of the CM Cabinet, when all members are new, it is recommended that members rotate off and on in a staggered fashion so that there is always a balance between fresh perspectives and seasoned participants
- agree to participate fully in ongoing CM Cabinet meetings and curriculum-mapping professional learning opportunities (e.g., book or video study, conference attendance, district training, school-site-specific training)
- serve in a dual role by being both a CM Cabinet member and a CM Council member, and participate in both district and school-site decision-making, implementation, and accountability processes
- gain a strong understanding and high level of confidence regarding all aspects and features of not only curriculum mapping but also the selected mapping system to reach the point of being confident and comfortable in conducting or aiding in mapping-system trainings or follow-up support
- assist district and school-site administrators, the CM Coordinator, and the CM Cadre in any aspect of implementation or ongoing strategic planning

Curriculum Mapping Council

For curriculum mapping to truly become sustained, it is critical that each school site in a learning organization establishes and maintains its own CM Council. A school site's CM Council consists of teachers, administrators, and technology support personnel, who represent all grade levels, disciplines, and support services. CM Council membership is approximately represented in a 1:5 ratio—one CM Council member to every five teachers. Council members become mentally and emotionally confident in all processes and procedures of curriculum mapping and the selected mapping system. Members participate in ongoing curriculum-mapping professional learning opportunities to become familiar with the districtwide implementation plans in order to help collaboratively design annual school-site action plans. CM Council members do the following:

- agree to at least a two-year service commitment; similar to the suggestion made for the CM Cabinet, after the initial implementation of a CM Council, when all members are new, it is recommended that members rotate off and on in a staggered fashion so there is always a balance between fresh perspectives and seasoned participants

- agree to actively participate in curriculum-mapping professional learning opportunities (e.g., book or video study, conference attendance, district training, school-site-specific training)
- assist, in an ongoing manner. a designated team of five or six mixed-group faculty members by helping them gain personal and collective understanding, including both the districtwide and school-site requisites for designing the various types of curriculum maps, writing quality maps, recording maps in the mapping system, and using the created maps and the mapping system's search and report features to help with data collection when conducting curriculum reviews
- commit to meeting as a council in person each month to

    o prepare or modify the school-site annual curriculum-mapping action plans
    o discuss site-based teacher, grade-level, or department progresses, challenges, and concerns, and if necessary, determine immediate actions or necessary modifications to the action plans based on the current pulse in relation to school-site and district mapping requisites
    o recommend immediate or future curriculum mapping or related professional development learning for the entire school, small groups, or individual teachers
    o plan for informal and formal celebrations of both the small steps and the giant leaps made regarding various aspects of the curriculum-mapping processes and procedures
    o assist school-site principal, other administrators, and fellow CM Cabinet member(s) in any aspect of implementation or sustainability that calls for personal or collective support

Potential Prologue Timeline

Figure 11.1 outlines a sample timeline for a prologue year. As with any initiative's timeline, monitoring and adjusting may be necessary during the course of a prologue year.

School principals and administrators are highly encouraged to be involved in both the CM Cabinet and a CM Council. Their understanding of all aspects of curriculum mapping plays a significant role in school-site-level success and sustainability. Principals who encourage teacher leadership (DuFour, DuFour, Eaker, and Many 2006; Fullan 2005; Marzano, Waters, and McNulty 2005; McEwan 2003; Wiggins and McTighe 2007) and carve out adequate time for teachers to be curriculum designers truly are successful in establishing curriculum mapping as a student-learning improvement model.

By conducting an engaging and well-thought-out prologue, a learning organization sets itself up for a higher chance of successful implementation and sustainability throughout the organization. It is important to build shared vision slowly and steadily during the prologue year.

All CM Cabinet and CM Council meetings are intended to be open to anyone who wants to attend. When a meeting is planned, the date and agenda should

Figure 11.1 Potential Prologue Timeline

Phase	Curriculum Mapping Coordinator	Curriculum Mapping Cadre	Curriculum Mapping Cabinet	Curriculum Mapping Council
First Phase: One to Three Months*	Self-selected or designated person begins personal and collaborative learning alongside CM Cadre	Self-selected or designated persons begin personal and collaborative learning alongside CM Coordinator		
Second Phase: Two to Three Months**	Instructs CM Cabinet regarding various curriculum-mapping processes so all members can begin to make implementation decisions and collaboratively develop a step-by-step districtwide action plan	Instructs CM Cabinet regarding various curriculum-mapping processes so all members can begin to make implementation decisions and collaboratively develop a step-by-step districtwide action plan	Selected by invitation or application, members begin personal and collaborative learning with CM Coordinator and CM Cadre's guidance and provide points of view and recommendations for collaborative development of districtwide action plan	
Third Phase: Two to Three Months***	Aids and supports CM Cabinet members' instruction to school-site CM Council members regarding curriculum-mapping processes and mapping system so school-site members can begin to develop school-site action plans based on districtwide action plan	Aids and supports CM Cabinet members' instruction to school-site CM Council members regarding curriculum-mapping processes and mapping system so school-site members can begin to develop school-site action plans based on districtwide action plan	Instructs school-site CM Council members regarding various curriculum-mapping processes and mapping system so school-site members, including appropriate CM Cabinet members, can begin to develop school-site action plan based on districtwide action plan	Selected by invitation or application, members begin personal and collective learning with CM Coordinator, CM Cadre, and school-site CM Cabinet members' guidance regarding curriculum-mapping processes and mapping system and develop a school-site action plan based on districtwide action plan

(Continued)

Figure 11.1 (Continued)

* Mapping systems may be investigated but not selected until the second phase, when the CM Cabinet members can also play a role in the investigation and final selection process.

**Intra-organization members discuss and determine
- what the first districtwide discipline focus will be, as well as plan a sequence for remaining districtwide discipline focuses, including traditional courses (e.g., mathematics, science, social studies, language arts), traditional specialists (e.g., art, music, physical education, library science, technology), distinctive disciplines (e.g., world languages, family and consumer science, automotive), and unique courses (e.g., senior school-to-workplace, mentoring, on-campus community college);
- what type of map will be incorporated during the first year of full implementation for traditional disciplines, traditional specialists, distinctive disciplines, and unique courses, as well as map expectations for special education (e.g., inclusion, pullout, self-contained);
- what map elements will be initially included (e.g., five common elements, one or more additional elements), which may vary slightly depending on type of map(s) chosen;
- map-writing wording, format, intra-alignment norm expectations;
- teachers-as-learners map recording expectations (e.g., recording one new element per month in the selected mapping system until all expected elements have been included, recording all expected elements at once), which may vary slightly depending on type of map(s) chosen;
- selection of mapping system, including purchasing subscriptions, or developing own system.

**Intra-organization members begin to
- practice writing map elements and recording map elements within the selected mapping system;
- explore the concept of breaking apart standard statements
- explore the concept of determining power standards for potential use when consensus or essential mapping

***All intra-organizations finalize and implement both the districtwide and school-site action plans, and members continue or begin to
- practice writing map elements and recording map elements within the selected mapping system;
- explore the selected mapping system's various functions related to (a) recording various types of maps as well as initial and additional elements, (b) adding or modifying course titles and information regulated to courses, and (c) using the search and report features and brainstorming how the features may be used to aid curriculum reviews and make ongoing data-based collaborative decisions.

be announced. If nonmember teachers, students, parents, or community members choose to attend (although meetings may take place during school business hours), they should be, if desired, offered a time to address the intra-organization members.

Mapping Mapping

Administrators often choose to map the mapping processes and procedures in relation to the districtwide or school-site-specific action plans by creating a curriculum map within the selected mapping system. While this form of mapping mirrors much of what is included in teacher-designed curriculum maps that address student learning expectations, the skill statements included in a professional development map may have a tendency to gravitate toward more of an activity statement than a true skill statement. Not only may administrators' or professional development directors' maps contain skill statements that, based on the measurable verb, express an event or an activity rather than a true skill; the recorded assessment performance or product assessments may not always include evaluation processes or criteria. Figure 11.2 is a CM Coordinator's Projected Map month.

Do We Need a Curriculum Mapping Consultant or Trainer to Help Us Create Our Shared Vision?

This is an often-asked question and is, in essence, tied to the other four critical components. I mention it here because curriculum-mapping consultants and trainers often play a role in helping a learning organization shape its desired shared vision. Many learning organizations choose to involve a curriculum-mapping consultant and trainer in the prologue and implementation phases because there is much to be cognizant of when first learning about curriculum mapping while having to simultaneously determine what is best regarding both short- and long-term action plans.

While curriculum-mapping consultants and trainers are available at national, state, and local levels, make certain during phone or in-person interview sessions that the person you are considering has a deep understanding of the complexities of Jacobs's (1997, 2004b) model. If a prospective specialist lacks such understanding, it will become apparent when he or she answers your preplanned questions. Likewise, the prospective consultant and trainer will ask questions of you that will be equally telling. It is best to discern early on whether the time, monies, and relationship building you plan to invest in this person will be well spent and worthwhile. Someone who is well-versed in curriculum mapping should be able to do both: consult by inquiry to provide ongoing directional advice based on the historical and current culture, climate, environment, and the reasons for wanting to begin and sustain a mapping initiative; and train by teaching and coaching small or large groups of teachers and administrators regarding the various aspects of mapping and the basic and advanced features and uses of the selected mapping system.

It is not recommended that you involve multiple consultants and trainers during the early learning phases, including the prologue and initial implementation. While most consultants and trainers adhere to the 10 Tenets of Curriculum Mapping outlined in Chapter 1, their interpretation and points of view regarding proposed implementation processes and procedures vary. During the early stages of learning, bringing in a variety of people who potentially have various viewpoints can create or intensify confusion. After the establishment years (usually into the third year), when the critical stages of implementation have passed, bringing in specialty consultants with expertise in assessment design, technology integration, instructional strategies, and other related topics is encouraged.

When interviewing, focus on finding a consultant and trainer who is a good fit for your learning organization's culture and needs. Consider the prospective

Figure 11.2 Curriculum Mapping Coordinator's Projected Map Month

Month	Essential Questions	Content	Skills	Assessment
April	*How does knowledge influence learners?* SQ How may curriculum mapping promote a continuum for students' acquisition of knowledge? SQ How may past cultures at each school site and in each district influence curriculum-mapping implementation?	**CM CABINET: SYSTEMIC CHANGE** A. Substantial Change: 5 Critical Components Resources --Curriculum Mapping Implementation Critical Components Matrix --Second-Order Change Document B. Quality Map Intra-Aligned Elements: Content, Skills, Assessments, Resources, Standards Resources --Sample Teacher Maps from CM conferences --How to Write Quality Maps Checklists --Map Element Puzzle	A1. Summarize orally initial interpretation of presence/absence of vision, skills, resources, incentives, action plan components based on matrix A2. Construct in writing parallel matrix to reflect specific concerns for district regarding implementation and level of administrative understanding A3. Appraise orally and respond in writing to mapping system task-force report on potential system purchase B1. Define quality orally as "map readers do not need map writer or writers present to interpret map data" B2. Analyze and distinguish visually sample maps reflecting quality versus moving toward quality elements B3. Summarize orally rationale for establishing districtwide quality map-writing norms	A1-A2. District's Critical Components Matrix A3. Mapping System Selection Confirmation B1-B3. Write-a-Month Map Simulation B1-B3. Meeting Discussion/Postmeeting Discussions

person's curriculum-mapping knowledge and expertise, comfort level with using various mapping systems, personality, and availability. During the prologue year a mapping specialist plays a significant role in training intra-organization members to function as a team and helping the members formulate the shared vision and develop action plans. Likewise, this person works alongside the cabinet and council members to inform and train all members within the learning organization during the first year of implementation.

Oftentimes a curriculum-mapping consultant and trainer is utilized for the first two to three years of a mapping initiative. During the prologue year it is not uncommon for this person to make district visits every month or two. For the first half of the full-implementation year, this person is often actively involved in teacher trainings, which may involve monthly or bimonthly visits depending on the confidence level of the cabinet and council members who conduct or plan the trainings. By the end of the second full year of implementation, a curriculum-mapping consultant and trainer is usually providing support from afar, with an occasional on-site visit for additional training for the CM Cabinet and Councils. This person's services are usually no longer needed by the end of the third year of implementation.

One final aspect regarding the concept of establishing a shared vision cannot be overlooked. Over time the shared vision will naturally evolve. Do not expect the initial vision to remain the same as a district and/or individual school site gains deeper understanding of curriculum mapping as a hub for focusing on engaged learning and dynamic professionalism (Jacobs 2007). As teachers and administrators spend time engaged in the mapping processes and procedures, they naturally desire to make additions or modifications to the established shared vision.

SKILLS

If *skills* is a missing critical component, there will be *anxiety*.

A skill is a proficiency, facility, or dexterity that is acquired or developed through training or experience. Necessary skills abound in conjunction with learning about the types of maps and the elements within a map, learning how to write a quality map, recording a map in the selected mapping system, using the mapping system for data retrieval and analysis, and conducting curriculum reviews. Any time someone is in the throes of learning something new that is multifaceted, professionally or personally, there will be moments of apprehension and anxiety (Jensen 2000). This is normal and should be expected and planned for accordingly.

What Will Our Teachers Need to Know and Be Able to Do to Design Curriculum, Write Quality Maps, and Use the Created Maps and Mapping System to Help Conduct Mapping Reviews?

The answer to this question is explained in detail throughout Chapters 2 through 9. The key is determining the correct order in which the teachers will be provided various trainings as well as conveying expectations regarding the various skills that need to be learned.

Whatever the correct order may be for a particular learning organization or school site, as mentioned previously, there must be a public announcement that no curriculum maps, map data, or review collaborations or conversations will be used for formal or informal teacher evaluations or punitive actions. It must be acknowledged up front that it does and will take time to build personal and collaborative curriculum-mapping skills and abilities. Teachers will be concerned about this right from the start given the fact that curriculum mapping is a mandated initiative. If there is even the remotest suspicion that maps will be used for teacher evaluation, do not be surprised when teachers begin to simply go through the motions or disengage altogether.

An important emotional point that needs to be recognized and addressed at this time is that some teachers may display what appears to be passive-aggressive behavior by not wanting or attempting to learn the expected skills in hopes that mapping will go away. This behavior is rarely insubordinate in nature; rather it is due to high stress given an often overwhelming number of currently implemented initiatives and expectations. As McEwan (2005) points out, "there is an attitude, even among some of the best teachers, that screams, 'Don't ask any more of me!'" (p. 97).

Remember that there is a symbiotic relationship between the five critical components. *Skills* is tied to *incentives*. If teachers do not quickly sense personal and collective purpose for using sacred time to engage in learning the necessary skills that they must know and be able to do, they will continue to be reluctant to buy in to both the initial and ongoing learning processes.

For some learning organizations, asking teachers to become the leaders in curriculum design may be a shift in current cultural practice and skill, especially if past or current curriculum decision making has occurred in a top-down fashion. Based on my observations, when the curriculum-design reins are handed over to teachers there is a potential for mixed results due to varying curriculum-design skill comfort levels:

- Some teachers will grab the reins and ask why they were not offered to them sooner.
- Some will have trust issues since they have never been offered the reins before and will not know what to make of it all when they are handed over.
- Some will not feel confident and will hold the reins with an awkward grip since no one has ever taught them how to properly steer.
- Some will immediately drop the reins because they do not see it as their responsibility to hold the reins or to steer.

In the preplanning phase it is important to focus on the point that Fullan (2001b) makes: we are not only dealing with a moving and changing target but also playing this out in a social setting. The social setting referred to here connects with Barth's (2006) four professional relationships. If teachers do not currently function using social skills that support collegial relationships, it may prove difficult to implement the collaborative nature of mapping in horizontal, vertical, like-group, and mixed-group curriculum decision-making environments.

Likewise, since curriculum mapping places curriculum design and decision making squarely into the teachers' hands, it is absolutely essential that school administrators are equally trained in the skills of mapping to support teacher leadership and working as a team. It is therefore wise to take a candid look at the present culture and dynamics of how each school site's teachers and principal function as a team (Senge 1994). If a principal does not currently exercise quality leadership and support, both covertly and overtly, which directly affects teacher leadership, then curriculum-mapping implementation and sustainability will be nearly impossible (Marzano, Waters, and McNulty 2005).

To best understand what skills are involved when learning to write a quality map, it is recommended that each principal have some firsthand experience in writing a map to gain insight into the enormous learning curve that confronts teachers during the first year or two of a curriculum-mapping initiative. Figure 11.3 shows an example of a principal who desired to embrace and internalize the complexities of mapping and writing a quality map. The principal integrated the skills involved in writing a quality map with documenting the school's annual Literacy Action Plans in the form of a Consensus Map.

Figure 11.4 is a sample map month of a principal who wanted to internalize what her teachers were learning about the process of writing a quality Diary Map. For her administrative map, she decided to subdivide the included data so that it represented her personal responsibilities as well as those of her teachers.

The critical role administrators play in establishing curriculum mapping as the new way of conducting curriculum business is important for sustainability. Principals must remain vigilant in working with teachers as they all learn initial and new skills related to various aspects of curriculum mapping. Highly effective principals support second-order systemic change best by understanding and valuing the change process, being willing to change themselves, procuring resources, using a situational approach, being able to handle uncertainty and ambiguity, respecting resisters, knowing that the power is within, trusting their teams, planning for short-term victories, and being motivators (McEwan 2003).

During the prologue, the intra-organizations' members are the first to become actively involved in learning the various skills needed to ensure that mapping becomes institutionalized. As the members engage in the learning process, they provide firsthand insight and advice that often affect the development of step-by-step action plans related to the initial and long-term skills expectations of teachers and administrators alike.

RESOURCES

If *resources* is a missing critical component, there will be *frustration*.

Resources can be represented in multiple ways. For example, the role of the principals mentioned in the previous paragraphs can be viewed as a resource.

Figure 11.3 Elementary Literacy School Improvement Plan Consensus Map—First Grading Period

Content (What teachers/school administrator must know)	Skills (What teachers/school administrator must be able to do in relationship to the knowing)	Assessment (How results of knowing/doing are evaluated in relation to student learning)
SCHOOL IMPROVEMENT PLANS FOR ENGLISH LANGUAGE ARTS		
A. Student Performance: Data Analysis Resources --ISAT School Performance Profile --IL Frameworks for Assessment Content Categories Table --Gates Test Results --IOWA Test Results	A1. Identify in writing statistical patterns of horizontal and vertical weaknesses and strengths by comparing and contrasting 3 years of data A2. List in writing targeted areas and appropriate state standards for improvement A3. Identify in writing disaggregate groups representing special needs in targeted areas A4. Prioritize in writing grade-level targets for improvement using IL Frameworks for Assessment and vertical articulation	A1-B2, C2-C4, D1. Monthly Action Plan Results Report (Evaluation: Student Learning Results) A1-A4. Target Area(s) Table (Evaluation: Group Consensus)
B. Standards: Coverage Breakdown Resources --Diary Maps --Standards Reports: Standards vs. Courses, Search for Missing Standards, General Search, Compare Courses, What Am I Missing?	B1. Analyze orally and in writing Diary Maps to determine frequency and depth to which standards are addressed in targeted areas B2. Compare and contrast orally and in writing horizontal and vertical alignment of Diary Map element fields in targeted areas	B1-B2. Mapping System Standards Analysis Report (Evaluation: Group Consensus)
C. Action Plan: Improvement Strategies Resources --IL Standards, Frameworks for Assessment, Performance Descriptors --Diary Maps	C1. Generate orally and in writing self-selected grade-level and personal research plan to identify best practices in reading using Internet links or personal resources C2. Report orally and in writing research-based recommendations and results of use for improvement in targeted areas	C1. FOR Grade-Level Research Planning Chart (Evaluation: Self-Assessment Checklist) C2-C4. Research-Based Strategies Report (Evaluation: Group Consensus)

Content (What teachers/school administrator must know)	Skills (What teachers/school administrator must be able to do in relationship to the knowing)	Assessment (How results of knowing/doing are evaluated in relation to student learning)
--http://www.isbe.net/ils/ela/capd.htm (English Language Arts: Classroom Assessments and Performance Descriptors—Index Page) --http://dese.mo.gov/divimprove/edprog/Bestpractices/Recent%20Best%20Practices%20Messages.htm (Recent Best Practices' Messages) --http://www.psea.org/article.cfm?SID=197 (PSEA Best Practices in Reading) --http://dese.mo.gov/divimprove/fedprog/Bestpractices/Web%20Resources.htm (Best Practices Web Resource and Publications) --http://clerccenter.gallaudet.edu/Literacy/about/reading.html (Priority: Literacy Best Practices in Teaching Reading) D. Student Works: Improvement Evidence Resources --Grade-Level Student Sample --Performance Assessment Indicators	C3. Identify orally and in writing grade-level student skills for improvement in targeted areas, lesson-plan recommendations to incorporate best practices/instructional strategies, performance assessments as indicators of improvement C4. Identify in writing modification strategies for differentiating instruction to address disaggregate students C5. Formulate in writing assessment criteria to determine impact on student learning C6. Determine in writing scheduled meeting dates for collaborative evaluation of student work samples D1. Evaluate orally and in writing student samples for designated target areas using performance assessment indicators (e.g., state rubrics/performance descriptors, staff-developed rubrics/checklist) D2. Formulate orally and in writing a revised plan of action based on student samples/assessment results	C5. Student Impact Assessment Plan (Evaluation: Group Consensus) C6. Action Plan Calendar (Evaluation: Completion Checklist) D1. Strategy Assessment Report (Evaluation: Student Learning Results) D2. FOR Revised Action Plan Chart (Evaluation: Self-Assessment Checklist)

Figure 11.4 Elementary Principal Professional Development Diary Map Month

Month	Content	Skills	Assessment
August	**READING** A. Houghton Mifflin Training: Grades K-1/Grades 2–3/ Grades 4–5 Resources --Houghton Mifflin Representative --Houghton Mifflin Teacher Guides/Grade-Level Materials **CURRICULUM MAPPING** B. School Site: New Teachers Orientation Resources --CM PowerPoint Presentations --Web-Based Mapping System	*Teachers* A1. Discuss scientifically based research related to reading series A2. Explore visually comprehension instructions included in series and supplemental resources to ensure student success in 5 dimensions of Reading First: Phonemic Awareness, Phonics, Fluency, Vocabulary, Comprehension A3. Explore visually components of reading program per grade level A4. Discuss importance of scaffolded instruction for ELL population A5. Plan in writing and apply integration of series strategies and best reading practices already established in classrooms *Myself* B1. Explain orally importance and relevance of curriculum mapping as a districtwide initiative B2. Explain orally and explore visually district standards-driven mathematics Essential Map per grade level B3. Discuss integration of Saxon Math with Essential Maps through designed Consensus Maps B4. Provide user accounts--teachers manually login/set up accounts, navigate manually through system B5. Justify visually and orally criteria for Diary Map writing norms B6. Attend districtwide New Teachers Orientation on diary mapping with our new teachers	A1-A4. Teacher Workshop Participation A5. Grade-Level Team Meetings/Administrator Walk-Throughs (Evaluation: Teacher Plans Ob/Checklist/Feedback) B1-B5. Teacher Meeting Participation B4-B5. Mapping System Hands-On Lab B6. Teacher Questions/Concerns Clarification

While the concept of resources can vary, three key resources that need to be in focus are personnel, a mapping system, and time.

Personnel

There must be a clear understanding of who will be one-time or ongoing curriculum-mapping trainers and coaches for each school site and throughout a learning organization, not only for the initial implementation but also for the months and years ahead. While some of the teachers and administrators involved in the prologue and retraining may become training personnel, there need to be discussions about training personnel for ongoing new hires each school year.

Training considerations must also address the fact that teachers, as learners, will learn at different rates. Therefore, teachers will be attending training sessions with varying degrees of prior knowledge about curriculum mapping and technology. Jacobs (2004b) addresses the need for differentiated staff development by warning that "one-size-fits-all staff development may cause faculty defections. . . . Adult professionals resent attending workshops that do not match their needs" (p. 134). Resources must therefore match the needs of the adult learners. For example, when initial or ongoing full-day professional development trainings are dedicated to learning about curriculum mapping, a learning organization may choose to divide the responsibilities (resources) for teaching minisessions among the CM Cabinet and Council members (as well as guest trainers, when appropriate) and give teachers the option of attending one full-day session or two half-day sessions based on individual needs.

When teachers are asked to attend initial or ongoing districtwide or school-site trainings, considerations should include (a) the size of the training groups in relation to who is meeting for what reason(s), (b) who is providing the trainings, (c) room size and availability, (d) presentation technology, (e) reproduction of handouts and other materials, (f) participants' access to computers and the Internet, and (g) paper or online training announcements that share the *why, when, where,* and *how long* information as well as any attendance prerequisite or preattendance requirements.

Mapping System

During the prologue and preplanning phase, it is important to remember that a mapping system is integral to embracing Jacobs's (2006a) coin-with-two-sides analogy. A selected mapping system must not only allow teachers to input map elements in various types of curriculum maps with ease but also provide teachers with easy access to one another's archived or current-year maps and include a variety of search and report features that enable teachers to use the maps for personal reflection as well as to search and compare the ongoing curriculum to aid and enhance related collegial dialogues and reviews.

Your learning organization may initially plan to subscribe to only a company's mapping system rather than the company's potential system suite, and that is fine. When and if it becomes appropriate in subsequent years, you may want to investigate what a mapping system company offers in terms of relational database resources that provide multi-integration of curriculum maps, high-stakes and teacher-designed formal and informal assessment results, and/or grading systems. The concept of system integration embraces Jacobs's (2004a) concept of curriculum mapping serving as

> a hub for planning future directions with new data. . . . [M]erging data sources will help us create new knowledge . . . this new knowledge can give us new solutions, and we will need corresponding new directions for staff development. In the future, curriculum mapping and its electronic format can lead us toward including a focus on student curriculum maps, where learners can document their own progress and can communicate that progress to teachers. (p. 136)

After a mapping initiative is well-established, some learning organizations begin to experiment and incorporate the use of Diary Map–student portfolio entries to provide feedback to teachers and give students an opportunity to be reflective and self-evaluate themselves as learners (Beckwith and Niguidula 2007). These schools and districts are exploring best practices related to interfacing the maps housed in the selected mapping system with students who are either electronically or by hand sharing their thoughts and insights connected to the planned and operational curriculum. While this may not be a part of an initial curriculum-mapping implementation plan, it provides insight into the reality of why shared vision and the other critical components naturally evolve over time.

Time

How Will We Guarantee That Teachers Have Adequate Time to Individually Map, Work Together on Collaborative Maps, and Conduct Reviews?

Fast-paced personal lives are often mirrored in fast-paced learning organizations. Teachers and administrators almost always feel strapped for time. Based on what you have read in the previous chapters, it is important to recognize the fact that curriculum mapping requires more time and effort during the first few years of implementation than in later years when mapping becomes established and embedded in the academic and social cultures.

As mentioned previously, learning organizations that reach sustainability are those that have literally restructured days, weeks, and months to provide student-free time for teachers to adequately design curriculum and assessments; review, revise, and refine the planned and operational maps; and meet regularly to horizontally and vertically study student work, make immediate intervention and extension decisions, and discuss current and future pedagogical practices.

Teachers who are consistently provided two to four one-third or half days per month, plus a full day every month or every other month, are much more settled and confident in using curriculum maps and other data sources to make ongoing curriculum decisions. Unfortunately, I have seen the opposite happen. Teachers are told to map but are not given any new or reconstructed time to do so. To function interdependently, teachers need adequate time to meet, preferably without having to write lesson plans for substitutes. If this is not honored or planned for upfront by administrators considering how to restructure time in the official calendar each year, and then truly honoring the reconstructed time, there will understandably be problems with sustainability. Teachers often become discouraged to the point of seeing no value in mapping and may even take their grievances to official levels.

I offer one final note regarding time and technology. Given the demands of teaching and learning in the 21st century, finding adequate time outside of in-person meetings may potentially be harnessed by meeting via e-mail or by using other forms of online technology forums.

INCENTIVES

If *incentives* is a missing critical component, there will be *resistance*.

Villa and Thousand (2000) state that "continued investment in staff through professional development, constructive feedback, engagement in decision making, and acknowledgment for successive approximations can serve as powerful incentives" (p. 113).

Knowing what mapping can potentially do for students and teachers is not enough. Teachers need intrinsic and extrinsic incentives to encourage them to pull away from their comfort zones, even if the zones are unhealthy for oneself or others, and move toward new behaviors and actions. As Pfeffer and Sutton (2000) comment,

> why is it that, at the end of so many books and seminars, leaders report being enlightened and wiser, but not much happens in their organizations? We wondered, too, and so we embarked on a quest to explore one of the great mysteries in organizational management: why knowledge of what needs to be done frequently fails to result in action or behavior consistent with that knowledge. We came to call this the *knowing–doing problem*—the challenge of turning knowledge about how to enhance organizational performance into actions consistent with that knowledge. (p. 4)

Getting rid of knowing-doing gaps within a school site or throughout a learning organization can only happen when those involved consistently revisit the shared vision and adequately feel like what they are doing differently makes a difference. Therefore, Villa and Thousand's (2000) mention of professional development, constructive feedback, engagement in decision making, and acknowledgment of successive approximations is critical to ensure that teachers feel emotionally and professionally that change is for the better. The concept of *successive approximations*, a method for estimating the value of an unknown quantity by repeated comparison to a sequence of known quantities, is simple in theory but not necessarily in practice. When applied to curriculum mapping, it requires teachers and administrators to slow down often and find small gains concerning where they once were, where they currently are, and where they still desire to be in relation to their shared vision, skills, and resources. Celebrating each small step, even the first-time entry into the selected mapping system, can be recognized as an incentive for moving forward even when those participating are not in their comfort zones.

Changing current beliefs from explicit or implicit resistance to focusing on individually and collectively doing what is necessary to improve student learning and instructional practice may take some time to achieve. Do not be surprised if it takes longer than you initially expect for teachers to buy in to the small incentives that lead to them feeling empowered by professionalism within a school or throughout a learning organization.

How Will Teachers See That Mapping Can Help Improve Learning and Instruction?

While trying to find common ground, agreeing on what is critical to ensure student learning success, and allowing teachers to experience professional satisfaction is at the heart of curriculum mapping, it is important that teachers intellectually and emotionally feel that their hard work and efforts are paying off early on in the mapping process. Fullan (2005) observes that

> there is a growing problem in large-scale reform; namely, the *terms* travel well, but the underlying *conceptualization and thinking* does not. This is an age-old issue in knowledge dissemination. There is a great deal of tacit and in-depth contextual knowledge that would be required to understand the lessons at work. . . . Furthermore, issues of holding people accountable and building communities of learners within and across scores of schools are enormously complex. (p. 10)

It will take time for teachers to move from feeling like learners being watched to being honored as curriculum designers and decision makers. For a time, some teachers may have difficulty seeing curriculum mapping as nothing more than the latest initiative du jour. Throughout initial and extended phases of a curriculum-mapping initiative, teachers and administrators need to be involved in a reflective process regarding what is working well and what may need to be adjusted. Reflecting, in and of itself, is a form of incentive. Senge et al. (2000) note that "an innovative personality knows that mistakes are stepping-stones to better understanding" (p. 237). Personally and collectively reflecting on what has taken place as teacher-learners, while continuing to develop understanding of the explicit and implicit benefits of mapping, is a critical aspect of the incentives component.

How Can We Ensure That Teachers Are Given the Opportunity to Develop an Intrinsic Appreciation of the Value and Purpose of Mapping Early On?

I will mention it again: Celebrate every small step along the way. Celebrate asking the hard questions about what it is that teachers truly want students to know and be able to do. Celebrate when a map is being written with quality.

Celebrate when teachers design a common assessment, use it, study their students' results, and determine the best immediate learning plan to aid those in need and those who are ready to excel. Celebrate when teachers conduct a seven-step review focus (which may not include the use of maps at an early stage of implementation) that increases their ability to solve a critical learning or environmental problem, issue, or concern.

All of these small celebrations collectively lead to improving student learning. Members of the intra-organizations may have to constantly remind teachers and themselves of the need to celebrate each step, especially during the first year or two of implementation. It is wise to go slow and steady. Proper implementation, including the use of the created maps as soon as possible to drive curriculum decisions, will help teachers make connections to all that they are learning, begin to intrinsically value mapping, and recognize its positive impact on student learning and performance as well as instructional practice.

ACTION PLANS

If *action plans* are missing critical components, there will be *false starts*.

Jacobs (2006b) points out that curriculum mapping may be a districtwide initiative, but teachers must own the model at the school-site level. Therefore, there are two levels of action plans. The first is the overarching districtwide yearly action plan developed and implemented by the CM Cabinet, Cadre, and Coordinator, which includes protocols and encompasses expectations for all the schools in the learning organization. The second includes each school site's yearly action plan, which is developed by the school-site CM Council. A school-site action plan incorporates the requirements set forth in the districtwide action plan while allowing for autonomy at each school site so that each school site can determine one or more issues, problems, or concerns it wants to address.

Be aware that there is no guarantee that all schools within a learning organization will move forward at the same rate of understanding and application regarding the various aspects of curriculum mapping and the use of the selected mapping system. A wide range of variables may affect this reality, including (a) proper initial and ongoing support training, (b) adequate time to personally map and meet collaboratively, (c) principal leadership, (d) teacher leadership, (e) collegial relationships, and (f) a familiarity with conducting reviews using the selected mapping system.

From Year Five to Year One, What Are Our Learning Organization's Step-by-Step Procedures, Courses of Action, and Goals?

I wish I could write out a pat step-by-step action plan to answer this question, but such an answer does not exist. In all my years as a consultant and trainer, I have never experienced two identical learning organizations, nor have I experienced two identical implementation plans.

As you begin to plan the implementation action plan process for a district or one school site, encourage the development team members to base the implementation steps and timelines on the following:

- the 10 Tenets of Curriculum Mapping presented in Chapter 1
- past, current, and desired future school-site and districtwide cultures and climates regarding teachers, administrators at all levels, and the relationship between the two
- the prioritized list of problems, issues, or concerns that mapping will be used to resolve
- the initial type(s) of curriculum maps to be created
- the selected mapping system's basic usage as well as search and report features
- the available technology support (e.g., computer access, bandwidth) when teachers throughout the learning organization want to simultaneously get online to record, revise, or refine maps
- the personnel who will be responsible for conducting any trainings
- adequate, board-approved early-release, late-start, or full-day no-student time to meet to discuss review focuses (or whatever time is available for teachers to learn about the mapping processes and procedures, record various types of maps, and independently use the selected mapping system)

When developing a districtwide or school-site action plan, backwards design is a popular way to determine what needs to take place when moving forward within the action plan's sequential order. Begin by addressing this question: What do we want our learning organization's curriculum and related environments to look like in five years given the various facets of curriculum mapping? Once this question has been answered by the appropriate intra-organization members, the team can start working backwards from the anticipated future five-year mark to the present. It is recommended when using a backwards-design process to first plan backwards by full school years, then by grading periods within each school year and finally by the month within each grading period. Please remember that the selected disciplines and type of maps may vary in the planning process based on feeder-pattern school configuration, desire for collaborative learning evidence, and number of teachers available to be involved in teams and/or task forces.

When the planners are ready to fill in the major and minor details based on the now sketched-out plan, do not forget to include the names of those responsible for specific trainings, implementation resources, celebrations, and various other types of accountability necessities desired during the first two years' monthly or grading-period implementation expectations.

Some learning organizations choose to create their action plans as curriculum maps and house them within the selected mapping system using appropriate course titles. All members of the learning organization then have easy access to the plans and can review action-plan map documentation from the two perspectives of planned actions versus what actually happens.

Are We Willing to Be Flexible and Modify Our Mapping Journey Along the Way?

Reading Chapter 12 provides insights into the need for flexibility and tenacity when implementing curriculum mapping as a second-order change model. I guarantee that whatever the action plans may be, they will need to be modified within the first year of implementation. While it is wise to be proactive and try to predict and plan from the onset what is perceived as problematic, it is often the unexpected that truly blindsides progress. If and when the unexpected happens, simply reevaluate where the implementation has been, where it currently is, and where it needs to go—then modify accordingly.

If small or large changes are made to any action plan, be certain that the changes are clearly and quickly announced and disseminated to all those affected. Failure to share such pertinent information in a timely fashion often hurts an initiative. The CM Cabinet and Council members and administrators play an active role in disseminating such information either by e-mailing the information or by announcing the modifications at an upcoming faculty meeting.

CONCLUSION

If a learning organization is truly committed to curriculum mapping as something that is here to stay, it is intellectually and emotionally wise to start slow and grow steadily in personal and collective understanding and application until implementation naturally gives way to sustainability and normalcy.

As explicitly stated and occasionally implied throughout this book's chapters, be ready for your curriculum-mapping implementation process to take persistence and courage. Jacobs (2004b) comments that "as a genuine 21st-century shift in our practice, mapping requires knowledge and courage" (p. x). And as John Wayne so aptly observed, "courage is being scared to death—but saddling up anyway."

REVIEW TASK

This chapter concludes with a personal and collaborative task rather than with a series of questions. Based on what you have read in these 11 chapters, plus Chapter 12 if you would like to read it first, privately sketch out a prospective backwards-design short- and long-range timeline detailing your suggestions for your learning organization's mapping implementation plan. When ready, get together with colleagues who have also personally sketched out a plan, and compare the plans' similarities and differences regarding the personal perspectives of you and your colleagues.

What Roadblocks
and Brick Walls
May We Encounter
Along the Way?

*It is not a field of a few acres of ground, but a cause that we are defending,
and whether we defeat the enemy in one battle, or by degrees,
the consequences will be the same.*

—Thomas Paine

I sat down in an aisle seat after boarding a flight from Philadelphia to Chicago. The gentleman in the window seat was engrossed midway through a sizeable book. The middle passenger noticed as well and asked, "What's your book about?"

He responded, "The American Revolutionary War." Following a slight pause, he looked up and added, "We won."

He shared with us that, although he knew the outcomes in advance, he wanted to learn more about the intricacies of actions taken in the various theaters. The communiqués in this chapter serve a similar purpose. While each portrays the intricacies of personal actions, collectively they have similar themes. These themes have been addressed in previous chapters, yet when expressed by those who have actually lived out the themes, they may solidify or add a new dimension to your understanding. May these practitioners' perceptions strengthen and enrich your learning organization's curriculum-mapping journey.

PRACTICAL ADVICE FROM PRACTITIONERS

Kathy Tegarden, Creighton School District Principal of the Year and a recipient of the Honeywell Silver Apple Award, understands systemic change. For Gateway Elementary School's curriculum-mapping initiative, Mrs. Tegarden conducted a successful prologue and implementation. She provided her 52-teacher staff with organizational support, incremental and ongoing professional development, and time structures conducive to both creating and reviewing curriculum maps. Nonetheless, roadblocks were encountered along the way.

Gateway Elementary School (K–8)

Phoenix, Arizona

Plain and simple, school improvement is hard work. My teachers and I had been knee deep in school improvement efforts since the authorization of No Child Left Behind. Curriculum mapping was originally explored and implemented to play an integral role in aligning our instruction and assessments to the Arizona state standards.

As the instructional leader I had to continually support this new effort and eliminate as many roadblocks as possible. When it comes to finding creative ways to sustain your school or district's curriculum-mapping initiative, you realize up front that there will be many challenges along the way. The three most challenging issues for us were establishing purpose, using technology, and the ever-present dilemma of finding time.

Establishing Purpose

Making a case for curriculum mapping can be one of the most important steps in getting your staff mentally prepared to accept this new challenge. I chose to start that process by educating myself. I attended several conferences and institutes that featured leading-edge presenters and current practitioners. I then brought along a small number of staff whom I knew other teachers respected and would go to in times of stress. My teachers really liked attending conferences where they could hear in person from other teachers, schools, and districts that found curriculum mapping to be an effective way of improving student achievement.

When we debriefed after attending conferences and workshops, we all realized that making a case for mapping wouldn't be easy or end with an initial sales pitch. We knew we had to include ongoing dialogue about why curriculum mapping is important and who curriculum mapping is truly designed to serve—our students.

Don't be surprised when you think things are humming along at a nice pace and then you find yourself once again defending the initiative. I remember one particular meeting when my teachers asked me if they could please stop diary mapping. We were under considerable pressure to improve our reading and math achievement scores, and everyone was feeling overloaded. I really wanted them to mentally connect diary mapping with what we were currently working on. At our next staff meeting I had them read through our state's school-improvement rubrics and asked them to highlight any indicator that related aligning curriculum, instruction, and assessment to the state standards. Needless to say there were a significant number of indicators that screamed out *curriculum mapping*. They got it! Once these mental connections were made, mapping moved forward in our school with a renewed commitment.

Using Technology

There are many advantages to using technology, yet there are two roadblocks you should be aware of during the beginning of your initiative. The first is cost. There are several effective Web-based mapping systems, and while the cost is reasonable, there are annual fees to consider. Obtaining grant or district funding to support the ongoing cost is helpful. Fortunately, our district adopted curriculum mapping as an essential tool for all teachers and has an annual budget for technology costs and support.

The second is realizing that your teachers will represent a range of technology savvy when you introduce the selected mapping system. I found that most young teachers took to using the mapping system without hesitation. My more experienced staff, especially those with little technology training, found curriculum mapping to be a double challenge—dealing with learning the mapping elements as well as learning new technology skills. I met this concern head-on by developing training sessions based on Jacobs's (2004b). Differentiated Staff Development Model—Low Tech/High Curriculum, High Tech/High Curriculum, Low Tech/Low Curriculum, and High Tech/Low Curriculum. Teachers who met the quadrant criteria were given specific times to map in our computer lab. The initial sessions were facilitated by our Tech Cadre, peer teachers with strong backgrounds in technology, the mapping system, curriculum, and curriculum mapping. With support from the cadre, district technology staff, and our curriculum-mapping consultant, we were able to get everyone comfortable with mapping online within the first half year of implementation.

Finding Time

I saved time for last, although it certainly is not the least important issue. As educators we are great at adding new things to our already hectic lives, but not as good at taking old things away. If you are an administrator you must be willing to let go of some things in order to give your staff adequate amounts of time to create maps and meet on a regular basis.

During the initial year or two, you will find that the learning process is more time intensive. Here are a few ways we found time to map:

- We chose to use a pool of guest teachers. These were substitutes who had worked extensively with our teachers and students, so we felt comfortable leaving our students in their care. Extensive lesson plans were not needed since the guest teachers were familiar with the style, daily routine, and mannerism of each teacher. Guest teachers took over class time for 60–90-minute blocks. This was accomplished for the most part by grade level. Initially, the released teachers were trained in each map element. Later they met to work on improving the

(Continued)

(Continued)

quality of the maps. Initial trainings were conducted by our consultant and aided by our Tech Cadre. Eventually the trainings were run solely by the cadre. This method supported our curriculum-mapping action plan's goal of establishing strong, in-house teacher leadership.

- About mid-year I reconfigured our weekly staff meeting's usage of time. I gave teachers the first meeting each month to individually create or edit Projected/Diary Maps. The Tech Cadre staffed the computer lab during this time in case anyone desired assistance. We found that teachers eventually needed less and less support as their mapping comfort level grew.

- During the second staff meeting of the month, teachers held (and still hold) vertical-team data reviews using the curriculum maps. While some teachers initially were resistant to recording Diary Maps, no one wanted to be the only one on a team to not have maps available for review. This proved to be an emotional time for some, who found it difficult to share what is *really* happening in *my* classroom. While curriculum mapping is not used for a teacher's formal evaluation, I found that a few teachers needed reassurance about this fact. Once they felt at ease with being open in their recordings, I saw what the mapping process is all about—teachers helping each other with strategies and activities to improve student learning. Oh, the powers of mapping!

- For the two remaining weekly meetings, our structure began to vary early on. Some teachers have a horizontal meeting to discuss specific grade-level and learning issues, while others meet in mixed groups. Sometimes we meet as an entire staff to focus on such topics as English language learners, vocabulary, or various learning strategies. Sometimes we simply gather to celebrate the teachers' and students' progress—both great and small.

Regardless of how or when we meet, our curriculum maps and other data sources are always in focus and play a continuous role in our curricular decision making.

No roadblock is too big or too tough to overcome if you are committed to doing what is in the best interests of the students. While the process may initially feel chaotic and sometimes painful, your staff will eventually develop a new way of viewing teaching and learning.

I have found that the teachers on my staff are much more willing to share ideas and have become open to learning from one another. We recently incorporated the concept of formalized professional learning communities that focus on data-driven decision making and setting meaningful student learning goals. We know this move is a direct result of our sustained efforts to align our curriculum and instruction through curriculum mapping and the use of our curriculum maps.

Good luck with your initiative! Remember to learn from others, preferably in person. Plan to attend a local or national curriculum-mapping conference. Interaction with other schools and districts is meaningful and motivating. It was during these times that we found our greatest inspiration for getting started.

Dr. Janet Boyle came to Center Grove Community School Corporation as the new assistant superintendent of curriculum and instruction. Previously Dr. Boyle had been a district curriculum coordinator and assistant high school principal at Ben Davis High School in Wayne Township in Indianapolis, Indiana. While there she worked extensively with Dr. Douglas Reeves and Larry Ainsworth, whose work on unwrapping standards and curriculum alignment greatly influenced her framework of curriculum design.

While curriculum mapping had been gaining momentum before her arrival, Dr. Boyle has played an instrumental role in establishing mapping districtwide through her advocacy of teacher-leader decision making, site-based professional development, and early-release mapping sessions.

Center Grove Community School Corporation

Greenwood, Indiana

Curriculum mapping in Center Grove Community School Corporation (CGCSC) has experienced its share of roadblocks and brick walls, but overall, we are doing well. Here is a little history and background to understand our journey:

- We are located just south of Indianapolis, Indiana.
- Formerly a rural school district, CGCSC has evolved into a suburban bedroom community of the Indianapolis metro area.
- K–12 enrollment currently includes 7,300 students spread among six elementary schools, two middle schools, and one large comprehensive high school, and we know our numbers will only continue to grow.
- Approximately 12% of our students are on free or reduced lunch.
- Over 90% of our student population is white.
- Our students' scores on state assessments are generally high.
- Approximately 80% of our high school graduates attend college.

Two years ago, four of our nine principals were new to their position, as were all of our central office administrators, with the exception of the superintendent and the technology director. Serving as the new assistant superintendent for curriculum and instruction, I soon discovered that despite strong test scores and a solid reputation as a good school district, our K–12 curriculum was, at best, a patchwork. No alignment or articulation had occurred on a systematic basis in any one school, let alone collectively. Teachers had a glancing familiarity with our state standards and did not actively use standards in planning instruction or designing assessments. In reality, most teachers taught what they wanted when they wanted.

With No Child Left Behind in place and Indiana's school improvement process in full force, it became clear that CGCSC would not be able to maintain the expected annual increase in strong academic performance unless (a) student performance data was continually analyzed by teachers and used in instructional decision making; (b) K–12 curriculum was fully articulated, aligned, and accessible to all teachers; and (c) effective professional development was site based to support the curriculum work.

(Continued)

(Continued)

In the year prior to my arrival, 20 secondary teachers were sent to the National Curriculum Mapping Institute. Teachers came back fired up. Unfortunately, no one from the central office had accompanied the group. Since there was no district direction or support, the following school year consisted of individual school sites moving forward in a variety of ways:

- The high school wanted a mapping system in place before beginning to map. It took a full school year to acquire a system, and during that time the initial excitement waned and momentum was lost.
- A new middle school had opened and was just getting established as a learning organization. Its staff chose not to begin mapping during this time.
- The established middle school's principal decided to have the staff diary map one preparation period within their discipline. The goal was to gain insight into the most common mapping elements.
- The six elementary schools were not formally aware of the curriculum-mapping process. They did not participate in any collegial conversations with each other, the middle schools, or the high school.

A key turning point for our district came when I was able to coordinate sending our superintendent, district curriculum director, eight of the nine principals, and myself to the following summer's National Curriculum Mapping Institute. Our goal in attending was to learn as much as possible. We spread ourselves out either independently or by twos or threes to attend the various breakout sessions. This allowed us to listen to a variety of practitioners and consultants. At mealtimes we gathered together and shared our learning. The entire experience bonded us beautifully. We collaboratively outlined an action plan for the next school year that included a more cohesive districtwide implementation and determined who we wanted to approach for consulting services.

Technically, the following school year became recognized as our first districtwide mapping year, even though two schools had attempted mapping in some manner for two years. Each school site formed a Curriculum Mapping Council, and the district formed a Curriculum Mapping Cabinet. For the first half of the school year, many cabinet members were tense, anxious, and uncertain, especially those newest to the curriculum-mapping concepts. A common complaint voiced was, "We don't have time to map *and* plan for classes *and* teach!"

Knowing well that curriculum mapping equals systemic change, we acknowledged where they were emotionally and worked through the uncertainties until everyone began to feel comfortable and have a clearer picture of the direction in which our district was moving. We also guaranteed school-site and districtwide support.

The district administrative team brainstormed ways to provide a three-fold time allotment structure for (a) ongoing curriculum-mapping professional development sessions, (b) time to map, and (c) time to conduct mapping reviews. After extensive work by stakeholders, including staff, parents, and, most important, our school board, we initiated districtwide weekly early releases for the second semester. The 45-minute sessions that this allowed were instrumental in successfully launching curriculum mapping at each school site. Each school devoted at least two early-release sessions per month to learning more about the curriculum-mapping process and providing teachers time to actually map and review their map entries with one another.

This process proved to be such a success in helping us meet our mapping goal of creating a K–12 teacher-designed aligned and articulated curriculum that our school board permitted us to provide weekly early-release sessions for the entire next school year. Based on collegial conversations within the Curriculum Mapping Cabinet, we selected mathematics as the first discipline for which to create K–12 Essential Maps based on individual Diary Maps, school-site Consensus Maps, and K–12 teacher-determined power standards.

We acknowledged then, and still do, that mapping is a process. We knew that we would not have a fully articulated K–12 curriculum in all subject areas for at least another three to four years.

So, what lessons have we learned that may help you in your curriculum-mapping journey? Here are several significant ones:

- **Building and district leadership must be in place early on to support the curriculum-mapping process.** Not only do all administrators need to have a clear grasp of the complexities of mapping and the mapping process; they also must be continually proactive at finding ways for staff to have adequate time to map, meet, dialogue, and reflect horizontally, vertically, and in mixed review groups. Site administrators must constantly encourage and allow teachers to become the leaders who move mapping forward. When school-site administration changes, it is critical that new administrators are provided immediate and adequate support in gaining insight and understanding into the complexities and processes involved in mapping. Their full participation in the current work, as well as future plans for their schools and schools throughout the district, is critical for sustainability.

- **Make adaptations when a roadblock or brick wall is encountered along the way.** Our consultant's first recommendation was to create cohesiveness throughout our district by forming a cabinet. The Curriculum Mapping Cabinet began meeting and has proved to be cohesive—with one caveat. Because cabinet members from the elementary schools came on board with no background knowledge, unlike the middle schools and the high school, we found it necessary to split the cabinet for a period of time to allow for this differentiation. We alternated between split and whole-group meetings and foresee the cabinet meeting continually as one entity in another year.

- **District-level technology support staff needs to be well versed in both curriculum mapping and the selected mapping system.** We chose to purchase a commercial mapping system. One surefire way to experience roadblocks is to not have a designated technology team readily available, whose members understand the concepts, complexities, and processes of mapping and can serve as liaisons between the schools, the district, and the selected mapping system company. Having site-based mapping technology people available to assist is wise. Encourage both district and site-based technology experts to conduct professional development training on the mapping system's basic functions and search and report features. This

(Continued)

(Continued)

training can be differentiated to meet the needs of those who feel that they are novices, those who are more advanced, and new hires to the district.

- **Although mapping is a site-based model, working cohesively toward common district goals is beneficial to the process.** When we started our full-fledged districtwide initiative, all six elementary schools began the learning process together. We found an overall acceptance and cohesiveness in them that we did not find in the secondary schools. Since the middle schools and the high school were in different places when mapping became official, they sometimes struggled with communicating a collective vision and determining a cohesive synergy. While they have always respected one another's viewpoints, their differences sometimes caused friction not present in the elementary schools.

- **Don't do too much at one time.** There are a variety of models and strategies that embrace curriculum design and improving student learning that integrate well with curriculum mapping. One problem we recently encountered was too many *-ings* at one time. Our middle school and high school teachers (many of whom serve on the Curriculum Mapping Cabinet) had attended trainings and workshops in and out of the district where they were collectively exposed to determin*ing* power standards, unwrapp*ing* the standards, unpack*ing* the standards, and break*ing* apart the standards. While each *-ing* is worthwhile and correlates to improving student learning, over time all the secondary teachers were trying to do them all at once, which caused understandable dissension. The Curriculum Mapping Cabinet met to discuss the situation and, after collegial conversation, made a districtwide decision that there should be one focus (determining power standards) given our current curriculum-mapping action plan goal of designing K–12 mathematics Essential Maps.

- **Celebrate the small successes.** No school or district celebrates enough, especially when it comes to small steps and small wins. We purposefully stop and take time to recall how far we have come. We proudly highlight advancements made in each school and throughout the district. Creativity plays a part in our celebrations. Two schools created videos to use for staff development, which other schools have in turn borrowed. One school's teachers designed a curriculum-mapping birthday cake for their principal, which led to cakes being sent to all the schools from the district office as part of an end-of-year celebration.

We have accomplished much more than expected in our district's formal implementation. We know that we still have much to do and much to accomplish. Mapping is slowly becoming the natural way of designing and refining our K–12 curriculum. We constantly remind ourselves that mapping is not about a product or arriving at a destination. Mapping is the journey. With our students constantly in mind, we are excited about our journey and hope that you will be equally excited about yours.

Matthew Shockley is the principal of Center Grove High School. His was one of the first schools to embark on a curriculum-mapping journey in the Center Grove Community School Corporation. The following is an informal conversation that took place between Mr. Shockley and two of his high school teachers, Jennifer Pickell, a science teacher, and Karen Agnew, a foreign language teacher. Their insights and honesty provide a genuine glimpse into how mapping is perceived by those most intimately involved in the work.

Center Grove High School

Greenwood, Indiana

Mr. Shockley: When mapping was first introduced at our high school, what was your initial reaction?

Ms. Pickell: Most of us were thinking "Here we go again." One of the biggest concerns was where we would find the time to do what was being explained to us.

Ms. Agnew: Honestly, I thought it was just another hoop we were going to have to jump through because somebody read a book, went to a conference, and got a wild idea. Some of us thought that it was just going to be a roundabout way to make us submit lesson plans.

Mr. Shockley: Based on what you just shared, Karen, I admit I was one of those who attended a conference. As an administrator it just made sense to start mapping. I tried to convey to our teachers that mapping is a terrific way to articulate our curriculum, find gaps and overlaps, and deal with other curricular issues. The maps would provide data and serve as starting points for conversations. Since we were working toward becoming professional learning communities, mapping and having maps seemed like such a natural tie-in to the concept of collaboration. Like you, Jennifer, I had a big concern about the time issue. How are we going to find the time necessary to properly attend to creating and using maps? As you know, we now have district-supported release time to map and conduct mapping reviews, and that has really helped. Since we started mapping before it was a districtwide initiative, what were some of your early struggles?

Ms. Agnew: I think now, looking back, which is somewhat difficult to do since it seems like a long time ago, we jumped into it all too quickly. If I can use a swimming analogy, we were trying to swim the butterfly before we even knew how to tread water. I felt like I was mapping before I knew what I was really supposed to be doing. And was I doing it right, or was I doing it wrong? A big frustration for me and others back then was that we did not see immediate results. We didn't see collaboration as a result. It took some time to realize that results were both the process and the decisions we made. Visual results did finally come farther down the road, but not having immediate ones got naysayers going and dampened the spirits of those around them.

Ms. Pickell: I totally agree with Karen. I basically grasped why we were doing this, but I honestly did not get the big picture of where it was all going. I struggled with the terminology because, at that time, it was not explained. We were just told to create maps. We found ourselves struggling with what that was supposed to look like and what each element was supposed to represent.

(Continued)

(Continued)

Mr. Shockley: Our assistant principal, Sandy Hillman, along with administrators and teachers from the middle school and the high school, attended the summer National Curriculum Mapping Institute just before the school year when we officially started mapping. You know they came back excited about the potential use of curriculum mapping. However, we did not have district representation at the institute and in hindsight that was a mistake. When I came to the high school it was apparent that we really needed support from the district level to aid in providing time and proper professional development. I admit along with you that when we, the administrators, asked everyone to start writing maps, it was a fiasco. *(Ms. Pickell and Ms. Agnew chuckle.)* We did not know enough about the nuts and bolts of mapping to effectively explain it to the staff. This left a bad taste in many teachers' mouths. This bad taste was quite difficult to overcome when we later began our work with mapping as a districtwide initiative. When did you find that mapping began to help teachers carry on conversations that led to improving student learning?

Ms. Pickell: Some department teams were already effective communicators, while others are not. My team, a Collaborative Content Team (CCT) that focuses on Chemistry and Physics, has been fortunate in that we have communicated well with one another for many years. What we found, though, was that by having map evidence of what we focus on individually in our classrooms was helpful when we needed to come to agreement concerning strategic learning and instruction. For example, once we learned the proper way to write the map elements and began to have quality maps, when conducting a review we noticed that we had quite a range of terminology to explain the same concepts in the various courses. Since our students switched teachers mid-year, we realized this was confusing for them and it instantly explained some of the classroom behavior we often saw. As a CCT we came to agreement on, one, specific terms and, two, specific sequences for explaining the concepts. We are so glad we did! Our students now have much more successful transitions, not only from semester to semester but also from the Chemistry course to the Physics course. While this is only one case in point, mapping truly has deepened our conversations and decision making on behalf of our students.

Ms. Agnew: As a foreign language teacher I have to share that the maps have made a big difference in how we approach grammar. As a department, since our courses are naturally sequential—Spanish One, Spanish Two, and Spanish Three—our team has always been communicative and collaborative. But we'll be the first to admit that we had been making assumptions for years about our students' learning prior to entering foreign language courses. Now that we had the ability to go into our mapping system and review the English courses' maps, not only at the high school but at the two middle schools as well, we discovered that English grammar is not addressed as it was when we were students in the 1970s and 1980s. This discovery immediately impacted our instruction. Rather than seeing grammar as review for our students, we now focus on it in depth and perceive it as new learning. We have found that being able to compare what students are learning in other disciplines by reading the maps is invaluable and has had a great impact on us as individual teachers and as a department.

Mr. Shockley: From a school-improvement perspective, writing across the curriculum has recently become our improvement goal. As you both know, we are going to be using the maps as data sources to see how writing is addressed. How often is writing assigned? How is writing being assessed? What types of skills are we formally teaching students in the various content areas? What writing skills are being supported across the content areas? We are designing a specific review wherein our CCTs will use the search and report features in our mapping system to evaluate our current status and determine what needs to be changed to improve our desired focus on writing. After reflections in each CCT, we will meet as a full staff to discuss each CCT's action plans and determine how we want to monitor our schoolwide progress.

Ms. Agnew: May I add one more thought? As teachers we sometimes assume our students know this or don't know that. If we think they should have known it and don't, we blame them or our fellow teachers. Mapping has really stopped the Blame Game. Having instant access to each other's maps and really knowing what is happening has made a big difference. This has actually helped morale since we no longer finger point. Instead, we solve problems.

Mr. Shockley: What is the one piece of advice you would give teachers or administrators just starting to implement curriculum mapping? Is there something you feel we did well or something you wish we had done differently?

Ms. Pickell: Karen mentioned earlier that we basically put the cart before the horse when we initially got started. My advice is to not go too fast. We tried to do it all at once and really struggled with the concepts of content, skills, assessments, resources, and standards all in one shot. If I could give advice, it would be to slow down before speeding up. To be effective, start by focusing on one element at a time so everyone can gain a clear understanding of what it means in relation to writing a map and mapping. When we did this in our second year, it really began to click in teachers' minds and made a big difference in the quality of our maps.

Ms. Agnew: I think if I went to speak to a school that was just starting I would tell them that slow and steady wins the race. Although we heard that mapping was a process, we didn't listen and dove right in—head first. We were frustrated by not immediately getting or having a finished product. It took us a long time to grasp that mapping is not about getting finished. You never will be. This was a huge mind shift for everyone, and still is for some. Also, remember to embrace the word *flexible*. If you have made a deadline for creating a drafted map or conducting a review and time encroaches on the ability to complete the task, deal with it, readjust slightly, and keep moving on. Be sure you listen to the teachers and their needs for support in learning how to map and the time needed to use the maps for collaborative discussions. Don't see mapping as a race to finish. Take your time and see it as a journey.

Mr. Shockley: From an administrator's perspective, I have three pieces of advice I would share. First, if at all possible, start by attending the annual summer National Curriculum Mapping Institute. It is by far the best venue to open your mind to the endless possibilities of what mapping can do for your school or district. It also provides insight into the basics you will need to get mapping started. While you are there be sure to network with others who have gone before you. Everyone is honest and open about what worked and what didn't. Be sure to talk to teachers as well as district and school-site administrators.

(Continued)

(Continued)

> Second, reiterating what you two just shared, do plan to take it a bit slower than what you first think you should do. Listen carefully to the input from lead teachers whom you have brought on board early to help make mapping happen. Build in checkpoints to find out what is going well and what is posing a challenge. Be flexible, never lose sight of the purpose of mapping, and always press forward.
>
> My third piece of advice is that technology is critical for making mapping successful and sustainable. The mapping processes cannot function properly without it. A Web-based mapping system enables teachers to have immediate access to everyone's classroom and makes it much easier to share and glean information without having to gather teachers together in person. Whichever mapping system you choose, make certain that you plan professional development on the uses of the system. Beyond the basics of how to create a map in the system, teachers must become familiar with its search and report features. They will be incredibly useful. Also remember that, just as learning about the map elements needs to be a step-by-step process, learning all that the mapping system offers should be taught to teachers in increments as well.
>
> Well, ladies, thank you for sharing your thoughts and insights.
>
> **Ms. Pickell:** Thank you!
>
> **Ms. Agnew:** Thank you as well. It has meant a lot to our staff that you and Sandy have been willing to really go down this road of learning about mapping alongside us. Your honesty makes us feel like we can be honest, too, and share our thoughts about the process. Many of us also really appreciate how you constantly encourage us to think outside the box and stretch us to find new ways to use our maps in our CCTs and across the curriculum.

During an open consultation time at a National Curriculum Mapping Institute, a group of teachers signed up to meet with me. I can vividly recall beginning with a circle of 12 chairs—one of which was empty on purpose. Steve Kovach, at that time a high school teacher, spoke on behalf of the assembly to get started with a list of group-generated questions. I could tell they had been doing their homework, as the questions were articulate and to the point. Upon returning home, this small team of caring educators eventually expanded mapping to become a districtwide initiative. Mr. Kovach, now the K–12 teaching and learning coordinator, and Cynthia Stevenson, the K–12 professional development coordinator, are currently serving as their district's Curriculum Mapping Coordinators.

> **Lakeville Area Public School District**
>
> **Lakeville, Minnesota**
>
> Lakeville Area Public Schools is a suburban school district with 11,000 students in south-central Minnesota. After having completed our second year of districtwide implementation, curriculum mapping is going perfectly—all 850 teachers have quality maps in our mapping system and are engaged in deep, collegial discussions about curriculum through the use of the maps.

Things just couldn't be better. And if you believe that, we have some swampland you might be interested in purchasing!

As with any systemic initiative, asking people to make changes has its challenges, curriculum mapping included. While our initiative is going much smoother now than our initial implementation year, we learned early on to recognize and accept that obstacles would come along. We have learned to find creative ways to address and solve them. We realize that our obstacles may feel like brick walls, but collaboratively we can devise ladders to climb over and move beyond them. By sharing our three greatest challenges, and the steps taken to resolve them, our hope is that you can preplan for (or entirely avoid) similar situations.

Brick Wall #1: A Leadership Information-and-Support Gap

Three years ago, 11 teachers, including the two of us, attended a National Curriculum Mapping Institute. We became excited about the possibility of putting curriculum mapping into action throughout our district. As a team we began planning how to facilitate our collective desire. We organized a Curriculum Mapping Cadre, consisting of teacher leaders from throughout the district who were committed to learning more—and we did! Our knowledge and understanding of mapping expanded. We readied ourselves to enlarge our cadre to 20 members and begin the process of introducing curriculum mapping to our district's 15 schools.

When we started introducing the concepts of mapping, we were met with skepticism because many thought this was the new initiative du jour. Even though we felt we had thoroughly done our homework, there were questions raised that the cadre felt it could not readily answer. Because of this some members became frustrated and stepped down. Those who remained continued to display a will and determination to the commitment that curriculum mapping was the right change for our district and our students and forged ahead.

What we found at this time was that the most difficult challenge was not the loss of some cadre members, but an error made at the onset of creating the cadre. We did not include the expectation that all school-site administrators needed to be an active part of the cadre to learn and grow along with us. Therefore, we did not have the administrative buy-in we needed. We learned the hard way that it is critical to have all levels of administrators on board and informed right from the start.

To overcome our leadership gap and create stronger teacher buy-in, we established a Teaching and Learning Council (TLC) at each school site, which was made up of building administrators and teacher leaders. Each TLC, similar to a Curriculum Mapping Council, participated in ongoing trainings to increase its curriculum-mapping knowledge and understanding. Eventually each TLC developed a specific school-site action plan.

The district provided support by increasing available funding and professional development release time. It also encouraged administrators to participate in regional or national curriculum-mapping training opportunities. Over time, the school-site administrators truly became excited about embedding curriculum mapping into established initiatives. They found ways to provide support for ongoing professional development, adequate time to map, and funding.

(Continued)

(Continued)

Recently we created a districtwide TLC, similar to a Curriculum Mapping Cabinet, that serves as a connecting point for all 15 TLCs and has become our nucleus for curriculum, instruction, and assessment decision making throughout our district.

Brick Wall #2: Time Allocation

This wall wasn't quite as tall as the previous one, but it still proved challenging. The bricks were mortared with a mix of (a) finding time to dedicate to learning the mapping process, (b) finding time to engage in curriculum-mapping reviews, and (c) addressing the constant need to train newly hired teachers and veteran teachers who initially were skeptical and now realized they needed to catch up because mapping was not going away.

Our ladder to scale this wall has proven successful. Preplanned, master-schedule release dates are publicly announced at the onset of each school year. The school-site TLCs plan around these dates with respect to personal mapping time and collaborative review time. TLC members periodically survey their teachers to find out current comfort levels for designing and revising maps, conducting collaborative reviews, and using the various search and report features included in our mapping system. School-site professional development workshops are then planned based on the survey results. Districtwide collaboration time is also scheduled annually so teachers can meet across grade levels and school buildings to share insights gained from comparison reviews of curriculum maps.

Brick Wall #3: Professional Growth Issues

We consider this brick wall our newest one, and it is proving to be simultaneously the most challenging and the most rewarding to scale. Now that we are entering our third year of formal mapping, we have discovered that we still have a wide gap in teacher understanding of mapping concepts. We still have teachers who need help in understanding the foundational concepts of writing a quality map, determining purposes for conducting reviews, using the mapping system's search and report features to support review purposes or focuses, conducting the actual reviews using the formal seven-step review process, and collaboratively determining strategies and structures that lead to improved learning.

Our latest ladder includes not only providing differentiated professional development but also supporting the natural transition from learning the rudiments of designing a map to *using* the maps to provide real-time data of our curriculum issues, including gaps, redundancies, high-level thinking expectations, and an increase in project-based assessments. We have enjoyed observing these new levels of engagement and collaboration. At the heart of this transition is the fact that mapping is becoming how we do business in Lakeville.

A Worthy Climb

We continue to work diligently to make certain that curriculum mapping becomes a solid cornerstone of our district's ongoing curriculum-renewal process. We know we will encounter new brick walls as our existing ones are scaled and overcome. Empowering teachers to craft their own ladders—the ladders of teacher leadership—to resolve curriculum issues and concerns is an important part of this process. Continual collaboration and improvement of student learning makes any brick wall worthy of the climb.

Jeanne Tribuzzi and Brandon Wiley share responsibilities as West Seneca Central School District's Curriculum Mapping Coordinators. Their dynamic leadership and communication skills have aided them well in implementing and sustaining a districtwide curriculum-mapping initiative. Even though they developed a strategic three-year plan from the onset, they have stayed attentive to potential roadblocks and brick walls. As problems surfaced they adjusted what they needed to do to keep the initiative moving forward.

West Seneca Central School District

West Seneca, New York

After starting a project to align our K–5 English/Language Arts curriculum, curriculum mapping was explored as a potential process and tool to enhance this project. We were not truly ready for how mapping would change the entire course of curriculum management in our district of almost 7,500 students and 640 teachers.

When we began to see its potential, we read Dr. Jacobs's books, attended various conferences, and purchased a mapping system. Soon we began a large-scale, districtwide mapping initiative. The philosophy of mapping made sense to many, but the amount of work and setup necessary to make it happen was greater than we originally thought. While we felt that we planned well, we did not envision some of the problems we initially encountered.

The following are a few points to contemplate that may help you in your planning process.

Shared Leadership Is a Must

We learned the hard way that key players, both administrators and lead teachers, must be involved throughout the prologue to support and sustain mapping. It was difficult to share the mapping vision with building administrators who were not originally involved and were trying to manage multiple initiatives. To bring them up to speed, we provided one-on-one and small-group learning opportunities and aided the initiation of the curriculum-mapping process at each administrator's school site.

We also learned that dictating to teachers how the mapping process will unfold without soliciting teacher leadership from square one is not wise. Getting input and feedback about what mapping can look like, what will work best, and after starting, what is and isn't working well needs to be carefully planned out with input from lead teachers throughout the district. Once we realized our error, we adjusted and immediately enlisted direction and recommendations from teacher leaders. For your initiative, consider the following upfront:

- Solicit both formal and informal teacher leaders from throughout the district. Develop a structured support network, including a district-level Curriculum Mapping Cadre and Cabinet and building-level Curriculum Mapping Councils. These organizations truly help guide the mapping efforts and allow for input from all levels. Also, be certain that administrators are included in these leadership organizations.

(Continued)

(Continued)

- Involve all constituents from the cadre, cabinet, and councils in the development and implementation of the district's curriculum-mapping vision and goals. When times get tough or the workload gets heavy, revisiting how mapping benefits student learning is important. The purposes for mapping need to be continually revisited with faculty members by referring back to the vision and goals during various meeting forums.

- Be certain that everyone involved in training and explaining the components and process of mapping to teachers is capable and comfortable with all aspects of curriculum mapping. The cabinet and building-level council members are valuable communicators and must feel capable and able to reinforce connections between the mapping how-tos and the district's vision and goals.

Curriculum Mapping Coaches

Developing common mapping expectations throughout the district is important. We realized that there needed to be consistency in this message. We asked specific teachers to be key leaders and trainers at each school site by serving as curriculum-mapping coaches. Teachers who accept this position are given in-depth training and a stipend for their additional learning time. We have found this to be a fruitful decision. These site-based experts have played a significant role in establishing and institutionalizing mapping throughout our district. When teachers have questions, the coaches can answer them in person and address their immediate needs and concerns. The coaches also help maintain a continual focus on one of our ultimate goals: designing and maintaining a vertically articulated curriculum.

Establish Norms

Before individual teachers are asked to map, make certain that the Curriculum Mapping Cadre, Cabinet, Councils, and, if in place, coaches have participated in establishing districtwide mapping element norms. Instituting common expectations for writing the elements and recording maps has truly enhanced the ability to read the collective K–12 maps and has made conducting reviews much easier. We found that our teachers appreciated having informational how-to sheets that reminded them what each element's wording, format, and intra-alignment needed to be given our established norms.

Our Curriculum Mapping Cadre members originally took turns traveling from building to building to meet one-on-one or in small groups with teachers to aid them in their mapping work. We found that you have to be realistic and know that teachers will, for a time, need constant reminders about what is involved in writing the maps and especially using the created maps. We continuously remind teachers that mapping is a process. Speaking of which, we suggest you create a digital place, such as a school or district Web site's home page, to share and post the mapping norms. The home page can also include a link to your mapping system for easy access. Posting ongoing information about your district's curriculum-mapping initiative is invaluable. We have found that providing public information is advantageous to keeping our mapping momentum moving forward.

We've Already Done This Before

One roadblock you may face is apprehensive teachers who do not want to buy in to curriculum mapping. Some will tell you that they already engaged in a process wherein they determined what the curriculum should be. While many teachers have been involved in some form of curriculum development in the past, Dr. Jacobs's model differs since it does not function based on static documents reviewed once every five to seven years. Maps are digitally stored, living documents. Old methods of storing curriculum never allowed for instant accessibility and virtual examination of vertical and horizontal curriculum needs and concerns using a specialized mapping system.

Apprehension may also come from teachers who are comfortable doing what they have always done. Based on test scores and the need for clearer K–12 articulation, we found that some teachers' comfort zones were not open to improving student learning or raising awareness of implementing state standards. To offset resistance, when you ask teachers to think differently about curriculum, make sure that you allow them to openly share their concerns and ask questions; doing so helps defuse resistance. Resistance is a common reaction to the fear of the unknown. As we mentioned earlier, having curriculum-mapping coaches helped tremendously in supporting the mental and professional changes that a mapping initiative causes.

Encourage all of your teachers to read curriculum-mapping books and articles, watch videos, and participate in online courses to reinforce the message about why mapping is important. We organized book studies and video groups that helped teachers and administrators internalize the concepts and processes of curriculum mapping.

That Frustrating Four Letter Word: *Time*

Initially we found that the most significant obstacle was finding time to create quality maps and collaborate based on using the maps. You must be creative in solving this dilemma. It may require changes in current procedures, practices, and structures.

During the first year or two, you will discover that teachers need more time than you originally thought to learn how to map the elements and conduct reviews. The initial learning curve in mapping is complex since there are two levels of learning. The first is learning to articulate one's curriculum in the form of a map, and the second is learning how to use the selected Web-based mapping system.

Technology can add a layer of frustration and time constraints. If a school or district's technology infrastructure is poor, time will be lost while teachers await access to the Internet and the mapping system. Slow connections and access speed translate into an incorrect message that curriculum mapping is a slow process. Mapping is as fast as the technology allows. Therefore, tapping into monetary resources to purchase faster computers and greater bandwidth may be necessary. Preferably, teachers should not have to leave their classroom to go online. If they do have to go to a computer lab or station, it should not be a great distance from the classroom; otherwise it can truly irritate teachers, and some resist mapping because of it.

(Continued)

(Continued)

Mapping requires using time and resources effectively. Traditional meeting times and grouping of teachers may no longer work well. Here are seven ways we learned to think differently about this issue:

- Provide release time for teachers with substitute coverage. During this time teachers can work on curriculum maps or discuss maps with colleagues.
- Structurally redesign the current schedule to allow for common horizontal and vertical meeting times per grade level, department, or feeder pattern school. This may affect both school-site and district scheduling structures. Building late-start or early-release days into the school calendar is one way to manage this need.
- Utilize curriculum and technology funding to provide summer mapping training and work sessions. Teachers typically are more productive and can focus more readily when school is not in session. Intra- or interschool teachers can be brought together to design or revise Consensus Maps or Essential Maps, or individual teachers can fine-tune personal Projected Maps or Diary Maps.
- Use current faculty and department meeting times differently. Try to end the typical business-meeting approach and give ownership of these meetings back to teachers to map and conduct collaborative mapping reviews. They will thus make decisions that almost always instantly impact their instruction and students' learning.
- Commit to a one-year focus wherein all building or district staff development time is focused on various aspects of the mapping process. This sends a strong message to teachers that mapping matters. On staff development days, each school site selects its mapping focus for the day. If possible, work with local educational agencies to develop professional development training that fits the various focuses. We have worked with our local West Seneca Teacher Center to develop a series of 10 curriculum-mapping minicourses. One course is titled "Content or Skill: What's the Difference?" Another course focuses on designing quality essential questions.
- Suspend the collection of formal lesson plans as a way to lessen the load for teachers. Although they are still expected to plan for instruction, our teachers no longer have to turn in weekly lesson plans to the building principal. We have found that quality Projected Maps and Diary Maps serve just as well to verify what actually occurs in classrooms. Some of our teachers have begun including best-practice lesson plans aligned to specific learning.
- Encourage teachers to include curriculum mapping as a component in personal action research. Our tenured teachers must complete 15 hours of action research every two years as part of our district's professional review Professional Study Plan. Many have selected curriculum mapping as part of their research project, which has added rich dialogue and conversation to our overall mapping process.

The Times They Are a-Changing

Bob Dylan said it best. Education is about change. Be prepared for your long- and short-range curriculum-mapping implementation plans to change, but remember that there is a delicate balance between determining what needs to be modified and what does not. Do take into account teachers' feedback and insights, but do not make changes based on a whim or the voice of only a few. In the case of the latter, everyone begins to lose faith and will comment that the initiative was never securely in place. Conversely, if what is written in a strategic plan is held onto too tightly without room for adjustments, energy and momentum can be lost.

Publicly celebrate small gains, not just the big wins. Celebrate the fact that everyone can log in to the mapping system independently, record a month with all the initial elements, add a new map element, or conduct a review.

Curriculum mapping has positively changed our schools and district into a collaborative, collegial environment. Roadblocks will continue to come and go, but we have seen firsthand the academic growth and progress our students— and teachers—have made and are excited to see where our mapping road leads. For West Seneca Central School District, mapping is here to stay!

Alice Learn, curriculum administrator for the Greater Southern Tier Board of Cooperative Educational Services, will tell you her last name speaks true of her mapping experiences. She has learned a great deal from being responsible for a variety of districts' curriculum-mapping implementations.

Greater Southern Tier Board of Cooperative Educational Services

Chemung County, New York

I facilitate curriculum development for districts headed by a regional service agency. I have facilitated curriculum mapping in four districts ranging in population from 800 to 4,500 students. Each of my endeavors has been a learning experience and has enabled me to grow professionally by gaining insight into all aspects of the curriculum-mapping process. Every experience has affirmed my belief in the value of curriculum mapping as a tool for communication and collaboration about what students should know and be able to do. What follows are some of the roadblocks I have encountered.

Plan, Plan, Plan

The more advance planning and preparation you can do, the better. During your prologue determine (a) why you are mapping, (b) who will initially be mapping, (c) what types of curriculum maps will be created, (d) what will be viewed as a quality map, (e) what types of reviews will be encouraged once

(Continued)

(Continued)

maps have been created, (f) how the initial and ongoing trainings will occur, and (g) who will be responsible for conducting various trainings. Jumping into curriculum mapping without extensive advance planning will give stakeholders, both teachers and administrators, the impression that this too shall pass.

Why Are We Doing This?

In the district I am currently working in, teachers have been mapping for three years. At times I still hear this question: Why are we doing this? Those leading a mapping initiative must have the answer to this question—for both the present and the future—and it must be conveyed multiple times and in various ways. When teachers begin to experience mapping in its entirety, they begin to answer this question for themselves. I find that teachers truly value mapping when they start conducting read-throughs and reviews.

Paper-and-Pencil Map Days Are Gone

Before mapping systems were introduced in the districts I currently work with, paper-and-pencil was the way of monitoring curriculum. This method worked well only for teachers directly involved in serving on a curriculum committee. To try to share the data, I took on the task of word-processing the paper-and-pencil maps. The documents were stored on floppy disks and kept in my care. The management was maximum work with marginal success. There was no easy access for all and no capabilities for conducting comparative searches. Thank goodness for online mapping systems! Providing teachers with instant access, relational databases, search features, and a variety of curricular reports truly helps teachers work collaboratively to improve student learning.

How Do I Write a Curriculum Map?

While many teachers are able to identify content, skills, and assessments within specific disciplines, I have found equally as many who struggle with this task. Teachers must have adequate training about what each map element represents and how to format and intra-align data in a map. Plan differentiated staff development to honor those at different levels of understanding. Providing appropriate examples will prove beneficial.

The most powerful trainers are the teachers themselves. One district I work with has curriculum-mapping facilitators (a stipend position) who receive specific training. I have seen tremendous improvement in the quality of maps as a result of the facilitators' coaching and encouraging small groups of teachers. They also make certain the message is clear that a curriculum map is never considered done. All types of maps are revisited and revised to include more detail or deeper data. The facilitators are truly cheerleaders and continue to be mapping trailblazers in this district.

Shouldn't I Copyright My Diary Maps?

As it should be, all commercial mapping systems allow collaborative maps (Consensus Maps, Essential Maps) to be replicated into a teacher's personal account. Most mapping systems have blocking features related to the copying of someone's Projected Map or Diary Map.

Our service agency designed its own mapping system wherein replication of a teacher's Projected Map or Diary Map is possible. Some teachers have doubts about this capability. Many have said things like "First, let me say that I worked hard on my personal map, and I don't want someone else to get off easy by simply copying it. Second, my maps reflect *my* students' learning, not someone else's students!" To overcome this roadblock, we asked our software designer to add the following statement to any copied map: "Map copied from (map writer's or writers') name." We also encourage teachers who copy Diary Maps (usually a teacher who is new to a school) to send an e-mail to the teacher who created that map and invite him or her to review the map after it has been modified to reflect the borrowing teacher's student learning. This has helped defuse copyright concerns and the feeling that someone is stealing one's work.

Another point that needs to be made is that some teachers initially fear that personal maps will be monitored as part of teacher-performance scoring. Administrators must be proactive and build trust to reassure teachers that maps will never be used for formal evaluation.

Finding Time to Map and Discussing the Map Elements Early on Are Critical

Be prepared for this issue. Most likely it will have financial implications. In a district I am working with, we offer teachers 10 hours of afterschool inservice credit per semester to work on Projected Maps or Diary Maps. After a block of inservice hours has been earned, teachers receive a stipend in addition to their base salaries. This district also offers release time from the classroom if a teacher is falling too far behind or is unable to take advantage of the afterschool hours. Since our Web-based mapping system can be accessed anywhere, some teachers prefer to work on their maps at home.

Writing maps is only one part of the mapping process. Reviewing maps frequently is important for sustainability. To do so, the maps must be written in a similar manner. In one district I worked with, we waited too long to conduct an initial read-through. We would have been fine had we conducted an initial read-through after only a month or two of writing all the map elements. Instead, after the initial element training, we instructed each teacher to create a Diary Map monthly for the entire school year before conducting the initial read-through. This caused a great deal of tension and frustration because poor map-writing habits had formed. Wide inconsistencies in wording and format made it difficult for teachers to read each other's maps. Some maps had too much data, others not enough. The teachers were not happy when we asked them to now adhere to the specific norms we shared at the beginning of the year. They all said that it would have been much better if they had been mentored throughout the year, rather than at the end of the year. It was a bit of a struggle to get them to break their established habits, but by the end of the following year the map quality had improved.

(Continued)

(Continued)

It's All About Teamwork

Having served as a curriculum coordinator in a variety of districts, I can tell you that initiating curriculum mapping is not a solo performance. It is a team effort based on collective actions. Select key team players, both administrative and teacher leaders. Take time to build work relationships as a newly formed team. Together, seek help and advice from others who have gone before you, and ask a lot of questions. Plan all phases of implementation in great detail. Trust the process, welcome problems, and solve them as best as your team can. Celebrate the small and big steps taken, and, most important, sustain curriculum mapping by continuing to work together!

The Diocese of Kansas City–St. Joseph's 1,357 teachers, representing 13,140 PreK–12 students in 52 schools, were about to embark on their curriculum-mapping journey. Because it was such a large-scale initiative, the diocesan Curriculum Mapping (CM) Cadre established school-site CM coaches. Each school was allotted two to four positions depending on teacher and student population, and the diocese provided the newly appointed CM coaches and building administrators with prologue training.

Brian Smith, an elementary and middle school teacher, provides a unique perspective regarding roadblocks and brick walls. With no insight into mapping, he was asked to be a curriculum-mapping coach for St. James Elementary School. While Brian struggled to make sense of curriculum mapping, he simultaneously struggled with trying to assist his principal and fellow teachers. His candor, both intellectually and emotionally, provides insight and inspiration to all who, like him, are willing to take risks.

St. James Elementary School

St. Joseph, Missouri

When I first heard the term *curriculum mapping,* I had no clue what it meant. Our diocese had no set-in-stone curriculum, and I couldn't figure out how maps fit in. I kept thinking it would simply be the latest initiative equaling a lot of work and a waste of time. Soon after my initial encounter with this term, I was asked by my principal to be a CM coach for our school. I was informed that the other coach would be a teacher who had, unlike me, attended the National Curriculum Mapping Institute during the summer. Reluctantly, I agreed.

We attended a two-day training session before the school year began that included 120 CM coaches and building administrators. During the first day I met a few more teachers who had attended the summer conference, but the majority of us had not, and we felt out of the loop. Our diocese's consultant started the training, and, honestly, all of the words were a blur: *curriculum mapping, content, skills, assessments, standards, Diary Maps, Consensus Maps,* and someone named Chris. I kept wondering to myself, "Is Chris this lady's husband, son, or someone she works with?" By lunch my head was

---

spinning. It was full of unfamiliar terms, and I was having difficulty processing it all. I thought for certain I had made an awful mistake. When I left the meeting, I consciously chose not to attend the second day. I truly felt the initiative would come and go. Isn't that the way everything works in education?

My fellow CM coach returned from the second day of training wondering where I had been. I confessed my feelings and concerns. She told me how she thought mapping would be good for our school and for the diocese. We sat down, and she explained the mapping process once again. I asked a lot of questions.

Eventually, after a few more weeks of conversation, asking questions, and rereading the provided training materials numerous times, the lightbulb suddenly went on! I felt in my heart and mind that mapping truly would be an insightful processing tool. Having our teachers record what was both planned and learned in real time made sense. Comparing these two databases as well as supplemental data sources would improve our students' learning. I couldn't wait to get mapping going!

Little did I know that while I now "got it," mapping was not easy to explain to others. Since part of my responsibility as a CM coach was to help teachers learn how to write and use maps, I began to hit some brick walls.

Providing Answers

The first one, which I did not expect, was how hard it was to have answers ready when teachers started asking difficult questions. There were times I felt it was the blind leading the blind. Not until I learned more about the process through additional training, e-mail exchanges with our mapping consultant, and participatory staff meetings during which we initially read through, reviewed, and revised our own maps did I finally feel comfortable with the complexities of mapping. With growing confidence I was better equipped to aid others in what they needed to know and do in order to accomplish our school's Year One mapping goal: writing a quality Diary Map.

Building Common Knowledge

A second brick wall came when I was trying to help teachers feel at ease with mapping the elements, including how the elements needed to be worded, organized, and intra-aligned. Based on each teacher's personal prior knowledge, I found that, as a staff, we had varying definitions of each element and how the elements related to one another. By reading various training handouts, working together as a staff, and having the freedom to contact our diocese's consultant to answer immediate questions, we eventually came to agreement and built confidence in writing quality Diary Maps.

Incorporating Technology

One technology brick wall that we hit pretty hard, while most other schools did not, was the fact that we were one of eight schools not yet included in the diocese's selected mapping system. This was due to the fact that each school had to purchase its own account, and we did not have sufficient funds at the time. I made a Microsoft Word table that matched the mapping system's template. Our teachers diligently created Diary Maps using the template, but there was an undercurrent of frustration at not being included in the system or being able to view other schools' maps.

(Continued)

(Continued)

My fellow CM coach, the principal, and I finally spoke to the parish office manager about helping us purchase a mapping system account, which eventually happened. Since we had begun our work using the template, it was a simple process for each teacher to cut and paste his or her Diary Map data into the system.

The mapping system truly made the biggest difference in getting everyone to literally see that mapping is alive and interactive. The system allowed us not only to read and review our own maps but also to interface with all the diocesan and community schools' maps in a matter of seconds.

Curriculum Mapping Is Ongoing

We were ready to go, but not home free. We still had a mental brick wall to overcome. Everyone kept wondering when we would be done. It took a long time to realize that curriculum mapping never ends. We had always had the mentality of working hard on grade-level or schoolwide projects and looking forward to the projects being done. Eventually we began to see that mapping is all about ongoing discussions, review, and revision to our maps. This revelation was definitely not something that happened overnight.

Finding Time

The last brick wall I'll mention relates to time and the reality that teachers' lives are busy. Finding time to work on our maps and conduct reviews has been challenging. We began to think differently about meeting by using several of our early-dismissal days to focus specifically on mapping. We started with learning how to write quality maps. Later we focused on how to use the mapping system's search and report features. We spent other designated half days and times reviewing maps for gaps and redundancies across grade levels.

We found review meetings worthwhile for locating problematic areas in our curriculum. For example, we discovered that Grades 1–3 teach a Plants Unit in the first quarter of the school year with no new learning from year to year. The conversations about this situation were inspiring and caused our curriculum to change. Maps were immediately revised along the lines of rethinking our instruction.

As a staff we were now hooked on mapping. No longer was it my fellow coach or me trying to find times and ways to meet or map. Instead, the teachers intuitively found times and best configurations for meeting and discussing our curriculum, both horizontally and vertically.

We are now in our second official year of mapping, and our teachers are doing quite well with the concepts and processes. We are reviewing last year's maps and updating our current year's learning while working on diary mapping a new discipline. Are we experts at mapping? No, but we have learned an invaluable lesson by taking risks and believing in the mapping process.

I am a CM coach who has learned much about myself, both personally and professionally, through mapping. I highly recommend networking with other teachers, schools, districts, and dioceses in your community, in your state, and throughout the country to share and learn from one another. Take it one step at a time. Curriculum mapping is about the journey, not reaching an end. And always remember the student in the empty chair . . . who, by the way, I finally realized is *Chris!*

Roadblocks and brick walls are a part of life. As these practitioners have honestly shared, implementing a second-order change model involves slow and steady successes mixed with moments of frustration, disappointment, and potentially even setback. To sustain a curriculum-mapping initiative, a learning organization must focus on a preplanning prologue, a step-by-step implementation process, and preparation for flexibility, tenacity, and vigilance.

Inscribe the words *in the students' best interest* on your curriculum-mapping banner. Then, regardless of what you may encounter along the way, keep waving your banner high.

Glossary of Terms

The following terms are grouped by topic rather than by traditional alphabetical order. The terms are also not listed alphabetically within each topic. Instead they are sequenced based on a typical introduction to teachers when implementing a mapping initiative.

CURRICULUM MAPPING

Curriculum Mapping An ongoing, calendar-based process involving teacher-designed operational and planned-learning curriculum, collaborative inquiry, and data-driven decision making.

TYPES OF MAPS

Curriculum Map Generic term to describe any type of map.

Diary Map After-instruction month or months within a teacher's personal map that represent students' operational learning.

Projected Map Before-instruction month or months within a teacher's personal map that represent students' planned learning.

Consensus Map A school-site planned-learning map designated by months or grading periods and designed by collaborative agreement. Alternative names include Master Map, Collaborative Core Map, and Benchmark Map.

Essential Map A districtwide planned-learning map designated by months or grading periods and designed by a districtwide task force. Depending on a learning organization's configuration, a diocesewide or countywide planned-learning map is also referred to as an Essential Map.

MAP ELEMENTS

Unit Name A word or simple phrase that broadly represents the specific learning within a unit of study.

Content What students must know.

Skills What students must do in relation to the knowing. A skill is not the same as an activity that provides practice for the skill learning.

Target A specific mode or modes related to how a skill statement's verb will be measured (e.g., Identify *in writing* . . . ; Justify *orally* . . .).

Descriptor Specific details pertaining to content or skill learning expectations (e.g., Content—Matter: *Solid, Liquid, Gas;* Skill—Identify aurally *accented syllable in spoken 3-syllable word*).

Assessment Student product or performance.

Evaluation Teacher or peer-student judgment tool (e.g., teacher observation rubric, checklist, grading scale) for a particular product or performance.

Formative Assessment Informal product or performance designed to provide student instant feedback for self-monitoring personal learning expectations' strengths and weaknesses. An alternative name is assessment *for* learning.

Summative Assessment Formal product or performance designed to inform student and others about personal achievement regarding learning expectations. An alternative name is assessment *of* learning.

Common Assessment A collaboratively selected or designed product or performance simultaneously administered and evaluated by all teachers teaching the measured learning. Teachers immediately score students' work and compile the results to discuss needs and provide immediate collective support to encourage and ensure student progress.

Same Assessment A collaboratively selected or designed product or performance administered at the discretion of each teacher. A teacher may or may not choose to collaborate with fellow teachers regarding students' personal results.

Benchmark Assessment A districtwide or school-site product or performance measurement. If scoring is not conducted by the classroom teachers, the scored assessments, not just the statistical figures, are returned quickly so that teachers can immediately use the results for curriculum review and instructional planning.

Resources Textbooks, manipulatives, supplies, tools, or other pertinent supplemental materials that aid or enhance learning expectations and instruction.

Standards Generic term for national, state, local, or self-generated proficiency targets.

Standard Statement A specific proficiency target.

Standard Statement's Level-of-Learning Expectation Coding term to inform map readers of students' learning progression regarding a specific standard statement.

- **Introduce** The first time students are exposed to any portion of a standard statement. This does not necessarily mean the first time a teacher introduces the learning expectations since a standard statement may occur in student learning over a period of two or more academic years. A standard statement can be introduced only one time.

- **Develop** Revisiting an already-introduced full standard statement or adding a new portion or portions to a partially introduced statement. This level is selected each time students are engaged in the statement's learning expectation until independent mastery of the entire statement is achieved.
- **Mastery** Students display consistent, independent application of all portions of a standard statement.
- **Reinforce** This level represents (a) any continuation or expansion of a standard statement that has been mastered or (b) an entire standard statement or any portion thereof being incorporated into cross- or interdisciplinary learning.

Strategies Specific method, model, or strategic criteria that enable students to improve their learning.

Modifications/Accommodations Reduction or expansion of learning expectations or assessments for general, special needs, or gifted students.

Activities Exploratory or reinforcing experiences that help students attain learning expectations.

Essential Question A conceptual question, which can be generalized, that frames a unit of study and influences learning expectations and assessment products or performances.

Supporting Question A conceptual question that incorporates terminology specific to a unit of study's theme or topic. A supporting question influences learning expectations and assessment products or performances.

ALIGNMENTS

Intra-Alignment An articulated connection between the elements included in a map's individual month or unit.

Horizontal Intra-Alignment Element coherency comparison throughout a map's school year of months or units.

Horizontal Inter-Alignment Element coherency comparison of multiple maps representing one grade level. Comparisons may be discipline specific, cross-disciplinary, or interdisciplinary.

Vertical Inter-Alignment Element coherency comparison of a series of grade levels' discipline specific, cross-disciplinary, or interdisciplinary maps.

SEVEN-STEP REVIEW PROCESS

This is a procedure for analyzing curriculum maps and/or other data, resources, or materials. A review may include the following team dynamics:

- **Horizontal** One grade level
- **Vertical** Across a series of two or more grade levels

- **Like** One discipline
- **Mixed** Cross- or interdisciplinary

The four team dynamics are often combined to best meet the needs of a planned review focus:

- **Horizontal–Like** (e.g., Grade 3 mathematics)
- **Horizontal–Mixed** (e.g., Grade 3 mathematics, science)
- **Vertical–Like** (e.g., Grades 3–6 mathematics)
- **Vertical–Mixed** (e.g., Grades 3–6 mathematics, science)

Step One: Collecting the Data A particular review's focus will drive the data necessary for conducting the review. The data may include one or more types of map and/or other data sources. Be aware that at times collecting the data related to curriculum maps may not include paper documents. When using the search and report features in a mapping system, the system performs the act of collecting data based on criteria entered and displays the results on the computer screen. Unless hard copies are desired for small- or large-group meetings, the collected map data and results can be viewed on a computer monitor. Again, depending on the review focus, there may be the need for collecting data that is in printed form, such as test results, survey results, or student work samples.

Step Two: First Read-Through Each review team member privately reads selected maps using one or more predetermined mapping system's features as well as, when appropriate, other pertinent hard-copy data sources based on the review focus. During this time of inquiry and reflection, each member records personal commentary notes.

Step Three: Small-Group Review A group of two to approximately eight team members focus on the collegial discussion of the preselected data related to the review focus. A designated recorder takes notes based on the individual findings and collaborative comments.

Step Four: Large-Group Comparison A meeting consisting of all the collective review team members who have first read individually and compared the small-groups' commentaries. During the large-group meeting, collegial dialogue addresses what may need to be started, stopped, modified, or maintained regarding curriculum, the learning environment, or other considerations based on the review focus and small-group findings.

Step Five: Immediate Revision If the large group comes to agreement on a resolution or resolutions with relative ease, decisions are noted and actions documented. If necessary, timelines are created and specific faculty members chosen to be accountability leaders. If the large group cannot come to agreement based on a need for more in-depth information, a task force is formed to conduct research. Timelines, the responsible person or persons, and dissemination of new information are determined.

Task Force A temporary team of teachers, and possibly administrators, best suited for the designated task(s). A task force is often formed to conduct research for a review focus or to collaboratively design Essential Maps. A task force is disbanded once the task or tasks have been completed.

Step Six: Research and Development The created task force investigates the large group's informational needs and periodically informs the large group of its findings.

Step Seven: New Review Considerations When the problem, issue, or concern has been resolved and appropriate actions have been carried out, the large-group review team is disbanded. A future problem, issue, or concern may warrant the same people being involved in another review or reconvening to revisit an earlier review focus.

COMMON REVIEW FOCUSES

Initial Read-Through This is a unique review focus that is not designed to review maps for student-learning inquiry. The purpose of this review is to support teachers and administrators who are learning to write quality maps. The review's dual focus includes (a) the correct use of wording, format, and intra-alignment writing norms and (b) ensuring a map's readability by people other than its writer(s).

Gaps Unplanned small or large deficiencies in learning expectations in a series of single-discipline, cross-disciplinary, or interdisciplinary courses.

Repetitions or Redundancies Unplanned identical learning expectations in a series of single-discipline, cross-disciplinary, or interdisciplinary courses.

Coherency A rigorous connection between aligned elements in a unit of study, in a learning month, or over a series or units, months, or years.

Timeliness Ensuring that learning expectations, environments, and tools are not outdated, including (a) resources such as textbooks, maps, and computers; (b) technology use such as Web-based research and electronic presentations or projects; and (c) studying of local, national, and global current events and breakthroughs.

Bilevel Item Analysis Analyzing a test item based on both the specific subject matter and the linguistic knowledge needed to comprehend the item's task.

CURRICULUM-MAPPING INTRA-ORGANIZATIONS

All intra-organization terms are appropriate for a multiple-schools learning organization. If a lone school is mapping, a Curriculum Mapping Council and possibly a modified Curriculum Mapping Cadre is sufficient.

Curriculum Mapping Coordinator Person responsible for the overall management of a curriculum-mapping initiative who serves as a liaison and key communicator between Curriculum Mapping Cadre, Curriculum Mapping Cabinet, and Curriculum Mapping Councils; administrators at all levels; board members; and the community.

Curriculum Mapping Cadre A team of approximately five to seven people, including the Curriculum Mapping Coordinator, who share the responsibilities of strategic planning and implementation. They also serve as the learning organization's curriculum-mapping resident experts.

Curriculum Mapping Cabinet A districtwide team consisting of teachers, administrators, and the Curriculum Mapping Cadre who represent the diversity of all grades, all disciplines, and support services. Cabinet members become proficient in the mapping process and serve as districtwide experts. The members participate in making ongoing districtwide mapping decisions as well as approving, developing, modifying, and expanding the large-scale learning organization's curriculum-mapping action plans. Cabinet members serve a dual role by also being members of a school-site council.

Curriculum Mapping Council A school-site-specific team of teachers and administrators who represent all grade levels, disciplines, and support services. Council members become proficient in the mapping process and serve as in-house experts. The council members support the districtwide action plans as well as collaboratively develop and implement school-site curriculum-mapping action plans.

MISCELLANEOUS TERMS

Learning Organization A generic term referring to an educational community such as a school, district, diocese, county, or college.

Operational Curriculum The learning expectations and assessments that actually took place in real time in a given school year.

Planned Learning Curriculum The learning expectations and assessments intended prior to the passage of real time in a given school year.

Breaking Apart Standards A procedure that aids teachers in collaboratively agreeing on the explicit and implicit learning expectations for each standard statement and translating these expectations into elements in a curriculum map.

Power Standards A collaboratively chosen subset of standard statements that teachers agree students must learn in depth to ensure student learning success.

References

Ainsworth, L. 2003. *Power standards: Identifying the standards that matter most.* Englewood, CA: Advanced Learning Press.

Ainsworth, L., and D. Viegut. 2006. *Common formative assessments: How to connect standards-based instruction and assessment.* Thousand Oaks, CA: Corwin Press.

Barth, R. S. 2006. Improving relationships within the schoolhouse. *Educational Leadership* 63(6): 8–13.

Beckwith, B., and D. Niguidula. 2007. Linking student digital portfolios to curriculum maps. Breakout presentation at the Thirteenth National Curriculum Institute, Park City, UT.

Black, P., and D. Wiliam. 1998. Inside the black box: Raising standards through classroom assessment. *Phi Delta Kappan* 80(2): 139–144, 146–148. http://www.pdkintl.org/kappan/kbla9810.htm.

Chappuis, S., R. Stiggins, J. Arter, and J. Chappuis. 2004. *Assessment FOR learning: An action guide for school leaders.* Portland, OR: Assessment Training Institute.

Costa, A., and B. Kallick. 2000. *Discovering and exploring habits of the mind.* Alexandria, VA: Association for Supervision and Curriculum Development.

DuFour, R., R. DuFour, and R. Eaker. 2005. *On common ground: The power of professional learning communities.* Bloomington, IN: National Educational Services.

DuFour, R., R. DuFour, R. Eaker, and T. Many. 2006. *Learning by doing: A handbook for professional learning communities.* Bloomington, IN: Solution Tree.

English, F. 1980. Curriculum mapping. *Educational Leadership* 37(7): 558–559.

English, F., and B. Steffy. 2002. *Deep curriculum alignment: Creating a level playing field for all children on high-stakes tests of educational accountability.* Lanham, MD: Scarecrow Press.

Erickson, L. H. 2001. *Stirring the head, heart, and soul: Refining curriculum and instruction.* Thousand Oaks, CA: Corwin Press.

———. 2002. *Concept-based curriculum and instruction: Teaching beyond the facts.* Thousand Oaks, CA: Corwin Press.

———. 2007. *Concept-based curriculum and instruction for the thinking classroom.* Thousand Oaks, CA: Corwin Press.

Friedman, T. L. 2006. *The world is flat: A brief history of the twenty-first century.* New York: Farrar, Strauss and Giroux.

Fullan, M. 2001a. *Leading in a culture of change.* San Francisco: Jossey-Bass.

———. 2001b. *The new meaning of educational change.* New York: Teachers College Press.

———. 2005. *Leadership and sustainability.* Thousand Oaks, CA: Corwin Press.

Gough, P. D. 2003. Creating a timely curriculum: A conversation with Heidi Hayes Jacobs. *Educational Leadership* 61(4): 12–17.

Heifetz, R. 1994. *Leadership without easy answers.* Cambridge, MA: Harvard University Press.

Hussar, W. J. 1999. *Predicting the need for newly hired teachers in the United States to 2008–09.* Washington, DC: National Center for Education Statistics.

Jacobs, H. H. 1989. *Interdisciplinary curriculum: Design and implementation.* Alexandria, VA: Association for Supervision and Curriculum Development.

———. 1997. *Mapping the big picture: Integrating curriculum and assessment K–12.* Alexandria, VA: Association for Supervision and Curriculum Development.

———. 2002. Integrated curriculum design. In *Interdisciplinary education K–12 and college: A foundation for K–16 dialogue,* ed. J. Y. Klein, 23–44. New York: College Board.

———. 2003a. Connecting curriculum mapping and technology. *Curriculum Technology Quarterly* 12(3): 1–8.

———. 2003b. Curriculum mapping. Keynote presentation at the Ninth National Curriculum Mapping Institute, Park City, UT.

———. 2004a. Curriculum mapping as a hub: Integrating new forms of data, decision-making structures, and staff development. In *Getting results with curriculum mapping,* ed. H. H. Jacobs, 126–137. Alexandria, VA: Association for Supervision and Curriculum Development.

———, ed. 2004b. *Getting results with curriculum mapping.* Alexandria, VA: Association for Supervision and Curriculum Development.

———. 2006a. *Active literacy across the curriculum: Strategies for reading, writing, speaking, and listening,* Larchmont, NY: Eye On Education.

———. 2006b. Wrestling with consensus maps: How to create meaningful anchors in the curriculum for your school or district. Keynote presentation at the Twelfth National Curriculum Mapping Institute, Santa Fe, NM.

———. 2007. The hub effect: Focusing engaged learning and dynamic professionalism through curriculum mapping. Keynote presentation at the Thirteenth National Curriculum Mapping Institute, Park City, UT.

Jensen, E. 2000. *Brain-based learning: The new science of teaching and training.* Thousand Oaks, CA: Corwin Press.

Kallick, B. 2006. Sustaining the mapping initiative. Keynote presentation at the Twelfth National Curriculum Mapping Institute, Santa Fe, NM.

Kallick, B., and J. M. Wilson. 2004. Curriculum mapping and software: Creating an information system for learning community. In *Getting results with curriculum mapping,* ed. H. H. Jacobs, 83–96. Alexandria, VA: Association for Supervision and Curriculum Development.

Kercheval, A., and S. L. Newbill. 2001. *A case study of key effective practices in Ohio's improved school districts.* Bloomington, IN: Indiana Center for Evaluation.

Knoster, T., R. Villa, and J. Thousand. 2000. A framework for thinking about systems change. In *Restructuring for caring and effective education: Piecing the puzzle together,* ed. R. Villa and J. Thousand, 93–128. Baltimore: Paul H. Brookes.

Lezotte, L., and K. McKee. 2002. *Some assembly required: A continuous school improvement system.* Okemos, MI: Effective Schools Products.

Marzano, R. J. 2003. *What works in schools: Translating research into action.* Alexandria, VA: Association for Supervision and Curriculum Development.

Marzano, R., and D. Pickering. 2005. *Building academic vocabulary knowledge: Teacher's workbook.* Alexandria, VA: Association for Supervision and Curriculum Development.

Marzano, J., D. Pickering, and J. McTighe. 1993. *Assessing student outcomes: Performance assessment using the dimensions of learning model.* Alexandria, VA: Association for Supervision and Curriculum Development.

Marzano, J., D. Pickering, and J. Pollock. 2001. *Classroom instruction that works: Research-based strategies for increasing student achievement.* Alexandria, VA: Association for Supervision and Curriculum Development.

Marzano, R., T. Waters, and B. McNulty. 2005. *School leadership that works: From research to results.* Alexandria, VA: Association for Supervision and Curriculum Development.

McEwan, E. 2003. *Ten traits of highly effective principals: From good to great performance.* Thousand Oaks, CA: Corwin Press.

———. 2005. *How to deal with teachers who are angry, troubled, exhausted, or just plain confused.* Thousand Oaks, CA: Corwin Press.

McTighe, J., and G. Wiggins. 2004. *Understanding by design professional development workbook.* Alexandria, VA: Association for Supervision and Curriculum Development.

O'Shea, M. R. 2005. *From standards to success: A guide for school leaders.* Alexandria, VA: Association for Supervision and Curriculum Development.

Pfeffer, J., and R. Sutton. 2000. *The knowing-doing gap: How smart companies turn knowledge into action.* Boston: Harvard Business School Press.

Random House. 2006. *Dictionary.com unabridged (v1.1): Know.* http://dictionary .reference.com/browse/know.

Reeves, D. 1996–2002. *Making standards work: How to implement standards-based assessments in the classroom, school, and district.* Denver, CO: Advanced Learning Press.

———. 2007. Ahead of the curve: Transforming research into action. Keynote presentation at the Solution Tree Assessment Institute, Denver, CO.

Schmied, K. 2004. A view that matters: Understanding essential questions. Paper presented at the 54th Association for Supervision and Curriculum Development Conference, New Orleans, LA.

Schmoker, M. 1999. *Results: The key to continuous school improvement,* 2nd ed. Alexandria, VA: Association for Supervision and Curriculum Development.

———. 2006. *Results now: How we can achieve unprecedented improvements in teaching and learning.* Alexandria, VA: Association for Supervision and Curriculum Development.

Senge, P. 1994. *The fifth discipline fieldbook: Strategies and tools for building a learning organization.* New York: Doubleday.

Senge, P., N. Cambron-McCabe, T. Lucas, B. Smith, and A. Kleiner. 2000. *Schools that learn: A fifth discipline fieldbook for educators, parents, and everyone who cares about education.* New York: Doubleday.

Stiggins, R. J., J. Arter, J. Chappuis, and S. Chappuis. 2005. *Classroom assessment FOR student learning: Doing it right—using is well.* Portland, OR: Assessment Training Institute.

Strangeway, M. 2006. Four reasons to map. Breakout session at the Twelfth National Curriculum Mapping Institute, Santa Fe, NM.

Tomlinson, C. A. 1999–2000. *The differentiated classroom: Responding to the needs of all learners.* Alexandria, VA: Association for Supervision and Curriculum Development.

Udelhofen, S. 2005. *Keys to curriculum mapping: Strategies and tools to make it work.* Thousand Oaks, CA: Corwin Press.

Villa, R. A., and J. S. Thousand. 2000. *Restructuring for caring and effective education: Piecing the puzzle together.* Baltimore: Paul H. Brookes.

Wiggins, G., and J. McTighe. 1998. *Understanding by design.* Alexandria, VA: Association for Supervision and Curriculum Development.

———. 2007. *Schooling by design: Mission, action, and achievement.* Alexandria, VA: Association for Supervision and Curriculum Development.

Index

Action-research teaching teams, 197
Administrator, role in curriculum
    mapping, 26, 27
Adversarial relationships, 8
Agnew, K., 265–268
Ainsworth, L., 199–200, 209–210, 211
Alignment
    horizontal inter-alignment,
        40, 156*f*–157, 285
    horizontal intra-alignment, 40, 285
    intra-alignment, 20, 21, 285
    intra-alignment coding, 85, 146, 147
    vertical inter-alignment, 285
    visual intra-alignment, 83*f*
Articulation review, 156–157
    overlapping vertical teams, 157*f*
    sample focuses, 156*f*
Assessment
    benchmark, 68, 284
    common, 284
    common *vs.* same, 69
    in Consensus Maps, 71
    definition of, 284
    in Diary Maps, 71
    in Essential Maps, 71
    evaluation *vs.*, 65–67, 107–108
    formal, 284
    formative, 67–68
    homework as, 68
    in Projected Maps, 71
    summative, 67–68, 284
    technology-based, 173
    writing elements for, 64–71
    year-long focus of, 64

Backwards design, 192, 254
Barth, R. S., 244
Benchmark assessment, 68, 284
Bilevel item analysis, 287
Black, P., 67
Bloom, Benjamin, 69–71
Bloom's Taxonomy, 70*f*–71

Boyle, Janet, 261–264
Breaking apart standards,
    199, 200, 201–209
    definition of, 288
    disaggregating standards, 201–202
    interpretation outcomes, 202–204
    Phase 1, highlighting process,
        204–206
    Phase 2, review of focuses, 206–207
    Phase 3, scaffolded/spiraled elements,
        207–209*f*
    Phase 4, adjustments, 209
    procedure, 204–209
    recording, 207
    standards statement, coding, 204*f*

Card shuffle debrief, 131, 144
Center Grove Community School
    Corporation, 261–268
Center Grove High School, 265–268
Change, second-order, 28*f*–29,
    245, 255, 281
Collegial forum, 6–9
Collegial relationships, 8
Common assessment, 69, 284
Compare-and-contrast learning
    continuum, 51–52*f*
Conceptual questions, for refining
    data, 188
    nouns/verbs and, 191
    structural formula, 191
    vs. direct-answer questions, 190
Conducting the Initial Read-Through
    DVD, 134
Conference/workshop, 29, 32, 34, 36,
    118, 137, 235, 258, 264, 270
Congenial relationships, 8
Consensus and Essential Maps
    articulation review, 156–157
    articulation review, overlapping
        vertical teams, 157*f*
    articulation review, sample foci, 156*f*

developmental considerations,
155–158
difference between, 145
See also Consensus Maps;
Essential Maps
Consensus Maps, 12*f*, 14, 19, 146–153
finding absences of standards in,
172–173
assessments and, 71
common initial map elements, 41*f*
conducting initial read-through, 147
definition of, 283
designing, 155
Elementary Literacy School
Improvement Plan, 246*f*–247*f*
elements included in, 146, 147
Environmental Science Consensus
Map Month, 160*f*
Grade 6 Library Science Consensus
Map Month, 162*f*
High School Communication Arts
Consensus Map Month—Year
One Versus Year Two, 147*f*, 148*f*
intra-alignment number coding
and, 146, 147
isolated teacher and, 150–152
mixed-group review of, 152–153
modifications/accommodations,
182, 184
resources and, 84
Social Studies Consensus Map
Month, 16*f*
use of existing maps to
write, 147–150*f*
See also Consensus and Essential Maps
Content
definition of, 283
writing elements, 45–50
Continent teaching, 117
Copyright issue, 276–277
Course name, writing, 91, 97
Curriculum
operational, 2–3, 288
planned learning, 2–3, 288
See also Review process, for
curriculum
Curriculum maps
comparison using, 31
definition of, 39, 283
level of detail in, 13*f*
visual comparison of, 13–19
vs. lesson plans, 19
See also Consensus Maps; Curriculum
mapping; Diary Maps; Essential
Maps; Projected Maps

Curriculum Mapper, 218*f*
Curriculum mapping
definition of, xv, 283
improper implementation of, 37
positive impact of, 37
tenets of, 3, 4*f*
Curriculum Mapping Cabinet,
236–237, 288
action plans and, 253
additional map data and, 182
Essential Maps and, 154
initial mapping and, 113, 118
map selection and, 34, 35, 36,
37, 219
as part of design task force, 228
preplanning and, 29–30, 156
Curriculum Mapping Cadre,
236, 287–288
action plans and, 253
map selection and, 219
as part of design task force, 228
preplanning and, 156
Curriculum Mapping Coordinator,
235, 287
action plans and, 253
map selection and, 219
as part of design task force, 228
preplanning and, 156
Curriculum Mapping Council,
237–238, 288
action plans and, 253
additional map data and, 182
initial mapping and, 118
map selection and, 34, 35,
36, 37, 219
as part of design task force, 228
preplanning and, 29–30, 156

Descriptor, content, 47, 48*f*
Descriptor, skill, 51, 58–59*f*, 206, 284
Design, map
initial map choice, 32–33
map selection examples, 34–37
mapping sequence,
appropriate, 32–37
preplanning time, 29–30
proper map name, using, 32
second-order change, 28*f*–29
teacher-designed curriculum, 26–27
trust and respect issues, 27–28
Develop (D) level of learning
expectations, 77–78, 79, 81, 285
Diary Maps, 2, 5*f*, 6, 11–12*t*, 13, 14
activities element, 184, 185*f*–187*f*
assessments in, 71

common initial map elements, 41*f*
definition of, 283
Elementary Principal Professional
    Development Map Month, 248*f*
Grade 7 Language Arts Diary Map
    Month, 179*f*
High School Visual and Performing
    Arts Diary Map Month, 128*f*
Intermediate Science Diary Map
    Month, 123*f*
Kindergarten Mathematics Diary Map
    Month, 183*f*
Life Science Unit Diary Map
    Month, 194*f*
Middle School Computer Keyboarding
    and Processing I Diary Map
    Month, 126*f*–127*f*
Middle School Physical Education
    Diary Map Month, 124*f*–125*f*
modifications/accommodations,
    182, 183*f*
non-normed excerpts, 90*f*
Prekindergarten Thematic Unit Diary
    Map Month, 185*f*–187*f*
Primary Mathematics Dairy Map
    Month, 121*f*
Primary Reading Diary Map
    Month, 122*f*
Social Studies Diary Map
    Month, 17*f*–18*f*
U.S. History Unit Diary Map
    Month, 195*f*–196*f*
vs. Projected Maps, 19
See also Diary Maps or Projected Maps
Diary Maps or Projected Maps
    difference between, 109–110*f*, 120
    due date, establishing, 112
    full disclosure and, 119
    implementation, 113–119, 115*f*–116*f*
    initial read-through,
        conducting, 117
    operational learning and, 110–113
    overview of, 130–131
    personal map writing and, 113
    recording Projected Maps, 118
    student-designed learning
        and, 112–113
    See also Diary Maps; Diary Maps or
        Projected Maps, preplanning;
        Projected Maps
Diary Maps or Projected Maps,
    preplanning, 131–137
    *Conducting the Initial
        Read-Through* DVD
Disaggregating standards, 201–202

Electronic meeting forum, 32
Element comparisons. *See* Alignment;
    Horizontal intra-alignment
Elementary Literacy School
    Improvement Plan, 246*f*–247*f*
Elementary Principal Professional
    Development Map Month, 248*f*
Elements, mapping
    activities, 20, 285
    additional map elements,
        common, 20
    alignment categories. *See* Alignment
    assessment, 20, 21, 284
    benchmark assessment, 68, 284
    content, 20, 283
    copying existing maps, caution
        about, 40–41
    descriptor, 51, 58–59*f*, 206, 284
    discipline for first districtwide
        focus, 21–22
    essential questions, 20, 285
    evaluations, 20, 284
    formative assessment, 284
    initial elements, common, 20
    initial map elements, 40, 41*f*
    modifications/accommodations,
        20, 285
    resources. *See* Resources
    same assessment, 69, 284
    skills. *See* Skills
    special education, 22
    specialist teachers, 22
    standard statement. *See* Standards
    standards. *See* Standards
    strategies, 20, 285
    summative assessment, 67–68, 284
    supporting questions, 20, 285
    target. *See* Target, proficiency
    unit name, 42–45, 44*f*, 283
    See also Writing elements
Empty chair analogy, xv, 152
Environmental Science Consensus Map
    Month, 160*f*
Environmental Science Essential Map
    Month, 159*f*
Erickson, L. H., 40, 69–70, 188,
    192, 200
Essential Maps, 12*f*, 13, 14,
    19, 153–154
    assessments in, 71
    definition of, 283
    designing, 155–156
    elements included, 41*f*, 154
    Environmental Science Essential Map
        Month, 159*f*

Grade 6 Library Science Essential Map
    Month, 161*f*
modifications/accommodations
    and, 184
Pinnacle Peak School District, 153*f*
resources and, 84
Social Studies Essential Map
    Month, 15*f*
See also Consensus and
    Essential Maps
Essential questions, for refining data,
    190–191, 194*f*, 195*f*–196*f*
Evaluation
    definition of, 284
    vs. assessment, 65–67, 107–108
    See also Assessment

FOR (significant formative
    assessment), 67
Formal assessment, definition of, 284
Fullan, M., 28, 232, 244, 252

Gateway Elementary School
    (K–8), 258–260
German I Diary Map Month,
    44*f*, 50*f*, 63*f*, 77*f*, 83*f*, 88*f*
Grade 6 Library Science Consensus
    Map Month, 162*f*
Grade 6 Library Science Essential
    Map Month, 161*f*
Grade 7 Language Arts Diary
    Map Month, 179*f*
Grassroots initiative, 232–233
Greater Southern Tier Board of
    Cooperative Educational
    Services, 275–278

High School Communication Arts Map
    Month, 147*f*, 148*f*
High School Visual and Performing
    Arts Diary/Projected Map
    Month, 128*f*
Homework, as assessment, 68
Horizontal articulation, 117, 233
Horizontal curriculum design, 46, 50*f*,
    206, 214, 215, 273
Horizontal inter-alignment,
    40, 156*f*–157, 285
Horizontal intra-alignment, 40, 285
Horizontal review
    group meeting, 6, 167, 245, 250,
        260, 263, 274, 280
    like-group, 286
    mixed-group, 174, 286
Hussar, W. J., 178

Implementation, Diary or Projected
    Maps, 113–119
    beyond first year, 118–119
    recording all elements from
        onset, 117
    recording elements incrementally,
        114, 115*f*–116*f*
    See also Implementation planning
Implementation planning
    action plan for, 253–255
    backwards design for
        steps/timelines, 254
    changes to, 255
    consultant/trainer for,
        241–243, 242*f*
    good to great, 233
    grassroots initiative, 232–233
    immediate/future concerns, 234
    incentives for teachers, 251–253
    intra-organizations and, 235–241
    issue-motivated initiative, 232
    mapping system and, 249–250
    personnel for, 249
    reasons for mapping, 233–234
    resources for, 245, 249–251
    responsible parties, 234–235
    shared vision of, 232–243
    skills needed for, 243–245
    steps and timelines for, 253–254
    systemic change and, 232
    time issues in, 250
Initial Read-Through Process,
    preplanning
    card shuffle debrief, 131, 144
    collaboration and, 142*f*–143*f*
    facilitator, 130–137
    forming small-group teams,
        131–132
    individual preread review, 133
    optional second round, 137–138
    packet, 132–133
    purpose/process/expectations, 132
    team member, 139–143, 142*f*–143*f*
Instant messaging, 32
Inter-alignment articulation, 146
Inter-alignment,
    horizontal, 40, 156*f*–157, 285
    vertical, 285
Intermediate Science Diary/Projected
    Map Month, 123*f*
Intra-alignment
    horizontal, 40, 285
    number coding for, 146, 147
    of vague *vs.* quality content-skill
        statement, 59*f*

Intra-organizations. *See* Curriculum
    Mapping Cabinet; Curriculum
    Mapping Cadre; Curriculum
    Mapping Coordinator; Curriculum
    Mapping Council
Introduce (I) level of learning
    expectations, 77–78, 79, 81, 284
Island teaching, 117

Jacobs, H. H.
    on bileval item analysis, 176–177
    coin-with-two-sides analogy of, 249
    on commitment, 255
    comparisons as diagnosis-prognosis
        relationship, 255
    on curriculum maps, 39
    on differentiated staff, 249
    empty chair analogy, xv, 249
    on gaps and repetitions, 170
    on knowledge/courage needs, 37
    on mapping as formal work, 2
    on planning time, 29
    seven-step review process of. *See*
        Review process, seven-step
    on student-friendly essential
        questions, 193
    on systems integration, 250
    on teaching skills, 40
    on technology, 217
    on technology-based
        assessments, 173
    on using maps to inform new
        teachers, 178
    on year-long focus of assessment, 64

Kallick, B., 28
Kindergarten Mathematics Diary Map
    Month, 183*f*
Knowing, defining, 45–46
Kovach, S., 268–270

Lakeville Area Public School
    District, 268–270
Learn, A., 275–278
Learning organization, definition of, 288
Like-group review, 6, 167, 245, 286

Mapping mapping, 240–241
Marzano, R. J., 2, 28
Mastery (M) level of learning
    expectations, 77–78, 79, 80,
    81, 285
McEwan, E., 244
McNulty, B., 28
McTighe, J., 192

Measurable verbs, 51, 52–53, 54, 56,
    57, 60, 70*f*, 192, 206
Middle School Computer Keyboarding
    and Processing I Diary/Projected
    Map Month, 126*f*–127*f*
Middle School Physical Education
    Diary/Projected Map Month,
    124*f*–125*f*
Mixed-group review, 6, 152–153, 167,
    174, 245, 260, 263, 286

National Curriculum Mapping Institute,
    262, 266, 267, 268
Nonmeasurable verbs, 53–55*f*
Noun-focused learning, 46–47
Nouns, for conceptual questions, 191
    Numerals *vs.* words for numbers in
        maps, 45, 45*f*

Operational curriculum
    definition of, 288
    vs. planned learning curriculum, 2–3
O'Shea, M. R., 200

Parallel play relationship, 8, 151–152
Pfeffer, J., 251
Pickell, J., 265–268
Pinnacle Peak School District, 153*f*
Planned learning curriculum
    definition of, 288
    vs. operational curriculum, 2–3
Power standards, 154, 288
    determining, 199–200, 209–214
    seven-step review for, 211–214
Practitioner advice
    adaptations, 263, 275
    Center Grove Community School
        Corporation, 261–268
    Center Grove High School, 265–268
    coaches, 272, 278–280
    copyright issue, 276–277
    districtwide vision, 264
    Gateway Elementary School
        (K–8), 258–260
    Greater Southern Tier Board of
        Cooperative Educational
        Services, 275–278
    Lakeville Area Public School District,
        268–270
    leadership, 263, 269–270,
        271–272
    mapping as process, 267, 268, 280
    mapping element issues, 272, 277
    multiple focuses, 264
    planning issues, 275–276

principal–high school teachers
conversation, 265–268
professional development, 262
purpose, 258–259
reasons for mapping, 276
schoolwide progress, 266–267
St. James Elementary School,
278–280
support, 266, 269–270
teacher apprehension, 273, 279
teamwork, 278
technology, 259, 263–264, 268, 273,
276, 279–280
time issues, 259–260, 262–263, 265,
270, 273–274, 277, 280
training, 262, 266, 267, 270, 274,
276, 279–280
West Seneca Central School District,
271–275
Prekindergarten Thematic Unit Diary
Map Month, 185f–187f
Primary Mathematics Dairy Map
Month, 121f
Primary Mathematics Projected Map
Month, 121f
Primary Reading Diary Map
Month, 122f
Primary Reading Projected Map
Month, 122f
Principal, role in curriculum mapping,
26, 245, 246f–248f
Professional development
training, 262, 266, 267, 270, 274,
276, 279–280
workshops/conference, 29, 32,
34, 36, 118, 137, 235, 258,
264, 270
Projected Maps, 12f, 13
assessments in, 71
common initial map elements, 41f
definition of, 283
finding absences of standards
in, 172–173
High School Visual and Performing
Arts Projected Map Month, 128f
Intermediate Science Projected Map
Month, 123f
Middle School Computer Keyboarding
and Processing I Projected Map
Month, 126f–127f
Middle School Physical Education
Projected Map Month,
124f–125f
Primary Mathematics Projected Map
Month, 121f

Primary Reading Projected Map
Month, 122f
vs. Diary Map, 19
See also Diary Maps or Projected Maps
Prologue, mapping, 29–30, 35
determining responsible
parties, 234–235
potential timeline for,
238–240, 239f–240f

Refining curriculum maps
activity data, 184, 185f–187f
adding data to established
elements, 184
backwards design and, 192, 254
conceptual questions, 188, 190–191
content-and-skills study unit,
191–193, 192f
direct-answer questions, 190
essential questions, 190–191,
194f, 195f–196f
essential questions,
student-friendly, 193
faculty member dual roles, 188, 189f
Life Science Unit Diary Map
Month, 194f
mapping questions, 193–197
modifications/accommodations,
182–184, 183f
strategies, 182
supporting questions, 190–191
U.S. History Unit Diary Map Month,
195f–196f
Reinforce (R) level of learning
expectations, 78, 80, 81, 285
Relational articulation, 156f, 157
Resources
definition of, 284
elements, mapping, 20, 284
standard statement, 284
textbooks as, 200
Review, mapping, 31
bilevel item analysis, 287
coherency in maps, 287
data-driven review, 163–170
gaps, repetitions in maps,
170–172, 287
horizontal, 6, 167, 245, 250, 260,
263, 274, 280, 285, 286
initial read-through, 287
like-group, 6, 167, 245, 286
mixed-group, 6, 152–153, 167, 174,
245, 260, 263, 286
multiple reviews, 170
ongoing nature of, 30–32

repetitions/redundancies
    in maps, 287
review meeting principles, 164*f*
teacher-examined curriculum
    and, 31–32
timeliness in maps, 173–175, 287
vertical, 167, 263, 274, 280, 285, 286
See also Review process, for
    curriculum; Review process,
    seven-step
Review process, for curriculum, 170–179
    absences in maps, 172–173
    assessments, 173–174
    bilevel item analysis, 175–177
    data adequacy, 172
    gaps, 170–171, 209
    integration issues, 172–173,
        174–175, 209
    new teachers and, 178
    repetitions, 171*f*, 209
    review focuses, 170–175
    timeliness, 173, 174–175
    universal commitment to using maps,
        177–178, 179*f*
Review process, seven-step, 166–170,
    200, 211–214
    preplanning stage, 167
    Step 1: collecting data, 168, 211, 286
    Step 2: first read-through,
        168, 211–212, 286
    Step 3: small-group review,
        168, 212, 286
    Step 4: large-group comparison,
        168–169, 213, 286
    Step 5: immediate revision,
        169, 213, 286
    Step 6: research and development,
        169, 214, 287
    Step 7: new review considerations,
        169–170, 214, 288
Rubicon Atlas, 218*f*

Same assessment, 69, 284
Scaffolded/spiraled elements, 207–209*f*
Schmied, K., 191
Schockley, M., 265–268
Second-order change, 28*f*–29, 245,
    255, 281
Senge, P., 252
Significant formative assessment
    (FOR), 67
Skills, 21
    definition of, 284
    descriptor for, 51, 58–59*f*, 206, 284
    vs. activities, 51–53

SMART (strategic, measurable,
    attainable, results-oriented, and
    time-bound goals), 36
Smith, B., 278–280
Social Studies Consensus Map Month, 16*f*
Social Studies Diary Map Month, 17*f*–18*f*
Social Studies Essential Map Month, 15*f*
St. James Elementary School, 278–280
Standard statement, level-of-learning
    expectation
    definition of, 284
    develop (D), 77–78, 79, 81, 285
    introduce (I), 77–78, 79, 81, 284
    mastery (M), 77–78, 79, 80, 81, 285
    reinforce (R), 78, 80, 81, 285
Standards, 20, 21
    collaborative interpretation of,
        200–201
    definition of, 284
    explicit *vs.* implicit expectations,
        203–204
    as proficiency targets, 200
    standards statement, sample, 201*f*
    translating to skill expectations, 55*f*
    See also Standard statement, level-of-
        learning expectation; Standards,
        interpretation procedures
Standards, interpretation procedures
    breaking apart standards, 199, 200,
        201–209
    importance of, 200–201
    power standards, defining, 209–210
    power standards, determining,
        199–200, 209–214
    power statement, worthiness of, 210
    variables in, 202–203, 212
Stevenson, C., 268
Stiggins, R. J., 67
Strangeway, M., 233
Strategic, measurable, attainable,
    results-oriented, and time-bound
    (SMART) goals, 36
Strategies, 20, 285
Successive approximations, 251–252
Summative assessment, 67–68, 284
Supplemental data. *See* Refining
    curriculum maps
Sutton, R., 251
System Design Task Force, 228–229
Systems Thinking Model, 28*f*–29

Target, in skill statement,
    51, 56–58, 56*f*, 57*f*
Target, proficiency, 55–58, 200
    aligned to assessment type, 56*f*

clarifying verbs with, 57*f*
definition of, 284
Technology
    commercial online mapping
        systems, 217–219
    Curriculum Mapper, 218*f*
    developing Web-based mapping
        system, 228–229
    featured commercial systems,
        218–219
    in-house software developers, 228
    learning organization support
        questions, 226*f*–227*f*
    mapping system questions, 221*f*–225*f*
    Rubicon Atlas, 218*f*
    selecting mapping system, 218–219
    system capabilities, 220*f*
    System Design Task Force, 228–229
TechPaths, 218*f*
Tegarden, Kathy, 258
Textbook, as resource, 200
Training, 241–243, 242*f*, 249, 262,
    266, 267, 270, 274, 276, 279–280
Tribuzzi, J., 271–275
Two review scenarios, 164–166

Udelhofen, S., 30
Uniform resource locator (URL),
    82, 84, 184, 217
Unit name
    definition of, 283
    for German I Diary Map Month, 44*f*
    recommended norms for, 44*f*
    sequential numbering system after, 43
    signifier after, 43
    writing, 42–45, 44*f*–45*f*
U.S. History Unit Diary Map Month,
    essential questions and, 195*f*–196*f*

Verb-focused learning, 46–47
Verbs
    clarifying targets with, 57*f*
    conceptual questions, nouns/verbs
        for, 191
    measurable, 51, 52–53, 54, 56, 57,
        60, 70*f*, 192, 206
    nonmeasurable, 53–55*f*
Verification *vs.* speculation, 3, 5*f*, 6
Vertical articulation, 21, 117, 172, 233
Vertical curriculum design, 46, 50*f*,
    206, 214, 215, 273
Vertical inter-alignment, 285
Vertical review, 167, 263, 274, 280,
    285, 286
    group meeting, 263, 274, 280

like-group, 286
mixed-group, 167, 286
Video conferencing, 32
Villa, R. A., 251

Waters, T., 28
Web addresses, writing, 82, 84
Web-based mapping, 7, 32
West Seneca Central School District,
    271–275
Wiggins, G., 192
Wiley, B., 271–275
William, D., 67
Workshops/conference, 29, 32, 34, 36,
    118, 137, 235, 258, 264, 270
Writing elements
    consistency in, 89, 91
    content, 45–50
    content, book titles, 47
    content, recommended
        norms, 48*f*–50*f*
    course names, 91, 97
    helpful hints, 89
    Intermediate Science Map Month,
        after revision, 96*f*
    Intermediate Science Map Month,
        before revision, 95*f*
    intra-alignment coding,
        50*f*, 85, 88*f*, 184
    Laundry List Map Sample
        Month, 94*f*
    non-normed Diary Map excerpts, 90*f*
    numerals *vs.* words for numbers, 45*f*
    quality map sample month, 92*f*, 93*f*
    unit name, 42–45, 44*f*–45*f*
    See also Writing elements, assessment;
        Writing elements, resources;
        Writing elements, skills; Writing
        elements, standard statements
Writing elements, assessment, 64–71
    assessment name, 64–65, 66*f*–67
    benchmark assessment, 68
    Bloom's verbs and, 69–71
    measurable skill verbs, 70*f*
    recommended norms, 72*f*–76*f*
    significant formative
        assessment (FOR), 67
    summative *vs.* formative
        assessment, 67–68
    use in each curriculum map type, 71
Writing elements, resources, 82–88
    adopted resources, 84
    Consensus and Diary Map
        comparison, 85*f*
    hyperlinks, 82, 84

intra-alignment coding, 85
recommended norms, 86*f*–88
Writing elements, skills, 51–63
descriptive *vs.* not descriptive,
language arts focus, 101–102
descriptive *vs.* not descriptive, math
focus, 99–100
descriptors, 51, 58–59*f*
measurable verbs, 51, 52–53, 54, 56,
57, 60, 192, 206
nonmeasurable verbs, 53–55*f*
recommended skills norms, 60*f*–63*f*
skill *vs.* activity, 51–53
skill *vs.* activity, math focus primary
grades, 103–105
as student centered, 60
target, 55–58

target, clarifying verbs with, 57*f*
target, in skill statement, 51
target modality aligned to assessment
type, 56*f*
various-discipline focus, upper grades,
105–106
Writing elements, standard statements,
71, 77–82
develop (D) learning expectation level,
77–78, 79, 81, 285
introduce (I) learning expectation
level, 77–78, 79, 81, 284
mastery (M) learning expectation
level, 77–78, 79, 80, 81, 285
reinforce (R) learning expectation
level, 78, 80, 81, 285
visual intra-alignment of, 83*f*

CORWIN PRESS

The Corwin Press logo—a raven striding across an open book—represents the union of courage and learning. Corwin Press is committed to improving education for all learners by publishing books and other professional development resources for those serving the field of PreK–12 education. By providing practical, hands-on materials, Corwin Press continues to carry out the promise of its motto: **"Helping Educators Do Their Work Better."**